The Southwest Center Series

Ignaz Pfefferkorn, *Sonora: A Description of the Province*

Carl Lumholtz, *New Trails in Mexico*

Buford Pickens, *The Missions of Northern Sonora: A 1935 Field Documentation*

Gary Paul Nabhan, editor, *Counting Sheep: Twenty Ways of Seeing Desert Bighorn*

Eileen Oktavek, *Answered Prayers: Miracles and Milagros along the Border*

Curtis M. Hinsley and David R. Wilcox, editors, *Frank Hamilton Cushing and the Hemenway Southwestern Archaeological Expedition, 1886–1889, volume 1: The Southwest in the American Imagination: The Writings of Sylvester Baxter, 1881–1899*

Lawrence J. Taylor and Maeve Hickey, *The Road to Mexico*

Donna J. Guy and Thomas E. Sheridan, editors, *Contested Ground: Comparative Frontiers on the Northern and Southern Edges of the Spanish Empire*

Julian D. Hayden, *The Sierra Pinacate*

Paul S. Martin, David Yetman, Mark Fishbein, Phil Jenkins, Thomas R. Van Devender, and Rebecca K. Wilson, editors, *Gentry's Rio Mayo Plants. The Tropical Deciduous Forest and Environs of Northwest Mexico*

W J McGee, *Trails to Tiburón: The 1894 and 1895 Field Diaries of W J McGee,* transcribed by Hazel McFeely Fontana, annotated and with an introduction by Bernard L. Fontana

Richard Stephen Felger, *Flora of the Gran Desierto and Río Colorado of Northwestern Mexico*

Donald Bahr, editor, *O'odham Creation and Related Events: As Told to Ruth Benedict in 1927 in Prose, Oratory, and Song by the Pimas William Blackwater, Thomas Vanyiko, Clara Ahiel, William Stevens, Oliver Wellington, and Kisto*

Dan L. Fischer, *Early Southwest Ornithologists, 1528–1900*

Thomas Bowen, editor, *Backcountry Pilot: Flying Adventures with Ike Russell*

Federico José María Ronstadt, *Borderman: Memoirs of Federico José María Ronstadt,* edited by Edward F. Ronstadt

Curtis M. Hinsley and David R. Wilcox, editors, *Frank Hamilton Cushing and the Hemenway Southwestern Archaeological Expedition, 1886–1889, volume 2: The Lost Itinerary of Frank Hamilton Cushing*

Neil Goodwin, *Like a Brother: Grenville Goodwin's Apache Years, 1928–1939*

Like a Brother

GRENVILLE GOODWIN'S
APACHE YEARS, 1928–1939

Neil Goodwin

The University of Arizona Press
Tucson

The University of Arizona Press

First printing

♾ This book is printed on acid-free, archival-quality paper.
Manufactured in the United States of America

09 08 07 06 05 04 6 5 4 3 2 1

ISBN 0-8165-2408-4
Library of Congress Control Number 2003116383

Like a Brother originally appeared as a double issue of the *Journal of the Southwest*, vol. 43, nos. 1 and 2 (Spring–Summer 2001) and is published by arrangement with the Southwest Center of the University of Arizona.

Publication of this book is made possible in part by a grant from the Southwest Center of the University of Arizona.

Contents

Acknowledgments

I am grateful to the people I have gone to for help in finding my way through the landscape of Apache culture. They shared their life stories and offered help, advice, and insight in assembling this volume. For help in reviewing the manuscript I am deeply appreciative to Paul Allen, Carlos Borunda, Catherine Bugbee, Jeanette Cassa, Al Fenn, Alan Ferg, Philip Greenfeld, Cline Griggs, Diana Hadley, Nick Houser, Berle Kanseah, Charles Kaut, Thelma Kindelay, Karl Laumbach, Ann McGarrell, Ray Nochita, Seth Pilsk, Alberta Rope, Nelda Villa, John Welch, Ben Williams Jr., Nick Zelinka, and especially to my wife Margot, my son Seth, and my *compadre* Barney Burns.

—NEIL GOODWIN

"I thought of you as my brother. Even if you are a whiteman but in my mind you are like an Indian."

—From a letter written to Grenville Goodwin by his Apache friend, Susie Wright of Bylas, Arizona.

Introduction

This book is a collection of pieces gathered around a central theme: the life and works of my father, Grenville (Grennie) Goodwin. They are for the most part only loosely connected, each part bearing a stronger relation to the central theme than to the others. This collection grew from writing the book, *The Apache Diaries: A Father-Son Journey,* published in May 2000 by the University of Nebraska Press. *The Apache Diaries* is focused on completing the compelling research that my father began in 1930 on the subject of the Sierra Madre Apache. That book, a conversation between his diaries and mine, is about the search for our own "Treasure of the Sierra Madre"; but it became as well my own search for the father I never knew. He died only months after I was born, and *The Apache Diaries* became a way for us to do something together and for me to begin to know him, but it was, I find, only a beginning. As this enterprise grew and I probed deeper into the lives of both my parents, I discovered that I was unearthing layers of my own life and history that I had never been aware of, and the experience has been transformative. My own life is being enriched as it might never have been without that diary: the key to it all.

This volume is a compilation of a chorus of voices. One voice comes from my father's unpublished field notes and diaries and from letters he either wrote or received. Another comes from my mother's diaries, her unpublished writings and letters, and the diaries and letters of her father and other members of the family. Since I draw on my own collection of papers, I have not footnoted the quoted material except in cases where the material has been published or is accessible in the archives of the Arizona State Museum in Tucson. There is a statement in the introduction to each chapter about the sources for the material quoted in that chapter.

Because this book is devoted to a better understanding of Grenville Goodwin, it is appropriate that the first chapter be a biographical sketch. Some of this material appears in the prologue to *The Apache Diaries,* but I have filled the biography out with material that has come to the surface since *The Apache Diaries* was published. As with so many of the stories I pursued in writing *The Apache Diaries,* chapter 2, "Captive Children," begins with brief notes that Grennie made about captive Apache children in Mexico. It picks up where he left off and pieces together the stories of three Apache children captured by Mexicans in raids on Apache camps in the Sierra Madre during the early decades of the twentieth century. Chapter 3, "Carmela" continues this theme, focusing on the life of one of those children and my efforts over the years to find out what became of her. These stories could be told only in part in *The Apache Diaries;* here they appear in full.

Chapter 4, "Jan and Grennie," begins as I finish reading Grennie's Mexico diary for the first time when I was twenty-three, utterly captivated by the story of the Sierra Madre Apache and equally at a loss to understand who my father was. As much as he tells me about his own search for the Sierra Madre Apache, he tells me nothing about himself or how it feels to have had the adventure of a lifetime. So I turn to my mother's written record—much more personal and, in its own way, more eloquent. In it I explore the relationship between my parents using my mother's poetry, paintings, and letters to help bring Grennie into higher relief.

As well as Jan knew him, there was a part of his experience that she could never fully share with him. Grennie's Apache friends wrote him some eighty letters, which he carefully kept, and my mother, knowing how precious and unique they were, kept them after his death. In chapter 5 these letters paint a powerful and poignant portrait of the daily life of Grennie's Apache friends and of their relationship with him. The Apaches speak through their letters so vividly that I can hear their voices and feel their simple dignity as they recount the often heart-rending tribulations of their lives. In order to create a broad perspective in this chapter, one that gives a sense of what the reservation as a whole was like in the 1930s, I have interwoven the Apaches' letters with entries from Grennie's daily diaries. As I did this, I realized I was beginning to hear my father's voice, or at least his point of view, more strongly than I had before. In the search for Grenville Goodwin, I was getting warmer.

In chapter 6, "The San Carlos Experience," I begin to dig deeper into Grennie's field notes and diaries. The latter were not personal in any way, shape, or form. He did not record feelings, emotions, impressions, or half-baked thoughts. Into his diaries went the things he noticed every day at Bylas and Calva, the two communities on the San Carlos Apache reservation where he spent most of his research time from 1928 to 1936: what was happening at the store, how the cattle were doing, who was in jail, who had a bad dream about ghosts, who was gossiping about whom, who was sick, who died, who had a baby, and a thousand other things. The diaries often provided the context for information more formally recorded in his field notes. Occasionally I would find a diary story that he had also told, with slight differences, in letters to my mother. As I immersed myself in this material, the detailed outlines of Grennie's reservation experience began to emerge before my eyes: what it was like to be Grenville Goodwin day after day, year after year at San Carlos. At the same time, especially after my meetings in late 1997 with people at San Carlos, I realized that there was a specific strand in Grennie's reservation experience that I needed to explore. He was powerfully and inexorably drawn to Apache spirituality, something that informs the most commonplace as well as the most sacred of activities. He became steeped in sacred knowledge, and I felt that an exploration of the way in which he recorded it—the patience, the respect, and the extreme caution—would allow me at last to sit almost by his side.

Having mastered—or at least having recorded in great detail—the encyclopedic complexities of Apache religion, he hands us a gift, something he knew all along, of course. Apache spirituality is expressed in the rhythms of everyday life: greeting the rising sun, making breakfast, saddling a horse, curing an injury, being good to one's family, telling stories, telling jokes, plowing the ground. The gift, in the form of chapter 7, is Grennie's simple description of a day in the life of an Apache family in 1936.

In the second to last chapter, "An Apache Ranchería," with a group of companions I return to Mexico and write what amounts to an archaeological epilogue to Grennie's original diary. Having located a large ranchería in the Sierra las Espuelas in the winter of 1997, we were able to spend only two days at the site. I was determined to return for an extended period in order to account for all the features that my father had recorded in 1931. Of the five dwelling clusters he had mapped, we saw only two in 1997. I wanted to find the others and to make an accurate map of the whole complex. Most of all I wanted a better understanding of what the people were really doing at this place. I felt I had only the most rudimentary picture; and Grennie, scientist that he was, spent all his time amassing a literal and exhaustive inventory without wasting so much as a word on interpretation, not to mention speculation. When I go to a site with one of my father's inventories, when I actually see how steep the canyons are, how little water there is, where the natural vantage points are; when I wade through the brush, smell the smells, get hot, get thirsty, get filthy, get drenched in sweat—when I do all these things, patterns emerge from his deadpan inventories and they take on nuance, relief, and eloquence. I was not to be disappointed in this case. ✥

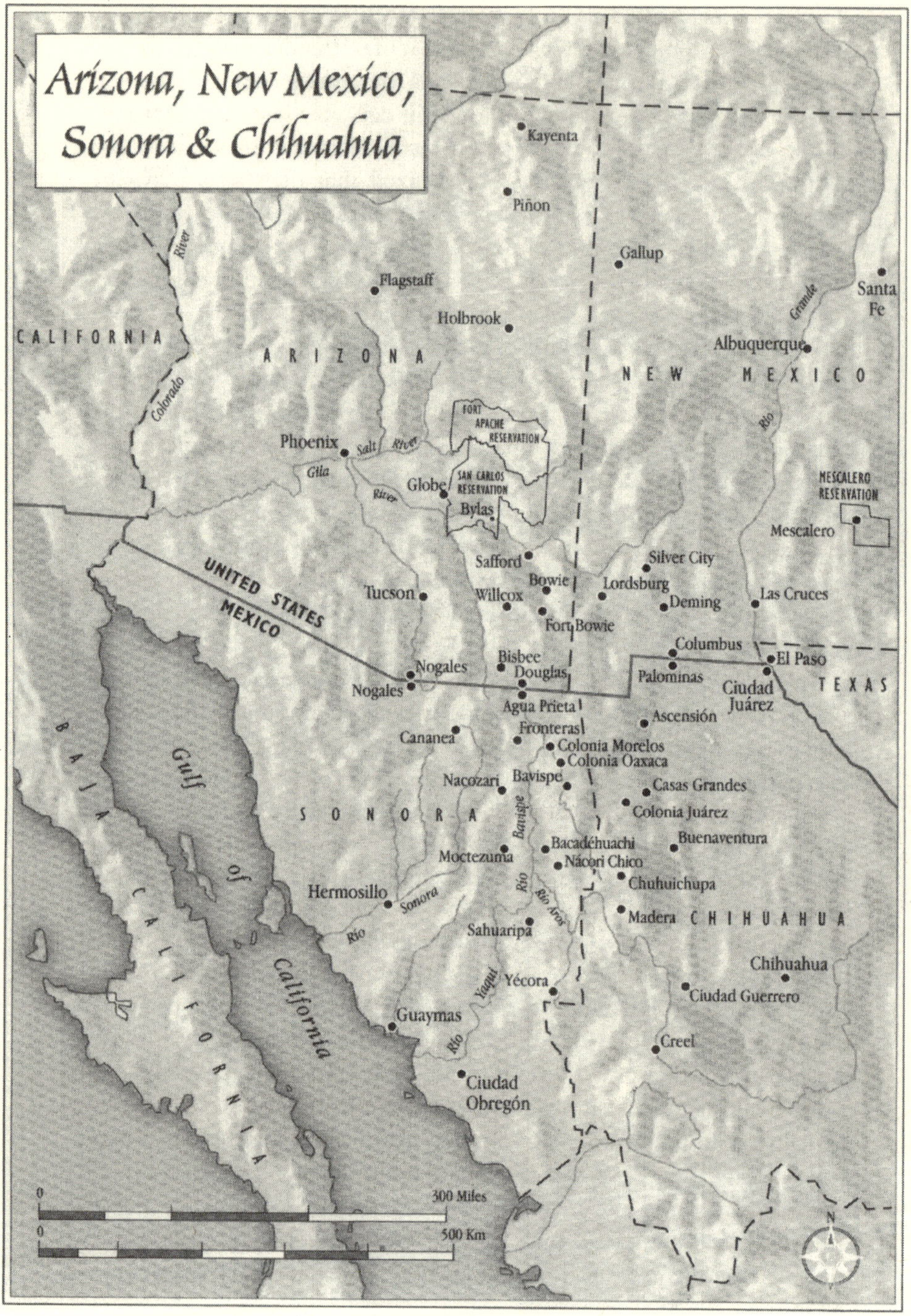

Arizona, New Mexico, Sonora & Chihuahua
Kayenta
Piñon
Gallup
Flagstaff
Holbrook
Santa Fe
Albuquerque
CALIFORNIA
ARIZONA
NEW MEXICO
Colorado River
Rio Grande
FORT APACHE RESERVATION
SAN CARLOS RESERVATION
Phoenix
Salt River
Gila River
Globe
Bylas
MESCALERO RESERVATION
Mescalero
Safford
Silver City
Bowie
Lordsburg
Tucson
Willcox
Deming
Las Cruces
Fort Bowie
UNITED STATES
MEXICO
Columbus
Bisbee
El Paso
Nogales
Nogales
Douglas
Palominas
Ciudad Juárez
TEXAS
Agua Prieta
Ascensión
Fronteras
Cananea
Colonia Morelos
Colonia Oaxaca
Nacozari
Bavispe
Casas Grandes
Colonia Juárez
SONORA
Rio Bavispe
Bacadéhuachi
Buenaventura
Moctezuma
Nácori Chico
Chuhuichupa
Hermosillo
Rio Sonora
Rio Aros
Madera
CHIHUAHUA
Sahuaripa
Gulf of California
BAJA CALIFORNIA
Chihuahua
Yécora
Ciudad Guerrero
Guaymas
Rio Yaqui
Creel
Ciudad Obregón
0
300 Miles
0
500 Km
N

Grenville Goodwin

Although Grenville Goodwin was only thirty-three when he died in 1940, he had published several papers and two books about the Western Apache. Soon after his death, his great friend, anthropologist Edward Spicer, wrote that Goodwin's landmark monograph, *The Social Organization of the Western Apache,* was "one of the most detailed and best-documented studies of Indian social organization."[1] His friend and colleague, Morris Opler, considered him "one of the most gifted and effective field anthropologists in the history of the discipline."[2]

Most of his anthropological colleagues wrote of him with similar praise, but I have heard that some could never forget that he was an amateur without formal training or degrees—gifted, but an amateur nonetheless. I have heard that some felt he got too close to his subjects, lost his objectivity, and recorded material that could not be used because it was either too private or possibly compromised by subjectivity. I have also heard that he is considered one of the most enigmatic and romantic figures in American anthropology.

GRENVILLE GOODWIN UNTIL 1929: MYTH AND REALITY

He went to live among the Apaches at such a young age, barely twenty, that they shaped him more than his own family did. My mother wrote of him: "He rebelled violently against his background and [the] eastern culture he was brought up in. He never wanted any of his friends to know . . . anything about his family and their wealth. . . . He was very shy with his own kind, but perfectly at ease with simple. . . people."

My father was a privileged Easterner who escaped to the West and rejected his high-born origins. In the 1920s long after the frontier was gone, the West was still a place to make a fresh start. In our family there

Grenville Goodwin and his first deer, El Paso Púlpito, 1930.

are stories hinting that he was rootless, rebellious, alienated, but also charismatic: a beloved infidel. It is hard to imagine a more discrepant product of the staid, patrician Hartford, Connecticut establishment than Grenville Goodwin.

Walter Lippincott Goodwin, my father's father, was what in the gilded age might have been called a "sportsman." He was the scion of a family business empire built on insurance and railroad fortunes. He was a Connecticut state legislator and was fond of polo, racehorses, fox hunting, shooting, and the late Victorian good life.

My grandfather's passion was horses. He had estates in Saratoga, New York, and Middleburg, Virginia: one for the racing season and one for the fox-hunting season. He owned a stable of thoroughbreds and was an avid shooter and angler. He made sure that each of his sons learned to ride a horse and handle a gun—skills that in some ways made my father's Sierra Madre adventure possible.

My father's parents were divorced in 1914, a time when divorce was rare and scandalous. His mother, Elizabeth "Betty" Sage Goodwin (after her second marriage to Meredith Hare, Elizabeth Sage Hare) counted herself among the movers and shakers of the New York avant-garde intelligentsia. She was one of the organizers of the New York Armory Show of 1913 and the granddaughter of one of the founders of Cornell University.

Hers was not a world of lightweight socialites, but my father rejected what he saw as the upper-crust pretense of this milieu. Nevertheless he fashioned his own world from much of what his parents offered. The family lived in what, for the members of this wealthy circle, was typical Edwardian grandeur. They had a brownstone in New York, a country place on the north shore of Long Island at Huntington, one near the beach at Southhampton, another in Aiken, South Carolina, and a summer house on a lake in the Adirondacks. Each of these places had a resident caretaker, and when the family was in residence a staff of several servants moved in with them. There was a cook, at least two chauffeurs, a butler, a scullery maid, an upstairs maid, one or two downstairs maids and, at the Huntington place, called Pigeon Hill, there was a full-time farmer, Steve Zelinka. An immigrant from Ukraine, he and his family moved to Long Island from Hartford in 1915 following the divorce of Grenville's parents. Betty installed Steve in a house on the property, where he and his wife and children lived for seven years.

Mr. Zelinka's son Nick became Grenville's closest companion at Pigeon Hill, and now at the age of ninety vividly recalls their shared boyhood. In a recent conversation with me, Nick remembered that Grennie, as my father was often called, always did things in the Indian way—or what he imagined was the Indian way, for during these years he was devouring a steady diet of boy's books by the likes of Ernest Thompson Seton and Clarence Hawkes—romantic adventures with animal and native heroes set in the Far North and the Wild West, articulating a classic frontier paradigm of rugged self-reliance and outdoorsmanship. Nick remembers walking through the woods, always carefully placing one foot before the other following Grennie's insistent example, as they went on their frequent camping trips in the woods around Pigeon Hill. The arrowheads on the farm were "as common as popcorn" remembers Nick, and they gathered enough to fill a bushel basket. The magical discovery of these beautifully crafted artifacts wove a durable warp into the fabric of Grennie's fantasy world and made it feel palpable. Little did he know in 1920 at the age of thirteen—though it might not have surprised him—that in ten years he would be living an adventure right out of one of his boyhood romances.

Grennie's father, two of Grennie's four brothers, and two of his uncles went to Groton and Yale. Grennie went to Groton himself at the age of fourteen but loathed it and lasted only a few months. Long interested in progressive education, his mother sent him to an experimental boarding school in Lake Placid, New York, but he was soon stricken with tuberculosis. The hot, dry climate of the West was the cure of choice for tuberculosis in those days. So in 1922, at the age of fifteen, my father was sent to rough it and recover at the Mesa Ranch School, a Spartan boarding school in Mesa, Arizona.

His mother had already discovered the Southwest and had a hunch that Grennie might take to it. She had a *pied-à-terre* in Santa Fe, where she maintained a high profile in its quasi-bohemian, left-wing intellectual world peopled by the likes of Elsie Clews Parsons, Edward Weston, Georgia O'Keefe, Ansel Adams, Mabel Dodge, Maurice Sterne, Tony Luhan, Robinson Jeffers, Max Eastman, Emma Goldman, and Frieda Lawrence. Betty would later live for periods in Colorado Springs, Colorado, where in the late '20s and early '30s, she was involved in the founding of the very progressive Fountain Valley School and the Colorado Springs Fine Arts Center.

My father made an initial recovery, but the tuberculosis was only dormant apparently. It returned at the end of his second year at the Mesa Ranch School, and though Grennie had to come home, he had fallen in love with the Southwest. The cultural and natural setting was what first drew him in, then he was drawn in deeper by the way of life—a way of life he thought might one day be his as well.

Betty next placed him in an upstate New York sanatorium where he spent a year recovering from tuberculosis, after which he entered the Gunnery School, a private boarding school in Washington, Connecticut. He spent his summers in Santa Fe with his mother and brothers, and immediately after graduation in the summer of 1927 he returned to the Southwest and, except for short visits, never lived in the East again.

One of his first undertakings in the summer of 1927 was an extended camping trip on the Navajo reservation, where he explored its many cliff dwellings and visited its remote trading posts to collect classic Navajo weavings and jewelry. It was there that he met a BIA (Bureau of Indian Affairs) policeman, John Hoffman, who was the first to tell him about the Sierra Madre Apaches. He noted the meeting in detail, never dreaming how it had nudged the trajectory of his life. Grennie had many interests, and he wanted to pursue them all—archaeology, natural history, anthropology, Spanish colonial history. So he spent two years exploring these fields, certain, it seems, that in one of them he would find his life's work.

One thing Grennie knew for sure: he wanted to live close to nature and in the outdoors. At first he thought he might have a future in forestry, so he signed on at a lumber camp at McNary, Arizona, on the northern edge of the Fort Apache reservation in the fall of 1927. Tuberculosis had weakened his health, and the demands of the lumberjack life were more than his constitution could withstand. He lasted only a couple of months, but living and working with White Mountain Apache logging crews gave Grennie his first prolonged contact with the Apaches. The next year he divided between extensive travel in the West and work as a park ranger at Frijoles Canyon in New Mexico's Bandelier National Monument—a region rich in cave dwellings and prehistoric sites.

By the end of the summer of 1928, he appears to have reached a decision to pursue his growing interest in archaeology. He moved to Tucson to be near the University of Arizona and its pre-eminent archaeologist, Byron Cummings, whom he had met while at the Mesa Ranch School. During the 1928–29 academic year he had a university student card. Though he took no courses he had, I suspect, somehow contrived to apprentice himself to Cummings.

Always ready to drop everything for adventure, it wasn't long before Grennie had left Arizona to join a cousin, Douglas Burden, for the winter in Ontario, to work on a film about the Ojibwe.[3] The trip to Canada was perhaps Grennie's first chance to practice ethnography in the field. As was his habit, he kept beautifully organized notebooks. One of them has page after page of Algonquin words and phrases; another is an illustrated inventory of Ojibwe woodcraft, hunting practices, and handmade artifacts such as snowshoes, birch-bark baskets, animal traps, knives, and canoes.

The following summer Grennie was back in Arizona with the Archaeology Summer School run by Byron Cummings to help excavate Turkey Hill Pueblo near Flagstaff. At the end of the summer he enrolled as a freshman at the University of Arizona for the 1929–30 academic year.

Although by now Grennie was well aware of the presence of Apaches in the Sierra Madre, it was not until late 1929 that he heard of a sensational crime they had committed in October 1927 about seventy-five miles south of the border near the tiny Mexican highland town of Nácori Chico. A group of Sierra Madre Apaches had attacked a family on a remote road, killing María Dolores Fimbres and kidnapping her son, three-year-old Gerardo.

The 1927 attack had received little or no publicity in American newspapers until the fall of 1929, when a large-scale manhunt and punitive expedition was organized with a base of operations in Douglas, Arizona. Suddenly the Fimbres tragedy and the Sierra Madre Apaches were receiving national newspaper coverage in the United States. The lure was irresistible. Grennie slipped away from classes at the University of Arizona and made for Douglas to interview those involved in the manhunt and to gather newspaper articles.

He spent Christmas that year at Coolidge Dam on the San Carlos reservation, passing his time at Rupkey's Trading Post, and beginning to make friends among the Apaches. Bert Rupkey, the manager of the trading post, told him that he had heard about the Sierra Madre Apaches from the people on the reservation, who knew them all too well.

The following summer, 1930, while at Fort Apache, Grennie heard that the Sierra Madre Apaches would sometimes roam as far north as the reservation to raid for horses and women, and by November he had resolved to go to Mexico to find out about them for himself. My father, still a freshman at the University of Arizona, had irreversibly entered the gravitational field of this epic story and had begun a diary to record his experience.

Although Grennie's interest in the Western Apaches dates from 1928, by his own account he spent the summer of 1930 as if he were trying to decide between the Navajos and the Apaches as a field of study. He worked behind the counter at Goulding's Trading Post near Kayenta on the Navajo reservation. And he appeared to have had a similar job at San Carlos—perhaps at Rupkey's Trading Post.

Following his November-December trip to Mexico to look for the Sierra Madre Apaches, he returned to the University of Arizona for the 1931 spring term. Then he headed directly for San Carlos and Fort Apache, having decided to leave the study of the Navajo to the many others already crowding the field and to study the Apaches, about whom hardly anyone knew a thing. At summer's end he returned to Mexico for a month and was guided to two recently abandoned Sierra Madre Apache campsites, which he thoroughly surveyed, photographed, and inventoried. He was the first and only anthropologist to see and describe these camps.

His head buzzing with his new discoveries and the knowledge that he was already breaking new ground, he returned to San Carlos early in 1932, his command of the language strengthened by his total immersion among Apaches on the reservation during the previous summer. Grennie spent virtually all of 1932 and most of 1933 among the Apaches. I wonder if it was during this period that he developed his habit of sleeping on the ground or the floor instead of in a bed. My mother said he always used to sleep Apache-style, flat on his back like a mummy. I was reminded of this when Charles Kaut, an anthropologist who followed in Grennie's footsteps in the 1950s, told me of a story going around the University of Chicago that "Goodwin wouldn't sleep on a bed, he preferred the floor."

By this time, Grennie was working as a research associate out of the University of Arizona and was embarked on writing a massive report on the Western Apaches, which was eventually to become *The Social Organization of the Western Apache.* Meanwhile he wrote another paper, delivered in May of 1933 at the American Association for the Advancement of Science (AAAS) meeting in Las Cruces, which was the beginning of his gaining a wider reputation in the field.[4]

By the end of 1933 tuberculosis struck again, and Grennie went to Colorado Springs to recover. He was away from the reservation until January 1935, an absence of well over a year. In the meantime he had completed a 490-page draft of *The Social Organization of the Western Apache* and had sent it to Dean Byron Cummings at the University of Arizona and to Morris Opler (an anthropologist studying other Apache groups) for comment. Eager to get back in the field, Grennie plunged into intensive research beginning in January 1935 and continuing through August 1936.

His only break was an early-1936 visit back East. Among other things, he renewed his friendship with Janice Thompson, and they resolved to meet again at the end of the summer. In August Grennie drove east and the two of them spent two months driving up and down the coast of New England, eventually deciding to head west together and get married.

After driving across the country—the first time my mother had been west of the Hudson River, as far as I can tell—Jan and Grennie were married in Holbrook, Arizona. They settled in Tucson, where Grennie continued with his work on *The Social Organization of the Western Apache*. There were occasional trips back to Bylas, especially in the winter, for the gathering of stories and other material that according to tradition could not be spoken of by Apaches except in that season.

Grennie was working on a number of other writing projects at the time, including *Myths and Tales of the White Mountain Apache* and several scholarly papers. He was keeping in touch with his Apache friends through letters and visits, and he was collecting examples of Apache material culture for the Arizona State Museum, the Laboratory of Anthropology in Santa Fe, and possibly for other institutions.

Jan and Grennie moved to Santa Fe in early 1938, where they remained until the summer of 1939, when they moved back to Tucson, living at the Evans School east of town. Grennie was given a position as research associate at the University of Arizona and was finalizing *The Social Organization of the Western Apache*. In the fall of 1940, feeling the need for more academic training, Grennie decided to take courses at the University of Chicago, and he and Jan moved to Chicago. By this time, a brain tumor, though as yet undiagnosed, was well advanced. Late in the winter it was detected and was surgically removed in March. Believing that the operation had been reasonably successful, Jan and Grennie made a planned trip to California in June, but he became irreversibly ill and died on July 30 in Los Angeles.

The Social Organization of the Western Apache was virtually complete at the time of Grennie's death. With assistance from a number of Grennie's colleagues, Jan brought the work to fruition and it was published by the University of Chicago in 1942. Since then several posthumous publications have resulted from Grennie's voluminous field notes: *Western Apache Raiding and Warfare*; *Grenville Goodwin among the Western Apache: Letters from the Field; Western Apache Material Culture*, and *The Apache Diaries*. Grennie's papers are in the archives of the Arizona State Museum, as is his extensive collection of Western Apache artifacts, utensils, clothes, and basketry.

These words from Ned Spicer, one of Grennie's closest friends, summarize his legacy as well as any:

> To Grenville Goodwin we owe most of what understanding we have of the way of life of the Western Apaches. The abundant literature on the Western Apaches, inspired in great part by the spectacular forays of Geronimo and his predecessors, is largely a literature of the men who fought the Indians and participated in the final relentless roundups. It is not a literature from which emerges a view of the values by which Apaches lived. But for the work of Goodwin we would have lost all opportunity to participate in the Apache world.[5]

Captive Children

two

"Captive Children" is a longer version of one of the chapters in my book *The Apache Diaries.* It appears in part 4 of that book following the conclusion of Grennie's Mexico diaries and begins to tell the story of my own search for survivors and captive children of the Sierra Madre Apaches.

Some background on these people is necessary to understand references in this chapter. The Sierra Madre Apaches were a people thought by most Americans to exist no longer. They were the last of the free-roaming Apaches, living in the traditional way—hunting, gathering, and raiding as they had for hundreds of years. With the surrender of Geronimo in 1886, all of the Apache bands were supposed to have been accounted for—either settled on reservations or, as were Geronimo and all the Chiricahua Apaches, in the custody of the U.S. Army as prisoners of war, permanently exiled from their homelands in New Mexico, Arizona, and Mexico. Only a few people knew there were Apaches who had never surrendered. Numbering perhaps as many as one hundred in the 1890s, they were made up of four groups. The most numerous were the *Ndéndaa'i* Chiricahuas, the southernmost of the four Chiricahua Apache subdivisions. Living entirely in the Sierra Madre of Mexico and never having spent time on American reservations, they would have been unknown to the U.S. Army or to reservation administrators. They were, of course, well known in Mexico, but once the massive campaigns of the 1880s were over and the infamous Geronimo was a prisoner, the relatively few Apaches that remained did not attract nearly as much attention. To their number were added six known members of Geronimo's band, who slipped away from the cavalry detachment that was escorting Geronimo and his people after they had negotiated terms of surrender with Lieutenant Gatewood roughly thirty miles south of the border.

In 1889, the Apache Kid, a notorious Western Apache outlaw, fled south to hide in the Sierra Madre, where he formed a gang comprised mostly of Chiricahuas. In addition, a small number of Western Apaches broke out of San Carlos in the 1890s and headed south into the Sierra Madre, perhaps joining the others already there. The old Western Apache scout, Sherman Curley, told my father of the many times he served with the army during the '90s in pursuit of "renegade" Apaches who were thought to have broken out of the San Carlos reservation or who had come north from Mexico to raid ranches in southern Arizona.

Mexican folklore is rich in stories of these people, stretching all the way from the border towns of Naco and Agua Prieta, two hundred miles south to Yécora and Sahuaripa where the Mountain Pima live. The stories are told even farther south than that—as far south as the Barranca del Cobre, Tarahumara Indian country.

Within twenty years of the surrender of Geronimo, settlers began to populate the Sierra Madre, and as they did so, they made more and more frequent contact with the Apaches there. Contact led inevitably to friction, and conflict soon broke out again. Tension built throughout the teens and early twenties, coming to a head in 1927 with a sensational murder and kidnapping near the village of Nácori Chico, about seventy-five miles south of the sister border towns of Douglas, Arizona, and Agua Prieta, Sonora.

While traveling along a remote mountain road in the Sierra Madre, a Mexican family by the name of Fimbres was attacked by a small group of Sierra Madre Apaches. The attackers killed the wife, María Dolores Fimbres, and kidnapped her three-year-old son, Gerardo. It was over in seconds. María was mounted on a horse, but her husband Francisco was walking and had fallen behind. He watched helplessly from one hundred feet down the trail. Immediately he mounted a massive manhunt in the mountains.

Newspapers on both sides of the border picked up the story, and it even ran in New York and California papers. While living in Tucson and beginning his work among the Western Apaches, my father heard of these events and went to Mexico with an experienced guide to find out about the Sierra Madre Apaches before they were all gone. It was said that Mexican ranchers were shooting them on sight.

After three years of fruitless searching, in April 1930, the Mexicans finally found and attacked a Sierra Madre Apache camp. A man and two women were killed, but there was no sign of the kidnapped boy, by now six years old and probably completely adapted to his life with the

Apaches. Two weeks later at the spot where the three Apaches were shot, Gerardo's body was found, killed by the Apaches in revenge.

News of these events spread quickly. It was soon open season on Apaches in Mexico—if they could be found. Elusive as the Sierra Madre Apaches were, reservation Apaches in the United States knew all too well of their existence. Chiricahuas at the Mescalero reservation in New Mexico were certain they knew who this group was: their relatives who had stayed behind in Mexico when Geronimo surrendered in 1886.

As this section begins, it is November 1932, slightly less than a year since Grennie's return from his last trip to Mexico. He has made a trip to Mescalero and is talking with an old Chiricahua Apache named Sam Kenoi. This chapter uses the format of *The Apache Diaries* in which the narrative is handed back and forth between Grennie's diary and my diary. ✣

GRENVILLE'S DIARY

Nov. 16, 1932, Mescalero Agency

Visiting here, I met Sam Kenoi, a *Ndéndaa'i* Apache. I told him about hearing about there still being some Chiricahua in the Sierra Madre and he was very anxious to know if I knew the names of any of them. He knew of them apparently and from what can be gathered, the renegades now in the Sierra Madre must all be *Ndéndaa'i*.

NEIL'S DIARY

Sam knows of their existence, even of one of the individual names (it was Adiłnadzi·d, mentioned in a later conversation) but apparently no more than that.

At this point Grennie assumes that all the Sierra Madre Apache are *Ndéndaa'i*, the southernmost of the Chiricahuas. In fact, there were some Western Apaches: some of them captured when the Sierra Madre Apaches raided San Carlos and Fort Apache in the early twentieth century; and some of them Western Apache renegades who had broken out of the reservation in the 1890s.

As much as the Chiricahuas at Mescalero might have wanted it, as of 1932 they have had no recorded contact with the Sierra Madre Apaches. For Sam Kenoi and other Chiricahuas, knowledge of long-lost relatives in the old homeland would mean hope for the end to a separation, long thought to be permanent; but that hope is growing dimmer, for the final act in the drama of the Sierra Madre Apaches is opening in Mexico even as my father and Sam are talking.

Since the fateful battle of April 1930 that claimed the lives of three Apaches and ultimately, Gerardo Fimbres, no sighting in Mexico has been reported. From the footprints left at the scene of the fight, the Mexican attackers could tell that there were survivors—most of them just children.

Following the death of Gerardo, the most hard-bitten of the Mexicans commit themselves to a campaign of extermination. The government has washed its hands of the matter. The Sierra Madre, as always, is outside the law, and it is open season on Apaches.

In April 1932, only four months after Grennie left Mexico, an Apache camp is discovered and attacked, blood is shed, and a child is captured. The news eventually reaches Bill Curtis (my father's guide and companion during his Sierra Madre trips in 1930 and 1931) and Bill's wife writes about it to Grennie. These letters have not survived, but notes that he wrote much later do.

GRENVILLE'S DIARY

Oct. 1935, Tucson, Ariz.

Saw Art Schrader [another of my father's friends from Mexico] in Tucson, on his way back to Douglas.

He said of the little Sierra Madre Apache girl who was captured by an American rancher near Nácori Chico and mentioned in letters from Mrs. Curtis, that it happened in this way.

The rancher was riding through a canyon in the mountains. He was quite high up on the side of the hill and as he happened to look down hill he saw a wickiup standing some ways below him. Wondering if anyone was in it, he dislodged a stone and rolled it downhill so that it went right through the wickiup. Out ran a woman and the little girl. The rancher with his high-powered rifle shot at the woman as she ran, hitting her in the shoulder and knocking her down. But she got up and ran on. The second shot killed her. The little girl ran up to her and cried over her. The rancher rode up to her and took the little girl home with him. Art claimed that he shot the woman to get the fifty-dollar bounty on these Apaches offered either by the state government or federal government, I don't know which.

NEIL'S DIARY

Nácori Chico

Although there is no evidence for a federal or a state of Sonora bounty on Apaches, the governor of Sonora had made it official: in the Sierra Madre, Apaches could be shot on sight in order to right the wrong of the murder of María and Gerardo Fimbres.[6]

The cowboy, who was actually a Mexican working at the American-owned ranch, brought the little girl here to Nácori Chico. It's 1996 and I am traveling with my good friend, Barney Burns, Mexican historian Nelda Whetten, and my son Seth; and we have come here to pick up the old, cold trail. Rodolfo Rascón, a journalist who lives here, has followed this story himself for years. He settles us in the plaza to listen to the old men who remember what happened. It was only a few miles west of Nácori Chico on a ranch called Los Laureles by the local Mexicans that the little Apache girl was captured. The ranch was owned by two Americans, Jack Harris and Jack Rowe.

Aristeo García, the foreman of Los Laureles, was the Mexican cowboy who killed the woman with the Apache girl. He brought the girl to Jack Harris and his wife Dixie, who adopted her and, I am told, named her Carmen. She was about three years old. The details of her capture written down by my father correspond with the other versions told and retold to us today in Nácori Chico. They also say that García was trailing stolen livestock when he came upon the camp, and that he shot the woman because he was alone and afraid that he himself would be in danger of ambush if she got away to spread the alarm. In written and oral history there are different versions, different justifications, some designed to make a folk hero out of García. Context aside, about one thing there is no debate: he gunned the woman down in cold blood like an animal. As I will find, there is more to the story of the capture. There were multiple gunshots, more than one captive, and the camp was torched.

GRENVILLE'S DIARY

June 1936, Geronimo, Ariz.

Bill Curtis and his wife stopped in to see me here. They spoke of the little girl who was captured from the Apache, the one whose mother was shot, described above.

They said that she was now in California, with the man and his wife. They, wishing to bring her into the U.S. from Mexico, had some trouble and had to legally adopt her before they could bring her over at Naco. She is beginning to talk English now. When first caught she just cowered in the room at the ranch house and would not talk, eat, or do anything. She was dressed in tanned cowhide and they took these clothes from her, giving her cloth clothes.

When they later brought them out and showed them to her again, she was evidently pleased and glad to see the clothes again. They could do nothing with her, and so sent for Lupe, the Apache girl in Nácori Chico. She came and tried to talk in Apache to the little girl, but could get no response whatever, and the little girl seemed more afraid of her than the others. However, she finally started to eat a little and after a bit seemed to be getting used to things.

NEIL'S DIARY

Nácori Chico

In Nácori Chico the old men show us where the Harrises lived and where, for a year, they made a home for Carmen. The family and the Apache child are vividly remembered, but no one seems to have any idea what became of them once they left for California.

In fact, many years ago one person did look for her—the Norwegian anthropologist, Helge Ingstad, after a 1938 trip to the Sierra Madre in search of the Apaches. He heard about her in Nácori Chico, and after returning to the United States, tracked down the Harrises in California where he conducted the only known interview with Carmen:

> They called me Bui [Owl Eyes].[7] There were only women and children in the camp—four young women and three children besides me. Nana decided everything, and she was very strict. We lived in caves and small huts made of grass. We were always afraid

that someone would come, so we moved often from mountain to mountain. One time Nana took me on her horse and we rode through a dark forest where I was hit in the face by a branch. I began to cry and Nana hid me in the mountains for a whole day, until she finally came back to get me.

We visited Indians who lived elsewhere. Once in a while some men would visit us, and one of them had great feathers on his head.

There was often talk about a white man who lived with the others in the mountain.

We ate mescal and dried meat, sometimes grass. We didn't have much—some skins, a knife, nails, a cup, that's about it.

We made clothes from leather and also wore moccasins.

Nana had just sewn a nice new dress for me out of leather, but then I was captured.

We dared not make any noise, but sometimes a woman sang me to sleep.

It was definitely not my mother though. I don't think that I had either a mother or a father.

I was often afraid. Nana was so strict, and I wasn't allowed to do anything. Once a little child cried very loudly and she held its mouth so that it died.

Every evening we got down on our knees and reached our hands to the heavens. All was quiet, no one said anything. But I don't know what God we prayed to.[8] ✣

Nácori Chico

This is the only time that something said by one of these Apaches has survived for us to read. Carmen's words describe a life so marginal and isolated that it is beyond my comprehension. From that, she is snatched abruptly into the world of the people who have killed her family, where she must learn a new language, eat strange food, wear strange clothes. Somehow she adjusts, the scar tissue forms: after all, Apache children—and for that matter Mexican children—have been doing so for two and a half centuries of bitter warfare.

Ingstad visits Lupe as well, and she confirms that there were small isolated groups in the mountains that occasionally saw each other. Carmen's memory that men came sometimes, one with a feather headdress, is intriguing, and it brings to mind the distinctive Apache turkey-feather ceremonial headpieces that Grennie collected among the reservation Apaches. The isolation Carmen describes is not the Apache way, for they depend profoundly on one another's company; but perhaps there is a precarious safety in this apartness. Misfortune befalling one small group might leave others undiscovered and therefore unharmed.

While we were talking to the old men in the plaza at Nácori Chico, Jesús Fuentes and Rodolfo remembered something Jack Harris told Fuentes's father years ago: Carmen married a man that she had met in Los Angeles, who may have been an engineer and was of Apache descent. Then they moved to Texas. Carmen would be about sixty-five now and it's possible that she is still alive. It's an electrifying thought.

She would be that exquisitely unique being, a sole survivor; but she appears to have vanished without a trace, which may be exactly what she wants.

In a more compelling scenario than a life in Texas, I have also heard that she and her adoptive mother, Mrs. Harris, went to Italy to live with another Harris daughter. As time goes by and the idea of Carmen in Italy takes up residence in my mind, I have this powerful waking dream.

It is so real that I can hear the cicadas and smell the burnt, ancient Italian earth. I am sitting in a deeply shaded grape arbor with a flagstone floor. There is dense planting all around, a large stone house to the left. Beyond the arbor, the land drops steeply into a valley and I am looking out across it to the other side, almost blindingly bright in the sunlight. In the foreground, seen only in silhouette, is Carmen, and she is telling me the story of her life, and all I seem to be able to think as I absorb her story is that she has somehow triumphed. Not only did she survive capture and wrenching displacement, but the trajectory of her life has achieved escape velocity from Mexico and the American Southwest and has taken her from the New World to the Old: new language, new customs, food, friends, perhaps even a little local distinction as the most unusual new arrival in some ancient Italian hill town.

This so vivid it has the power of reality and I call the American Embassy in Rome thinking that U.S. citizens might be registered there. Not in the embassy, I am told, but in local consulates. There are only six, so I begin calling and am able to reach them all. Registration of American citizens in Italy is elective, I am cautioned. In any case, the information is confidential. Can I find out, at least, if there is a Harris registered? Okay, I'm told, but only a yes or no. A long wait. International telephone static. Anxiety that the line will go dead at any moment if no one is talking. I mutter to myself just to show some sign of life in the phone connection. The answer comes back. No. No Harris. Six times. Carmen is beginning to feel like my own long-lost relative. Even if I find her, how much, I wonder, would she welcome me, not to mention the prospect of reunion with American Apaches? It's not something that I can assume she would desire.

Just like Sam Kenoi and Sam Haouzous in the 1930s, the reservation Chiricahuas of today hope for reunion with their long-lost blood kin in Mexico. For the Apaches in Mexico, if any are left, it is more complicated. They may well want to stay lost, as perhaps Carmen does. There was at least one who did, a little boy who was captured in the same year as Carmen and who spent much of his life trying to keep his true identity a secret. ✣

1963, Tucson, Pascua, the Yaqui settlement

Pascua is a small Yaqui Indian settlement within the city limits of Tucson. Every spring these people perform an Easter ceremonial that lasts for four days, and I am here with friends and family. Someone introduces me to Tom Hinton, an anthropologist who spent several months in 1955 and 1956 scouring the Sierra Madre of Sonora for traces of these Apaches. All he found were stories, with one exception.

Tom met a young Apache man named Julio Medina, who was captured as a boy in early July 1932, three months after Carmen, under even more violent circumstances. When Tom met him, Julio was working as a clerk or bookkeeper in a large pharmacy in Hermosillo, completely assimilated twenty years after his capture. Hinton was introduced to him by a mutual acquaintance, and Julio agreed to talk to Tom under one condition: Tom was never to publicize his Apache identity or his whereabouts. One time the wrong people had discovered his true identity and it had ruined his life.

The boy had fallen in love with a Mexican girl whose family learned of his Apache blood. The family instantly forbade contact between Julio and their daughter. To be an Apache in Sonora is to be an untouchable, and Julio did not want anyone ever again to know who he was.

HINTON'S DIARY

Bacadéhuachi, June 17, 1955

A school teacher from Bacadéhuachi, Lorenzo Robles, said that Julio is an intimate friend of his.

He says that Julio likes to drink mescal. He said that on one occasion they were drinking and talking and Julio, who was a little drunk, said, "You all tell me how grateful I should be for being raised like a civilized Mexican. *Pues no me agradació nada.* [I can't feel grateful for anything.] If I had my way I would be up there in the sierra fighting right now." (Robles says there was real malice in his voice.) Robles told him he did not really think he would want to be up there with the broncos living like an animal. Julio answered that he would rather be there. "I have one great desire—that would be to put a knife between the ribs of all those who killed my mother and my people there in the sierra and I would start with Manuel Madrid."[9]

NEIL'S DIARY

Tucson

Julio was captured by Nácori Chico ranchers determined once and for all to wipe out the Apaches. They had set out to avenge a murder apparently committed by Apaches who, two weeks following Carmen's capture, caught a Mexican cowboy in the mountains and killed him with stones.[10]

On what is described as "an errand of extermination," in late June of 1932, a posse of fifteen is formed, made up of men from Nácori Chico and Bacadéhuachi and led by Ramón Hurtado and Manuel Madrid.[11] They gather at the ranch of one Isidro Mora, who lives well up in the mountains, east of Bacadéhuachi. Rodolfo Rascón says that some of the men were "really bad."

The party of men from the two towns, Nácori Chico and Bacadéhuachi, split into two groups and spend three days in heavy rain searching in vain for the Apaches. They then regroup and make plans to search alternate areas. Again they split up and spread out. On July 1 the group comes suddenly upon an Apache camp with eight people—mostly women and children. The Apaches try to flee, but it's too late and the Mexicans are everywhere. The camp is a killing ground. One woman, about forty years old, one about thirty, and a girl about twelve are killed outright. At least two, possibly three, get away. One is the mother of one of the children: she drops him and flees, uninjured. One is an old man, badly gut-shot. The Mexicans try to follow his trail of blood, but as he flees, the man pauses to scoop up the dust where his blood spills and throws it into the bushes. The Mexicans lose the trail, but they say they are sure he will not live long.

Some remember that there was another fugitive: a girl of about fourteen or fifteen who is also seriously wounded, but escapes into the mountains for twenty days, it is said, then comes to the town of Bavispe for help. They take her in, try to heal her, but she won't eat, and finally she dies.

They say in Nácori Chico that she was very beautiful, maybe even an American captive—a recollection that has surfaced several times in these interviews. It's a striking detail, the memory of her beauty, intriguing in its contrast with the blood lust. Is it remotely possible that time and folklore have for some Mexicans softened the collective recall of these Apaches, transforming at least one of them into an exotic Rima-like creature? Or perhaps she's appealing as a corrupted beauty, a truly fallen angel. This mystery woman may hardly be real at all, but she has become part of the story. At the site of the massacre the dust settles. Among the blood, the lifeless forms, the scattered possessions, and the ringing silence are three stunned and terrified Apache children: one boy, a three-year old girl, and her twin brother. Her hand was nearly severed by a bullet, and it has to be amputated in Nácori Chico.[12] Her twin brother's foot is hit, two toes lost. The twins are taken in by Ramón Hurtado and his family, and they are baptized Rosa and Geronimo Hurtado.[13] They do not survive the year. They contract dysentery or some other disease, and are unable to eat what the Mexicans feed them. According to one of the stories Tom Hinton gathers, the boy deliberately bites through one of his own veins, severing it and thereby bleeding to death.[14] When I consider this, I think what a deep river this stream of folklore is. This act of terrible determination by such a young child is equally compelling whether imagined or factual.

If true—and the child would have to have been older than three—what a ferocious imperative to be embedded in a being so young and so unformed. Or rather: the boy may have been young but was by no means unformed. I wonder, could this have been something he was trained to do: elect death before Mexican captivity? Or was it simply a last instinctive act, desperate and defiant, beyond reason or choice—an act of utter, final, abandoned hopelessness?

If not true, the story is an intriguing act of Mexican imagination, fully resonant with the Mexican view of Apache ferocity. Even if recognized as apocryphal, this story would transmit a fundamental, accepted truth in the villages of the Sierra Madre: that there is something in the Apache being that is simply beyond the experience of the Mexicans. But in their folklore, Mexicans find the humanity of the Apaches as compelling as their "savagery," as if, like the seventeenth-century Jesuit and Franciscan missionaries before them, they saw a human soul locked inside every Apache.

As other Apache captives before them, the twins are baptized at once. A lot has changed in a hundred years. In 1832 there was a bounty on Apaches in Mexico, and a child's scalp would have fetched $25 in Chihuahua City, his soul ignored. Now it goes to God. Taking in the children, caring for them, and bringing them to Christ after murdering their families, it must have been devoutly hoped, would gain some moral ground for the men who did it. When the children died, they were duly buried in the old cemetery of Nácori Chico—now gone, the graves lost.

Of the three children, the only survivor is Julio, perhaps two years old, unharmed. He is unable to walk because his body is deformed from being carried constantly on his mother's back.[15] Julio is taken in by the Manuel Madrid family of Nácori Chico. It is said that Doña Negra Madrid Moreno, aided by Lupe, prescribes an old folk remedy. It calls for placing Julio inside the stomach of a freshly killed cow and administering a potent regime of herbal medicines. Julio's deformity is apparently corrected. He somehow survives what the other two could not and begins life with the family of Manuel Madrid.[16] ✣

Cumpas, Sonora

After a few years with the Madrid family, Julio is taken in by another family, the Medinas of Cumpas. The people here summon fragmentary memories of Julio: he was different from Mexicans, his face was different, he had a large head, was very brown and he talked *muy mocho*—with a heavy accent.

When Tom Hinton met him Julio was a bookkeeper at a large pharmacy in Hermosillo. Now we hear that Julio was also a lawyer, a teacher, and a mechanic—reinvented in the Mexican rumor mill, taking on a new life as his story was told and retold. Julio, named for the month in which he was caught, seems more and more a phantom. He was real once, but has become a wisp of folklore. It's only because of Tom's brief encounter with Julio that I have more than a name—and it wasn't even his real name. Most people think he moved from Hermosillo to the vicinity of Obregón, a town two hundred miles farther south, perhaps, they say, to settle among the Yaqui Indians who have always lived there. Some say he became an alcoholic and, while drunk, fell into a canal and drowned. All passion spent. Some say he was a teacher—a very good one—and that while on a trip to Mexico City in 1962 with his students, there was a traffic accident in which Julio died.[17]

When I hear this story a kind of exhaustion sets in, knowing that part of this journey will never be finished. As each one of these lives snuffs out, something is lost forever, except for the stories. They develop a life of their own as they evolve into myth.

GRENVILLE'S DIARY

January 8, 1934

Last summer or spring, another little girl about eight years old was caught by two Mexicans. They kept her tied on the end of a rope that was fastened to a tree. A friend of mine down in Mexico offered a hundred pesos for her, but before he could get in touch with the Mexicans who had her, she had died. It is hard to imagine how wild these people are.[18]

NEIL'S DIARY

Bavispe

Bill Curtis and Art Schrader are the only Mexican contacts my father maintained, so I assume that one of them is the friend who tried to ransom the little girl. But who is the girl? In the Bavispe Valley I have heard of no captive girl taken in the spring or summer of 1933. Is this a lost story that somehow fell through the net of local folklore so that no one alive today knows anything of her? If so, it hints of the many secrets the sierra must hide: Apaches encountered, captured, killed, and never spoken of.

I know of only one possibility for tying this story to a known captive: the beautiful fifteen-year-old Apache girl of whom they spoke in Nácori Chico. She came to Bavispe, badly wounded and desperate for help. The people of Bavispe did what they could for her. She refused to eat and died from her wound. That was all that anyone knew in Nácori Chico.

However, when we ask about this story in the streets of Bavispe, the people tell us that there was an Apache girl, a much younger one, brought here uninjured in 1932. Then they say to go across the plaza and talk to Francisco Zozaya. We do, and soon we are joined by his elderly cousin, Emiglia Samaniego, and together they tell us the story of the little Apache girl and Billy Bye.

Bye was a Norwegian who came to Mexico via the United States. He lived alone with a pack of dogs in the Sierra Tasahuinora, a wild mountain range east of the village of Bavispe. He came often into the village of Bavispe to see pretty María Rascón who lived there, and to take her to the dances during festival days. Francisco says that he lived in a deep canyon where he had built a tree house in an immense cottonwood. He always slept in the tree house with one or two of his dogs while the rest slept on the ground below the tree. No one knew with certainty why he chose to live alone in the mountains or what he did there. He grew some crops, and the people of the village believed he had a gold mine. He is also remembered by people in Colonia Juárez, a town on the other side of the mountains. They say he was a trapper.

No one knows what he was—only that he spoke Spanish well. He lived so far back in the mountains and in such isolation that, in the places he inhabited, his was the only locally remembered human presence, so those places now bear his name. On the most detailed topographic maps of the area, places that once had Indian names are now called Arroyo Bill or Cerro Bill.

When the secretive gringo appeared in Bavispe one day in late July of 1932 with a nine-year-old captive Apache girl he had caught in the mountains, it caused a sensation. Bill had been hunting, as was his custom, with his dogs. They were following a scent and he heard them ahead, out of sight, barking the way they always did when they had something treed. He came upon them and found they had driven a small girl into the lower branches of a tree. He called them off, tied them up, and coaxed the girl out of the tree, though she could not understand anything he said. She was extremely thin. She wore a pair of buckskin moccasins and a leather skirt. She had been gathering plants to eat when the dogs came on her, and the plants were on the ground under the tree. There was no one else. She was alone and she was very thin, probably starving, so Bill decided to bring her into town. He named her for the month and place of her capture: Julia Tasahuinora.

The little Apache boy, Julio, had been captured some seventy miles to the south and about two weeks earlier. Maybe nine-year-old Julia was a survivor of the carnage at Julio's camp and had managed to cover those seventy Sierra Madre miles in a couple of weeks, but it's doubtful. Still, she was extremely malnourished when Bill Bye found her. Was that because she had been on the run, too pressed or frightened to find food? Was she part of a group of orphaned children, too inexperienced to forage for themselves? There is no way to know if she was completely alone or if she was part of a larger group. Francisco Zozaya believes that there was at the time a large group of Apaches in the Tasahuinora and that Julia was of this group and had been only temporarily separated from them when caught.

Throughout Julia's first night in town, she made owl calls and other kinds of animal cries. Emiglia closes her eyes and the summoned memory still has the power to jolt her. She talks through waves of emotion, remembering that Julia's hair was straight and long and shiny when it was later washed by one of the village women. Her arms were very thin and there was nothing she would eat. When we asked her what her face was like, Emiglia put her hands up to the side of her face and drew back on the corners of her eyes. Oriental eyes: the epicanthic fold, so common to Apaches, found also in the faces of Julio and Carmen.

Bill wanted to adopt Julia but had no way to tell her so. Emiglia remembers that Bill had devised a plan for communication, but she did not know what it was—only that he was going to take her somewhere else. Bill and Julia left town and she was never seen again in Bavispe. But in Mesa Blanca, a remote mountain settlement, we hear the rest of the story from a woman named Manuela Chafino whose grandfather was part of it himself. ✥

Mesa Blanca, Chihuahua

Manuela's story is more like an epic.

Bill Bye appears in Mesa Blanca in 1918. Almost as soon as he arrives, he sets up his outlying farm in the Tasahuinora, an area at the time said to be "full of Apaches." Growing corn is not the only thing he is doing there; he mines gold. In the village they say he could not possibly do this without the permission of the Apaches. In fact they are sure he is in collusion with them. He makes the ten-hour ride to his camp from Mesa Blanca once a month with two men who work on his cornfield while he goes to his gold mine, a couple of hours farther on. Each evening he rejoins the men at camp near the cornfield. He stays three days, comes back to the village with the two men, then rides for two days all the way to Douglas to deposit his gold, and rides all the way back to the village. It is a killer schedule, but they say he does it every month.

Manuela repeats the familiar details of the capture of *la apachita*, and she knows the name Bill gave her, as they do in Bavispe. What they do not know in Bavispe is what Bill did when he left with Julia Tasahuinora. But now we learn that he brought her here to Mesa Blanca because of Manuela's grandfather, Jesús Chafino. Jesús was Bill's plan for communicating with Julia, for it was common knowledge in Mesa Blanca that Jesús was an Apache himself. He was a captive, Manuela tells us, from the 1880s who had been adopted by a Mexican family in Chihuahua City.[19] In those days it was not all that unusual: Apaches were often taken captive. But for us this is astonishing news—the first time we have ever come across a known descendent of an Apache in Mexico. My eyes are riveted on her face, knowing now that she is at least one-quarter Apache. She is a handsome woman of sixty-five with a short, stylish haircut. Her skin is quite dark, but her features are not particularly Apachean. Trained in basic health care, she has also taught in the local elementary school. She is the most knowledgeable person about village history. She said that, like everyone else, Bill knew that Jesús Chafino was an Apache and Bill was hoping he could talk with Julia. He did, but Julia told him only a little. She said that there were others in her group (how many she would not say), and when she heard Bill Bye coming, she thought it might be some more of her own people, but then the dogs ran at her, and she was so afraid she went up the tree. By then the others she was with had run off.

She had been gathering wild onions of some kind and had on a buckskin dress and moccasins. She was so thin when Bill found her, he decided to bring her in to keep her from starving to death. When Bill brought her to Mesa Blanca, she would eat nothing but bone marrow, scooped from bones she would break with a rock. Bill wanted to adopt her, but the local authorities said that Chihuahua state law required that he bring the orphaned Indian into Casas Grandes.

Manuela tells us that Bill complied with the law and that Julia stayed in the house of the *presidente* of the town of Casas Grandes, where she was baptized Julia Tasahuinora while the disposition of her case was under consideration. Bill hoped for the best, but he was relieved of responsibility for Julia and returned to Mesa Blanca certain he would never see the girl again. ✤

Colonia Juárez

Herman Hatch and his brother Roy, both knowledgeable, elderly Mormons, are telling us what they remember about the little Apache girl:

When the authorities assumed jurisdiction over Julia's case, the Hatch brothers remember clearly that she was placed in the Casas Grandes jail. Word of her capture spread. The brothers wanted to go see her—along with most of the rest of the town—but their father would not permit it. He would not let them go to stare at her like a caged animal. They say she snarled at people, would scratch, bite if she could, and she would hide in the corner allowing no one to see her face. She would not or could not eat the food she was offered, and she did not live to leave the Casas Grandes jail. They say she was buried in the Casas Grandes cemetery; but no one knows where, and there is neither a death certificate nor a baptismal record to be found.

Word of her death filtered back to Bavispe, and a doctor there guessed that she might have been overcome with stress and malnourishment and died from heart failure. Emiglia and Francisco remember how insistent Bill was in wanting to take Julia with him to Colonia Juárez, and they say it was a tragic mistake: the people of the town should have kept him from doing that.

This story has more than one wrenching end. Bill went back to his home in Mesa Blanca. If he ever went back to the Tasahuinora, no one in the village remembers. Having captured an Apache child, he might not have been safe from their vengeance. He planted fields nearer town from then on and in April 1938 married a woman from Bacerac. The following November Bill was found face-down in his bean field, shot once in the back. At first we thought it might have been the Apaches, but Manuela says it was not—only that village people were afraid of Bill. Other villagers know more and tell us he was trying to start a farmer's cooperative that was going to be a challenge to whomever held the local monopoly on selling equipment and supplies to the farmers. Bill was a threat to be eliminated. At the end of Julia's ephemeral life is the realization that we may now know all we will ever know about the Sierra Madre Apache children: Julio, and Julia. But Carmen, taken by the Harrises to California, is unaccounted for, and I can't get her out of my mind.

Mr. and Mrs. Sherman Curley, White Mountain Apaches, Grennie's close friends.
(Courtesy Arizona State Museum, negative #18243)

(Left) The Apache girl Bui at the time of her capture in 1932. (Photographer unknown)

(Right, above) The Apache, Lupe, 1940; captured in 1912 in the Sierra Madre. (Photo courtesy of Nelda Villa.)

(Right, below) The Apache captive boy named Julio Medina, about 1950, Hermosillo, Sonora. (Courtesy of the Arizona State Museum, Dr. Thomas Hinton Papers)

Carmela

chapter three

We—that is, Barney Burns, my wife Margot, my son Seth, and his wife Kathy Doherty—have been camping in Mexico, exploring one of the abandoned Apache camps visited and surveyed by Grennie in 1931. All trace of Carmen has apparently vanished, but the possibility that she is still alive somewhere keeps us from giving up on her.

Barney is an archaeologist, historian, founder of Native Seed Search, and trader to the Tarahumara and the Mayo Indians of Chihuahua and Sinaloa. We always go on these Sierra Madre Apache trips together. His memory for the scraps of information about these people that we have gathered over the years is encyclopedic.

As with chapter 1, this chapter is an earlier and much longer version of a chapter in *The Apache Diaries.* It tells of the search for the last of the captive Apache children and of the remarkable surprise that waited for us at the end of a very long trail. ✣

NEIL'S DIARY

Agua Prieta, September 13, 1995

While back in the Sierra Madre in Chihuahua, Barney heard a scrap of information that has lodged in a crevice of his mind. It was told to us as only a vague memory, but it may be our last chance to pick up the trail of the captured Apache girl adopted by Jack and Dixie Harris. Someone who once knew Jack told us that he had sown some wild oats south of the border and that he had a son named Enrique Harris, who married a Mexican woman in Agua Prieta. This woman now owns and operates a cafe. We feel that if we can find her, we might be able to learn something about Carmen.

We are entering Agua Prieta, about to cross the border and return home. Barney is certain he once saw a sign over a cafe in Agua Prieta with the name Harris on it. Driving through that dusty town, Barney spots the Tienda Harris, swerves off the road, and parks among the bellowing 18-wheelers. When we go in and make inquiries, we are told that this Harris is not the right Harris, but there is another cafe nearer town operated by the granddaughter of a woman named Harris. That is our next stop. A young woman there says she thinks her grandmother might be the one we are looking for and tells us where to find her. She even has a telephone. We go there but there is no one home. We are all dubious anyway. She might have been married to Jack Harris's Mexican love child, but why would she ever have had any contact with his legitimate family in California with whom Carmen lived? It seems a wild goose chase, but it is the only lead we have, so over the next year and a half Barney tries in vain to make contact with Enrique's wife by visiting when in Agua Prieta and by telephoning her. She is never there, never answers the telephone or the door. ✣

Agua Prieta, January, 1997

It's been a long year and a half since we first heard about Enrique's wife but, passing through Agua Prieta once again, we try. There's no answer as Barney knocks on the door and waits. He comes back wondering where she could be—she's never home. Margot says the man in front of the house next door might know something about her. Barney comes back with the name of the woman's daughter and the location of the small convenience store where she works. Maybe the daughter will know something.

We find the Abarrotes Chihuahua a few blocks away: a bustling little neighborhood convenience and grocery store with customers coming and going constantly. The man behind the counter has no idea what we are talking about, but disappears and comes back in a moment with a perfectly round woman with a pleasant face. She knows exactly what we are talking about: *la apachita*. She is Jack Harris's great-granddaughter and insists on taking us at once to her mother. On the way she explains that her mother is always at home but never answers either the telephone or the door.

Not wanting to overwhelm Magdalena de Harris, we wait in the car while Barney and the daughter go in.

This part of Agua Prieta is grim: dust blows, stray dogs run free, abandoned cars on flat tires squat in the street and in dooryards. Big flatbed trucks piled high with wrecked cars go in and out of an immense junkyard at the end of the block. There is another part of this town that is very different—a place where there are large, elegant houses, some quite modern, and some big, handsome, old territorial houses. But Agua Prieta is mostly a border town with decay at the core and with ragged edges of abandoned shacks and failed enterprises that define a surrounding dead zone before the desert begins.

The dusty streets of Agua Prieta hold many of the secrets buried in this story. The people who populate and impel this epic all seem to have had a *pied-à-terre* in either Douglas or Agua Prieta. The bars and back alleys of these sister border towns are the places where much of the folklore was born as participants brought news from the hinterland to people who otherwise would never have known what happened. The story of the Sierra Madre Apache follows many arcs, and most of them are tangent to my own here at Agua Prieta.

Barney emerges with a notebook full of information about the Harris family and the descendents of Jack, though no direct leads on Carmen. One of the first things we find out is that Jack and Dixie named her Carmela, not Carmen or Carmina, as so many have said. Barney has learned that both Jack and Dixie have died, but that Dixie had a daughter, Anna, who used to live in Italy and France, and who was apparently married to a well-known Canadian artist living in Bloomington, Indiana. She remembered that they owned a house there at one time. She once received a post card from Anna when she was in France where, Magdalena remembers, Anna's husband's paintings were on exhibit. She remembers Anna's married name and that she used to live in Tujunga, California. She even has the street address. She also remembered that the Harrises had a Spanish-speaking neighbor who collaborated with Jack in the writing of articles for publication. Magdalena says that there are supposed to be a couple of unpublished book manuscripts by Jack—one, perhaps, in the Douglas library.

A search of the Douglas library turns up nothing. The only solid leads point us to Tujunga, where the anthropologist Helge Ingstad must have found the family and interviewed Carmela.

The information on Anna Harris is better than nothing, but the fact that there is no word of Carmela, except for her name, is discouraging. Carmela, according to all accounts, has married and could live anywhere—but probably not Italy, I am now thinking—and Anna, world traveler that she has become, has in all likelihood settled in Europe where she and her husband live the expatriate life, certainly out of touch with Carmela.

It also occurs to me that Carmela may not want to be found, especially by someone like me, wanting to haunt her all over again with the terror of her capture. Still, I decide to keep looking. There are public records: birth and death certificates, marriage licenses, property deeds, census records. There is the immense Mormon Family History archive. And it all takes a great deal of time.

I write to the Los Angeles County Marriage Bureau. A month later I receive a Photostat of the 1946 marriage license of one Carmen Harris, a waitress, to one Franklin Swope, a bartender, both of the white race. 1946. Carmen Harris and Franklin Swope. I've met them before, but in the cheap, seedy bars in the dark underbelly of the Los Angeles of Raymond Chandler, Ross MacDonald, and James Ellroy. I write to the LA Marriage Bureau again and ask if they can look further, because maybe they have sent me the first one they found and have looked no further.

In the meantime, I get a genealogical computer program that lists marriages and deaths. I find my grandfather and two uncles, but no Carmen, no Carmela, no Carmina, no Dixie, no Jack. I get a national telephone directory computer program, find myself, a few friends, but no Anna.

I find a Native American Bulletin Board Service on the World Wide Web and post a message for Carmen or Carmela Harris. I find a lot of people who believe they are descendants of Geronimo, but no Carmela.

The LA County Marriage Bureau writes back to say there was no Carmen, Carmela, or Carmina Harris married there between 1950 and 1959, so please try the State of California Bureau of Vital Statistics in Sacramento. I do. From Sacramento I get a reply saying I have made the request on the wrong form; proper form enclosed for resubmission.

Months go by. In the meantime I decide to write the Tujunga Chamber of Commerce (not being incorporated, the area does not have a City Hall) for the property deeds for the Harris address and abutters between 1933 and 1945. A city directory would even be better—one that gives names and occupations and lists everyone, even those without telephones. The Harrises wouldn't live there anymore, but maybe their neighbors would remember them, maybe the man who wrote with Jack would be there, or his children would be. I'll try anything, but I am running out of options.

It's a long shot, but I telephone Bloomington, Indiana next. At the registrar's office in the City Hall I reach a pleasant lady by the name of Tessa. In the California megalopolis all I got was an endless series of menus of touch-tone options. Never once was I able to speak to a live human being. Tessa is a live human being. I can even imagine what she looks like—the way you do with a character in a radio soap opera. She has personality, a future, a past. Most of all, she has patience and compassion.

I tell her my problem: is there any way to find if someone owned any property in Bloomington, or even in the surrounding county, during the 1960s? I told her the name of Anna's husband, that he was a painter, a schoolteacher, possibly a Canadian. Tessa said she would look, and I believed her.

Time goes by. Nearly a month later, I call Tessa back to see if she has had any luck. She had, she said, already gone through one set of county records—the huge books two feet by three feet and three inches thick in which deeds are recorded—and was about to start searching another set. She has found one deed with the right last name but the wrong first name. She will keep looking. It was taking a little longer than expected she said, and she was doing it in her spare time. Go Tessa, I thought.

Weeks go by. The Tujunga Chamber of Commerce writes to say there are no city directories of Tujunga, and for deeds I have to write to the City Hall of Los Angeles, as Tujunga is part of LA.

Then I get a letter from Tessa, in neat longhand on lined notebook paper, clipped to Photostats of two property deeds. She says, "These were all I was able to find. The first name of the husband is wrong, but these were the only deeds in the county records under that last name. It's an unusual last name, so there were only these deeds, both in the name of the same couple."

The man's first name is James, not Gregory as Magdalena said. His wife's name is Anna, middle initial H. My pulse goes up a tick or two. Anna H. is like a gleam in the bottom of a hole. These must be the right people. But the deeds are thirty years old, the trail still thirty years cold. I call Tessa, and faithfully, as if to answer my phone calls is her purpose in life, she is there.

How, I ask, can I find out more about these people James and Anna? Tessa refers me to the Indiana Room in the Bloomington Public Library, where I am to ask another helpful librarian named Reann for a city directory.

She does better than that. She recognizes the name, says James was a fairly well-known painter, and that she will send me some information about him. A few days go by and a letter arrives from the Bloomington Library with James's curriculum vitae. Last heard of, he was teaching art at Washington University in St. Louis in 1981. There is a grown son. James is an alumnus of Indiana University. The trail is now only sixteen years cold.

I'm on the phone to Reann, asking for more information about James, especially current whereabouts. I am exercised. Reann is very calm; she can tell I need steadying.

She says, "Try the alumni office at the university."

She gives me a name to ask for. Soon I am talking to a Hoosier lady who has, I can tell, enviable blood pressure. Is James in her records?

"Yes. May I ask why you would like to have his address?"

"Very well. . . ."

"There does not appear to be a privacy request on his record. Would you like his address at this time?"

"Would you like his telephone number as well?"

I feel a stab of momentary apprehension as I wonder what kind of reception I would get from James or Anna. Is she alive, still married?

"Yes, please. Address and phone number, please."

I have a house in South Royalton, Vermont—more or less the middle of the state. I've had it for thirty years.

James and Anna, the alumni office tells me, live in Newbury, Vermont, thirty miles away as the crow flies, over on the Connecticut River—been there for years. I've probably been by James's and Anna's house once or twice. In fatalistic Mexico, they might just nod gravely, understanding that such things are meant to be and are to be expected from time to time. The coincidence leaves me almost numb and breathless.

I stare at the phone, pick it up, and call. A soft, complex, cultivated voice answers.

"I'm not sure if I have the right number," I say. "I'm doing some historical research. Is your name Anna?"

A pause, almost like a held breath, as if she had been waiting a long time for this call. . . . "Yes. Ann actually."

I begin: my father . . . Mexico . . . Apaches. . . .

Her voice: "Oh yes, you mean my sister Carmela."

It pours out. Their childhood together, the years in California, the years in Italy, and finally Carmela's death there in 1976, the same year Barney Burns, Tom Naylor, Misse Smith and I found the Apache camp in the Chita Huecas.

I tell Ann about my "waking dream," talking with Carmela in Italy. Under a grape arbor, I say. . . .

"Yes, says Ann, it was a pergola covered with clematis and wisteria."

"It was very shady."

"Yes."

"We could look out across a valley where the sun on the hills was very bright."

"Yes. It was the other side of the valley of the Upper Tiber River."

"There was a cool, comfortable stone house nearby."

"Yes. Our old farmhouse. I am so moved by this. . . . This is so moving. . . . When she died it was horrible."

"There's so much. Can I come and talk with you about Carmela? Can Margot come? Can Seth and Kathy come? They are all part of this."

"Yes. Yes, of course." ✜

Newbury, Vermont

Ann meets us gravely at the door of her big, boxy colonial house in the country outside the village of Newbury. James is nowhere to be seen, but he's upstairs working. She did not know what to expect any more than we. She is precise and scholarly. She is a professional translator of novels and poetry, able to go back and forth between English, Italian, and French. I try to put her at ease by staying away from Carmela and the Harris family for a short while. I tell her all about my father and his diary. I give her two of his books. I let her buy time so she can proceed at her own pace.

"I was dreading this," says Ann, surrounded by family photographs and papers. "Mother kept all this stuff with her in Italy and then in the nursing home after that. I haven't looked at any of this since Mother died. I was afraid it would remind me of those awful years."

She is busy with the photographs, going through them too fast for us to keep up. The business of recalling Carmela is laden with emotional burden because it also recalls the slow disintegration of Dixie Harris in a St. Louis nursing home.

Ann crosses some inner threshold and begins traveling back through time, hovering first over one picture then another, encountering faces, voices, smells, and banished memories for the first time in years. Mama, Dixie, slender, almost frail in jodhpurs and boots under a palm tree.

"She was part Cherokee and part Mandan, you know."

Papa, Jack. He's roguish, solid, capable looking. An adventurer.

"That's him in his Jack Nicholson pose. He had this different life south of the border. Very macho. Did what he wanted to. Had all these rough friends—Mexicans, Americans, miners, soldiers, pilots, all kinds. Fought alongside Yaquis in the Mexican Revolution. He was a machine gunner. He was a Hollywood stunt man. That's how they met. Mama was working for Selznick in Hollywood.

"Oh, here's Carmela. Her high school graduation picture. The fountain at our house, at the beach. Oh. And these are pictures she made living in Italy. She liked to take pictures of things that didn't look like what they really were.

"There's one album that's gone—the one you'd want the most to see. Oh, the pictures in it. I don't know who took them. The camp after Carmela was caught—burnt houses, a dead woman, things scattered everywhere. Carmy never forgot the gunshots and the fire. She remembered the fire, couldn't forget it. It was her grandmother, the dead woman was, she thought. But she didn't really know who it was. It was who took care of her."

Pictures taken in an Apache camp after an attack! I never dreamed such pictures might exist. There's not a chance, Ann says, of finding them. The album disappeared in the Saint Louis nursing home. There was a man there, another patient, who stole things from Dixie, Ann found out later. He might have taken it. Who knows? It's gone now.

Another near miss, I think, like my father's almost going to Nácori Chico in 1930 or 1931; almost meeting Lupe and Fimbres; almost seeing, photographing, drawing the artifacts from Apache Juan's camp; almost meeting that little Mexican boy from Pacheco captured by the Apaches—almost so many things.

Ann closes her eyes and summons up the memory of the photographs.

"I see burned things. There is a brush hut, sort of a lean-to that is mostly burned, but there is enough left to see how it was done. Poles leaning together, a lean-to covered with branches, but all burnt. The wood is charred. There are trees in the background. The ground is rough. There's a body. Carmy's grandmother, I guess. She's lying on the ground in a fetal position, like this."

Ann lowers her head and tilts it slightly, brings her hands up to one side of her face. The pose lasts only a moment, but she looks peaceful, asleep. It's a subtle and graceful mime and somehow utterly convincing in its evocation of the dead woman. Like all children, Ann once pored over the old family albums, and then she would come to the Apache camp massacre photos, amid other photos of old friends, new automobiles, faithful horses and dogs, beloved homes; and when she came to those, they drew her in, fascinated, unable to connect this scene with her own life experience, though knowing at the same time that this scene was one of the pivotal events in her own life. From this scene came her sister, Carmela.

Eyes still closed, Ann talks, uncoiling slowly from the fetal position, as if in slow motion.

"The old woman has long, straight hair, almost completely black. She's lying down, so it's all to one side. She's wearing something dark. A dark dress or something. Her face is old. It's all lined and old-looking. There are things scattered on the ground—maybe artifacts, but I can't tell. It was my mother's most precious album. I don't know how it could have been lost."

"What happened then?" I ask. "How did Carmela come from that burnt-out camp into your family?"

Ann tells us the whole story as she heard it from her mother and her grandmother.

"Jack was away, leaving Dixie alone in the village of Nácori Chico. There were several men in on the attack and they had liquor. After killing the old woman and burning the camp, they came back to town, drunk, with three children."

"This," I say, "is the first I have heard of other children being taken along with Carmela."

"Oh yes. There were three."

Dixie was convinced, rightly or wrongly, that the children were in grave danger. She thought the men might actually kill them—and these were men she knew. Dixie, who was a seemingly demure Southern belle from West Virginia, took over. When the raiding party came into town with the children, Dixie apparently faced them down in the plaza.

She was determined and she commanded a certain unassailable respect. People often came to her with an illness, thinking she might have some medicine. She told the men that she was going to take charge of the children. They needed medical attention. She and her housemaid Chu carried and bustled them into the house and barred the door. Dixie armed herself with a loaded rifle and made sure the men knew she had a weapon.

Now what? She couldn't keep the children like this indefinitely. Jack was not due to return for several days.

There was another American in town with a truck. She got a message to him and he came to her house. She convinced him that he must hide two of the children on his truck and drive them to Hermosillo, the state capital. Once there, he must take them to a convent whose name she gave him. He was to tell the nuns who the children were and that they were the children's last hope, that the sisters would be doing God's work if they saved these orphans.

While trying to figure out how to protect the children moment by moment, Dixie had also been soul searching. Before summoning the man with the truck, she had reached a momentous decision. The third little girl was older than the others, and her fear and hostility tore at Dixie's emotions. Dixie and Jack had been married several years and were childless, and Dixie thought there was something wrong with her—that she was unable to bear children. So she decided to adopt this terrified Apache waif.

Dixie summoned a local official, very likely Dolores Fuentes, the town mayor, dictated a statement, and had him sign it. The statement said that Dixie and her husband Jack had legally adopted the Apache orphan. She hoped it would give to her determined act of motherhood a certain official seal of approval and that it would be good enough to get her across the border when the time came to leave Mexico. Once in the United States, they could disappear.

Dixie and Jack named her Carmela and did their best. Ann does not remember hearing much about the first year. Bill Curtis wrote to my father that Carmela just cowered in the corner of the house at first, refusing to do anything. She was given new clothes and her old Apache clothes were taken away. Lupe came and tried to speak to the girl in Apache, but Lupe frightened her more than anyone else. After a while Dixie gave Carmela her Apache clothes back, and that made her feel better.

Saving Carmela from death was as powerful an experience for Dixie as giving birth. She loved Carmela fiercely and it brought about a sea change in Dixie. Within the year she was pregnant. Dixie and Jack and Carmela left Mexico so that Ann could be born in the Douglas hospital.

They moved back to California where Carmela and Ann grew up together in a magical, fanciful, protective Italianate mini-palazzo in a Los Angeles suburb. Dixie and Jack had to save Carmela's life once again in California. She had contracted polio in Nácori Chico. There was no cure, but with care she recovered with only a slight limp. She was tiny all her life—hardly over five feet tall and one hundred pounds.

Ann remembers that Carmela was the only Indian kid in their white-bread school, so when the other kids tamed the West in make-believe, Carmela was always on the losing side. Ironically, only she knew what it was really like.

For a long period Ann and Carmela were taught at home, so that they never had to leave their house to go to school. Ann says that Carmela was a sickly child and that the California public school system provided teachers at home for housebound children. When Carmela emerged and went back to school, she made lasting friends. One of them was Italian and Carmela was devoted to her, and through this good friend she saw the contours of another country, another culture, another realm.

Photographs. . . . Carmela, twelve, posed in the garden at home by an ornate fountain, in stylish slacks and blouse, wavy, sophisticated hairdo, her concentrated gaze skewering the camera. Carmela, fifteen, perched on the railing of a beach house in bobby socks and skirt—a regular teenager. Carmela, eighteen, her beautiful, exquisitely Apache face grave, deadpan, betraying nothing, but there's no repose there.

While she talked or listened, Ann says, she had a way of looking at you with such intensity that it was as if the rest of the world did not exist. It was flattering but it could also be unsettling if you did not know her. And laughter. She had an infectious laugh with a life of its own that could spread through a group of people, bringing them all to helplessness. And suspicion. She trusted hardly a soul, did not encourage boys, thought romance might be fun in the abstract, but did not like to be touched. She was most devoted to Dixie and lived with her always.

Jack Harris would come and go, living in Mexico for long periods while on business or just living life in the raw. Dixie always took him

(Upper left) Carmela in about 1941, Tujunga, California. (Courtesy of Ann McGarrell)

(Middle left) Carmela's high school graduation picture, about 1948, Tujunga, California. (Courtesy of Ann McGarrell)

(Lower left) Carmela and Ann Harris, California, about 1935. (Courtesy of Ann McGarrell)

(Backgound) The Harris house, Tujunga, California. Ann and her grandmother, Lola Semple, seated, the window of Carmela's bedroom above. 1942. (Courtesy of Ann McGarrell)

back and Ann never lost her fascination with him. She visited him in Mexico more than once. He took her back to Nácori Chico, where she met Jack's old friends and her Mexican half-brother Enrique, who was "incredibly handsome." Ann remembers that in Sonora, every once in a while, an old Yaqui Indian would come up to Jack in the street, take his hand and, remembering him as Obregón's machine gunner, say, "*Buenos días, mí coronel. Yo estuve con Usted en la guerra.*"

I tell Ann that in Nácori Chico no one knew where Carmela was—or rather, that they were telling us conflicting stories of her marriage and her home.

Ann says, "In Nácori Chico they knew perfectly well where we lived. Ramón Hurtado and the Gabilondos and others came to visit us in Tujunga. Carmela was an illegal alien and there could have been serious trouble—physically as well as emotionally—if she were discovered."

Ann thinks these conflicting stories we heard might have been red herrings drawn across Carmela's trail to confuse people. Ingstad found her—almost certainly with help from people in Mexico—but he was careful not to say where she lived.

I tell Ann the story of how I found her.

But for a lucky break in the dust of Agua Prieta, and a few more along the way in Bloomington, I might never have found you.

"I'm hard to find," deadpans Ann.

On the other hand, I might well have met her eventually in Vermont; we have several friends in common it turns out, and it's easy to imagine discovering each other in some casual, startling way. It's equally easy to imagine a near miss like two streaking asteroids closing on each other, passing, then rushing apart never to meet.

Surrounding Carmela were all these walls that insulated her from the rest of the world. To begin with, in a sense, she didn't exist officially. She was schooled at home in a magical house enclosed by big trees; the code of silence in Nácori Chico among the Harris's friends made it almost impossible to find her in later years. On the other hand, Jack and Dixie made no secret among their own friends in California of Carmela's provenance. Ann remembers overhearing with Carmela her parents talking about the massacre, the capture, and the rescue. As frightening as it was for Carmela to hear the recitation of the events, the more profound effect was that it reminded her that she might never be able to put that massacre behind her. The memory of the sudden, shattering terror, the shots, and the fire was indelible. When her world broke apart, it had marked her forever, just as different massacres had marked the other survivors, Lupe, Julia and Julio.

Carmela remembered a few things, says Ann, from the old days, and she used to tell Ann about them. Her Apache name was Bui, and she remembered a few Apache words, written down and preserved by Dixie. The old lady who took care of her used to take her out at night when it was clear and they could see the stars, and the old lady would tell Bui stories about the stars.

When Bui was caught she was wearing a tanned leather skirt and moccasins, and she had a little bag around her neck in which there was a deck of leather cards, "like tarot cards," says Ann.[20] A string of small wooden beads and a drum were also recovered from the campsite. Jack gave the drum to a friend in California. The other things supposedly were all given to the Southwest Museum in Los Angeles, but no record of them can be found there.

Dixie saw to it that the cards made a prominent, if anonymous, cameo appearance in a Hollywood film. While she was head of research in David O. Selznick's office, she had the cards used in the opening credits of John Ford's *The Searchers.* (I recently watched *The Searchers,* and at least in the version I saw, there were no cards.) If director John Ford had known the story behind the cards, would he, I wonder, have made another movie casting John Wayne as Jack Harris in Mexico, rescuing an orphaned Apache girl, then dealing rough justice to Mexican bandits, and finally meeting his match in fiery, willful, darkly beautiful Lupe, the other Apache captive in Nácori Chico?

Ann got married and, with her husband, lived for long periods of time in France and Italy. Carmela went to college and became a nurse, but she never left Dixie and her magical childhood home in Tujunga. Savvy, smart Dixie continued to work in the industry in Hollywood, supporting the family while Jack tried to make his fortune, largely in mining, staying for longer and longer periods in Mexico—both in Mexico City and in Hermosillo.

For about twenty quiet years Carmela lived this way, working as a nurse. From time to time she had made contact with Native American groups, especially while in school, where she vividly remembered a Mrs. Standing Bull. But she apparently was hesitant to do more. She could have sought out some way to contact Apaches on American reservations, but she didn't.

Jack and Dixie saw themselves as custodians of her Apache identity, even as she was trying to put it behind her and create a new one. Jack always insisted that all the Apache artifacts from Mexico be kept together. He always told Carmela that if she ever wanted to return to Mexico to try and contact her people, he would help her. As far as he knew, Carmela, Julio, Lupe, and the few things they had brought out of Mexico were all that remained of her people. Ann vividly remembers the grim prospects envisioned by Jack for the Sierra Madre Apaches.

"Extermination," Jack said.

Extermination was what the Nácori Chiqueños were bent on.

Carmela was afraid of Mexicans all her life. She saw the Hispanics in Los Angeles as The Enemy. Even though the Harrises had friendly visits from the people of Nácori Chico, a return to Mexico must have been an unsettling prospect. And what could she have expected from any Apaches hiding in the mountains, even if contact could be made? The same thing that awaited Lupe if she had ever tried to rejoin her people—certain death?

Ann says that Carmela never knew what she was.

"I'm not Indian," she would say. "I'm not American. I'm not Mexican. Maybe I'm all of them."

Carmela never knew who she was or where she belonged, except perhaps with Dixie, at least until the day of her terrible accident. That changed everything.

It was while lighting a gas oven at home with a match. A wall of flame enveloped her: Carmela's worst nightmare. Months of painful skin grafts to her shoulders and chest left her weakened and unable to continue nursing. At the same time Dixie decided it was time to retire from the movie business. It was 1972. Jack had died ten years earlier, and there was no reason not to take Carmela and move to Italy to join Ann and her family.

So the Apache orphan, born in the Sierra Madre wilderness, captured by the assassins of her family, and by this time the sole survivor of her small band of people, emigrated to Perugia, where she lived in a stone farmhouse and watched the Umbrian countryside bake in the sun from the shade of her wisteria- and clematis-covered pergola.

She adjusted to this final and most dramatic displacement in her life with equanimity. No, it was more than that. It brought her inner peace. She used to say that she was meant to come to Italy, that it was foreordained. In a way being in Italy surprised her not at all. She got a

Eurail pass and saw Europe. She took up photography, watched the landscapes and the ancient cities, and made pictures of the things she saw in them.

And finally she and Dixie moved to a beautiful apartment in Rome, where she walked the streets, loving the sense of history. She was in her mid-forties, having an adventure, in a sense home at last, when she died quite suddenly. An accident. She simply fainted in the house one day, fell, and struck her head a fatal blow. It was over in a second.

"I think," says Ann, "that my mother took Carmela's death harder than any other death: harder than her own mother's, harder than Papa's."

Ann talks through welling tears.

"She was her daughter. She had saved her life, she had brought her all this way, against all odds. Carmy was still young. Her life was incomplete. There could have been so much more."

Was she really the last one? There were fewer and fewer, finally just children and women, then none, then persistent rumors and an upwelling of myths-in-the-making. In the 1930s my father was by no means the only one yearning to confront the mystery.

Jan and Grennie

chapter four

"Jan and Grennie" was written as a single, very long chapter in an early draft of *The Apache Diaries.* In the published version of that book, I used only the first half. In this, the original version, "Jan and Grennie" begins immediately following the end of the second and last of Grennie's Mexico diaries. His diary ends abruptly on November 9, 1931, with the terse postscript, "Leave for Tucson and home now by way of San Carlos. This ends the second trip to Mexico and the Sierra Madre country."

At the end of Grennie's adventure in Mexico, many questions are left unanswered. One, of course, is the question partially answered in the preceding two chapters. Those two chapters form a single continuous narrative, and since they flow directly from the quest begun by Grennie's Sierra Madre diary, it seemed best to lead off this series of essays with them and tell the stories of the captive children before moving on.

The other unanswered question in my mind as I finish reading the Sierra Madre diary and recreating Grennie's Sierra Madre adventure is the question of who Grenville Goodwin really was. "Jan and Grennie" and all of what follows focus directly on Grennie, his work at San Carlos, and my pursuit of the answer to this question.

"Jan and Grennie" is at one level a love story: it is about my parents. The chapter begins with a meditation on my father's experience in Mexico and on my efforts to come to know him by reliving some of that experience. The conclusion I reach is that, as important as that experience has been, I have gotten as close to Grennie through the Sierra Madre Apaches as I will ever get. To go any further, I must turn to my mother and invite her to teach me about him so that I can see him through her eyes and see into their very private world and the experiences they shared in their brief three and a half years of marriage.

Jan and Grenville Goodwin, Santa Fe, 1938.

NEIL'S DIARY

1962, Mount Kisco, New York

I finish the diary and I look up, look around. It's the same room, it's still raining, still November, and only a few hours have passed, but I feel as if I have returned from a distant place. And I went there with my father.

No one's here. Not my father, not the Apaches. Just the view out the window. The story might as well have ended in mid-sentence. It's almost like a death, where nothing happens next. But it's not a death. Plenty happens next; it's just that telling the rest of the story is more or less up to me.

In the late fall of 1931, at the somewhat tender and normally impulsive age of twenty-three and a half, my father decides not to return to Mexico for a third, fourth, or fifth trip of adventure with Bill Curtis—or on his own for that matter. Instead he returns to his rented room over the gas station run by Mr. and Mrs. Knowles just off the reservation at the settlement of Geronimo. He begins what will become five years of fieldwork on the reservation. He spends his days visiting with Apache friends at the nearest reservation community of Bylas, asking them the Apache words for the objects, the ideas, and the social fabric that make up their world—asking how they do things, listening to people talk, making more friends, building trust. And this is how he spends his time: days at Bylas and nights in Geronimo.

Apaches have a way of giving people descriptive nicknames. While at San Carlos in late 1996, I spoke to one lady who had heard of my father, and she said, "Oh, yes, there was this Apache, Neil Buck, who used to hang around with this tall white guy. He had a name. It was 'White Man Talks.'" Then she said she knew an Apache named Grenville Wright, who told her there was a white man he used to call grandfather. This is the son of Mrs. Jewett Wright, who wrote a letter to my father in 1937 saying he was like her brother.[21]

My mother often said that my father felt that there was not enough for him to learn at the university for him to spend much time there. So, except for a few courses he took at the University of Arizona, he essentially went from high school to Indian country, and that was his higher education. While conducting fieldwork at San Carlos and Fort Apache, he accumulated a library of the seminal anthropology texts so that he could read the masters and learn craft, theory, and context. He developed professional connections with colleagues and conducted his research under a loose affiliation with the University of Arizona.

My mother also said that he was ambitious.

Ambition. Of course.

When I heard that, certain things fell into place. Love of learning is one thing, but ambition—that's hunger. That's a fire in the belly. My father wanted to make his mark. He started with the Navajos, but the field was crowded. The Western Apaches were *terra incognita*. No one really knew anything about them. After the U.S. Army gave up control of the Apache reservations shortly after the turn of the century, the Apaches were virtually ignored by the government. There was little or no attempt on the part of the BIA to assist the Apaches in developing the vast natural resources of the San Carlos and Fort Apache reservations. Employment was for the most part off-reservation, through big cattle ranches that leased land on the reservations, or by massive public works projects, such as dam and railroad building.

The reservation was economically depressed, prospects were not encouraging in the late 1920s, and outsiders would not have been especially welcome. But an enterprising individual, an individual who knew what he wanted, an individual who knew his destiny, an individual whose identity was not only extremely portable, but in some important ways unformed—such an individual might be able to enter the Apache circle if he had the patience—and the ambition.

As much as my father was drawn to the drama and the romance of the Sierra Madre Apaches, he also knew it could be a wild goose chase—that these people could not be his life's work. Once he began at San Carlos and Fort Apache, he was faced with an overwhelming amount of work, trying to record everything that a handful of very old Apaches knew while they still lived and had the energy and the recall. Time was running out, for they were the only ones who carried the old, pre-reservation culture. They were his library. They were also his future.

As he and the Apaches came to know each other, the professional line blurred, without ever quite disappearing, while trust built over the years. Trust may have been another reason to put the Sierra Madre Apaches on the back burner. Except for stories about the Apache Kid's raiding forays for women at San Carlos and Fort Apache, my father wrote nothing about people from San Carlos going to Mexico, though the outbreaks of the 1890s had been only forty years earlier.[22] There must have been many people on the reservation with personal knowledge of those who left in the '90s, or even later, and of whether they ever came back.

It is difficult to read Grennie's description of the Espuelas camp and not theorize about the possibility of a smuggling operation in jerked meat and livestock running between San Carlos and Mexico as late as the mid-1920s.[23] If that were the case, it is unlikely that anyone at San Carlos would tell my father anything about it. It is unlikely that he would even ask. Anyone involved would be an outlaw in two countries. On the other hand, he might well have heard things about such escapades without ever writing them down. To write them down would be to risk eventual, accidental disclosure and loss of trust—the only coin he had.

The whole subject might well have been a most delicate one—even taboo. If reservation Apaches were slipping across into Mexico for stolen livestock and meat, they would have attained great status among their people and would have been carefully protected by kin and by friends. They would also have been vulnerable to gossip and loose talk. For my father to pursue the subject would have been seen as prying. So, in tight control of what must have been a burning curiosity, he waited until the stories came to him, writing the safe ones down, such as the ones about the Kid, but keeping the secrets to himself, if they were told.

My father's mother once said that his trips to the Sierra Madre were the most exciting things he had ever done. I think that at some point he realized this too. I think he was also deeply moved personally and emotionally by the story. Among the specific instructions in my father's will regarding the bequest of possessions and collections, two things stand out vividly in my mind.

The first has to do with one of his Western Apache friends. He wrote: "To Charley Sago, an Apache Indian living at Bylas, Arizona, three hundred dollars because of the promise I once made him near Soldier's Hole. This is to take effect only if I do not get him to Washington before I die." He was always doing things like that—taking the Apaches on trips, bringing special gifts.

The other provision was that among all his field notes, manuscripts, and ethnographic collections, the Sierra Madre diary alone was to remain always in possession of his family, never to be given to an archive or museum. It was his way of saying that it was a treasured experience—perhaps unlike any other in his life—as it has been in mine.

I have gone as far as I can trying to get to my father through the Sierra Madre Apaches, but it's not enough. As much as he wrote, and as much as can be read between his lines, I feel that for him, writing was only the barest kind of notation for recording the literal word.

His writing betrays almost nothing of his interior life or even what interest he had in his own interior landscape. My mother is a different story. Hers was an examined life. For her, writing per se was a way of self-expression, self-exploration. She could barely contain her feelings.

Only my mother can take me further, and she's not here. I would ask her such simple questions and I would say, "Just imagine him and tell me what you see."

She wrote me once that, when we lived at the ranch, she used to talk about him to me all the time, to keep his image strong.

A LETTER TO MY MOTHER

I remember the things you said, but we need to go over it again. There is so much I missed, so much you know and never told me. But you kept all these papers and now I know why:

Letters from my father to you.

Letters from the Apaches to my father.

Biographical chronologies of my father written by my grandmother and by you.

Your journal for 1935 and 1936.

Your father's diaries.

Photograph albums from the 1930s and 1940s.

I have read all of these many times before, except for your journal. I read the journal mostly to find factual information: places and dates I can fit into a detailed chronology of my father's life, thinking I knew all I needed to know about you. I should have known better. You never cease to affect and touch me with the turmoil of your passionate inner life and the way it is poured out in these pages.

You are nearly foundering in a sea of self-doubt. You had always counted on finding your way through life with your art, but you seem to have lost something. You don't feel you can do it anymore and are desperately discouraged. I can turn to almost any page and find it full of anguish. In the fall of 1935 you went alone to Bermuda for several months to draw and paint and get away from the confining life of Boston, hoping for . . . I don't know what.

Jan's Diary, September 20, 1935

> One must continually carve one's way, carve out the shape of life from the blank rock.
>
> Will the time ever come when I can say to myself—At last!
>
> The din of the toads at night. The heaviness of the night—the stickiness. The head is heavy and dull—one cannot think—to move is an effort . . . The only desire is to sleep, sleep, sleep. The sky piles with hot clouds. Where is the relief? . . .
>
> What is the way out of the tangle of my thwarted life?
>
> With such an aching I remember Sark. What if I had stayed?

SARK

In 1933, you had gone alone to Sark, an island in the English Channel, to paint and draw. There you spent the happiest half-year of your life, working hard and well, falling in with an amusing, eccentric bunch of kindred-spirited English artists—and falling in love, I am quite sure—or you were at least fallen in love with.

The Artists

In cormorant dark
We twisted many keys
Down corridors of potted trees
And hanging grapes,
Trying various entrances and escapes.

Eyes seeing as jewels see,
With facets' flash,
An instant's multiplicity.
Hands poised to execute, excel
With diamond precision,
Tendon and bone the strongest
When most delicate,
Defined with line and curve
The pride of rock,
The baleful, earthen face.

Having breathed deeply of too keen an air
We journeyed back to family parlors
Of gas-blue flames in suffocating rows.
A hand bewildered, faltering with a cup
To brush away a crumb,
As grey, mole-faces peered from threadbare hair,
Not knowing from what climates we have come.

Whenever I think of the fact of your marriage to Grennie and my birth, it is as easy as it is foolish to think of it all as preordained: "I am, therefore I was meant to be." But, of course, I was anything but. Yours and Grennie's paths forked again and again after they first crossed at his brother's wedding in 1929.

You must miss Sark and the good times you had there. I believe you had more fun in those months than you had ever had. You write in your journal after being away from Sark for two years: "And when there are only three or four people in the whole world that matter to one, why does one go away from them?"

SEEING GRENNIE, 1932

I am sure you are referring to your friends in Sark and are without any understanding of why your life is turning out the way it is. I somehow doubt if you also mean Grennie. You may well be in touch with him, though there's no mention of it in your journal.

In journal passages from July 5–9, 1934, six months after returning from Sark, you write vividly of a trip on a three-masted coal schooner you took with your mother and younger sister up the coast of Maine from Bar Harbor to Grand Manan Island. Buried in the first day's entry is this tiny fragment: "On we went with a perfect breeze right behind us—watched the cliffs of Bar Harbor slipping by—tried to find the place G. and I were, but couldn't."

The only reason I am sure that by "G." you mean Grennie is that in a letter he wrote to you in early 1936, he refers to an island in Maine where you went together. It was probably Mount Desert Island, just off Bar Harbor. You give no hint of the way in which you remember him, but just the act of looking for the place where you met on that rocky shore must have brought the scene to mind. Was that rendezvous as disquieting and exhilarating as your first meeting in 1929 at Grennie's brother's wedding? Grennie had come back East briefly three years after that wedding. He remembered you and had gone to a good deal of trouble to locate you in Boston or Maine and then physically to reach you. He came over from Cornish, New Hampshire. Even today there is no easy way from Cornish to Bar Harbor. For three years he had been on your mind, and you on his, albeit out of sight.

In late 1935 you barely knew each other and both had other things, other people in the forefront of your minds. You told me that you believed during these years of intensive work on the reservation there might have been an Apache woman in Grennie's life. That road not taken fascinates me just as yours in Sark during 1933 does. Of course, either one of those roads would have meant that I would never have happened.

SEEING GRENNIE, 1936

You are back in Boston by early February 1936, and you have an apartment at 100 Charles Street in Boston. You write: "The new room—100 Charles. Gulls and pigeons—the frozen river—painting again—settled with all my things around—a lovely room."

Then, with no warning that he is expected, or that you have been corresponding:

> Grennie here—Feb. 20–21.
> Things seen, things alive—
> Sitting over the harbor—
> The black-tipped gulls—the green and red and black tugs—
> Two hours under yellow blanket
>
> G. was delighted with everything I saw and felt intensely. We sat and talked there for hours—and walked along—shapes of black boats heaving—cracked ice under the piers—like a creature breathing—the ice caked posts—like white columns—shapes of warehouses—people in the shops and bars.
>
> A talk in the Ritz bar—a talk at lunch—dinner at the Russian Bear—walking back—skaters in the garden—under the lighted city—the cutting of skates in the cold. Dinner at South Sta. talking and talking as if we had known each other forever. Time flew—talking and reading and looking at pictures in studio.

Van Gogh exhibition—yes—but—Egyptian lady in granite. We were enthralled.

After Grennie leaves: "Thrilling with painting as never have before . . . Our purpose is the mold into which we pour our lives."

Then, a poem:

What will become of my lovely toys—
Most lovely was the moon,
And flowers strewn upon the snow,
And all my stars, the tales of pale folk—
Now with the sun, the fiery axle of my wheeling days?

I think you were both lonely—you from work, discouragement, and ragged partings. Grennie from his own self-sufficiency and the recurring culture shock each time he crossed the Apache reservation boundary. The Apache world was the one he knew best, but because of his professional discipline, knew he could not be of it, could not really join it. But I think he felt awkward, ill at ease, almost alien in the white world.

You both must have been astonished that you were capable of touching and of being touched so deeply. You begin to correspond and within a month make plans for an extended summer holiday together in the East.

LETTERS FROM BYLAS

March 28, 1936, Bylas, Arizona

Dear Jan,

It's about half moon tonight, with a clear dark blue sky and lots of stars. In the west a polar blue with just a little rim of yellow on the horizon where the sun went down. I wish you were here. . . . I wonder where you are and what you are doing now. It's just a little over a month since we saw each other now. The possibilities of this summer are always in my mind. Don't forget, it stands as far as I am concerned.

I don't know what became of the letters you wrote to him, but you gave me his letters in 1980. I treasure them. As I reread them now, after seeing your journal, I see new contours in your lives.

Grennie is finishing nearly eighteen months of continuous fieldwork at San Carlos and Fort Apache. He lives in a tiny room over a store in Geronimo, Arizona. But, I'll let him tell it:

> I wish you could see Geronimo. It is a very amusing place, and the one where I stay. . . . It is a sort of port of missing ships here, and the old men from far and wide seem to concentrate in the vicinity. There are many more old men than young, and I guess the reason is that the place is a "has been," nothing doing here any more. The town is made up of one tourist camp and small store and filling station combined, a second filling station and small store combined, a third filling station and part-time dance hall combined, a garage, and one cafe. That's all.
>
> The cafe is run by Mrs. Knowles with whom I board and room. Mr. Knowles is a staunch and bitter Republican and denounces the "New Deal" vehemently.

At the bottom of page 5, after more description of the town, the Knowleses, and the characters that gather around the cracker barrel in the store, he says: "Here I go, on and on about the things here, and there is no reason for their being interesting to you, so I better stop."

Most of his letters contain an apology like this. Is this supposed to be a shambling kind of self-deprecating politeness? Does he think he is being self-indulgent in talking about himself and his world? Is he being coy? Slightly testy? For someone who is otherwise so straightforward, these moments of almost childish awkwardness are revealing: they are painfully courteous and unnecessary. The absence of emotional reaction, of subjectivity, in the Sierra Madre diary doesn't really surprise me anymore. Such elements are missing not just in the interest of scientific objectivity, but also because I think my father believed that the expression of feelings, at least on paper, was somehow unseemly.

The writing styles of the two of you are so different. Yours is headlong, resonant, dark, vivid, supple, literary—packed with imagery and searching, above all with yourself. You are a minor chord; Grennie, major. He sees and writes about primary colors, you see infinite shadings, a painter's palette: fuchsia, burnt sienna, salmon, umber, vermilion.

My father's writing is so straightforward and literal and concrete that he may also have thought it was not up to your standard of expressiveness. But I think you were riveted by every word. He was telling you about a world that was as real to him as it was exotic and intriguing to you. Perhaps you also hoped to bring him out into the open farther than he would come of his own accord. As I read his letters, I think you may be succeeding.

He usually sends some pressed flowers and always asks about your work, saying, "There are so many questions I want to ask you." He asks you to send him a photo of yourself—and says this: "My, but if I could see you. If you were 200 miles away instead of 2000, it wouldn't be so bad. The other day I looked up the price of a phone call from Safford to Boston (Safford is the nearest place—27 mi.) and the price isn't prohibitive at all, so you may hear from me some day."

He writes a simple, spare description of an Apache funeral, so moving and vivid, it seems fresh to me every time I reread it. You must have been able to picture it just as I do:

March 14, 1936

> You remember the old woman whose photo you liked? Well, the husband of her daughter died of pneumonia. It was he who had the cycle of songs used in the girl's puberty ceremony. Now he is gone and they say there is no one who knows all the songs left in this district. He was going to tell me part of it this spring.
>
> Two mornings ago they were just starting the journey to the burial ground. Everyone liked this man so there were a lot of cars in the procession. In the lead was the dead man's brother's new tan-colored pickup truck, with the coffin in the back and the close relatives riding with it. Behind came the rest, down the narrow little lane between the fields, up over the highway slowly, under the railway bridge. . . . It doesn't sound to you like much of an Indian burying party maybe, but it was very Apache, in spite of its modern accouterments, and impressive. It was the twentieth century to all outward appearances, except for one thing: a man in a black hat, in blue [jacket] and blue denim pants, riding a black horse bareback, in front. I don't know if the horse was killed at the grave or not. In old times they used to do it.

He writes you on March 21:

> Jan, you have always been aware of commonplace things and taken pleasure from them. What you say about my having helped you along those lines is a great compliment, but one which I really don't believe is deserved. You wouldn't be the person you are

unless you noticed things like that. But nevertheless, what you say makes me very happy. I wish I could see the van Gogh pictures with you again. It helped so much, you being there, to help me see the beauty in them.

I know exactly what you mean about remembering colors and forms. They almost live in your mind, don't they?

It's such fun to get your letters Jan, and you really seem happy in them. You don't know how much you've done for me. You say things are fresh for you. They are for me also.

I wonder if Grennie starts seeing the colors and shapes of the landscape around him in a different way. Descriptions like this remind me of the way you would see things, though the hues are still pretty primary:

> The big mountain that lies close to the west, it has several peaks, but there is one, the highest, that looks as if it was reaching up into the sky for something, eternally. The Apaches call this mountain by a name which means "painted white," and they say the reason is that long ago three old women went up to the foot of it and painted themselves all over with white earth there. Beyond this mountain to the west, the horizon was all yellow and orange. Over the mountain were a very few thin, hard, ridged clouds which turned gradually from a deep dull purple to a light rosy pink, then back to a dull gray as the sun sank lower. The mountain itself was blue-black with its ridges running down like great steps against the horizon, into the valley. When the sun had gone way down, it turned from this to a dark misty blue and you could see the darkness rolling up in the east, where it was already night. I wish you could be here.

He goes on to describe a new technique he is trying for writing down what people tell him. He has always done it in longhand, but now he is trying something he "never had the courage" for. He is going to try touch-typing while people talk to him. He listens while they talk in Apache and simultaneously translates, typing in English.

He has filed down some of the symbols on the keys of the typewriter—rarely used ones—to make the complex diacritical marks for writing Apache words he doesn't want to translate. Neil Buck is always there as an interpreter to help with difficult words, precise meanings. "Am still pretty slow and shaky in taking dictation in Apache, but bit by bit speed is coming," he says.

You always said that he had an extraordinary capacity for learning skills. He could make anything with his hands, you said. He could play a couple of musical instruments, was a skilled draftsman, could start a fire without matches, and could shoe a horse. He was always afraid he might lose the use of his right hand, so he practiced writing with his left. When bedridden with tuberculosis in 1933, he was afraid he might lose his eyesight and learned Braille.

Being able to get it all down verbatim was crucial. What the people said to him was his raw material, and the speed at which he could write an absolute control on progress—and the summer was coming fast.

May 24

> I am working six hours a day, and then in the evening it takes almost two hours to straighten the day's notes out. Am going to try and keep up this speed right along if possible, so as to finish off the work as soon as I can. You know why.

By the time June arrives, he has nearly finished his work and the pace relaxes. He describes life around the Neil Buck camp: the bead-covered glass bottle given to him as a present by four-year-old Katie Buck, his special friend, "a funny, half-bold half-shy little girl" who loves to dance, who has just gotten into some rouge and is decorating herself and her little sister; Mrs. Buck going about the business of gathering wood and cooking; her father, a very old man who sleeps by his wickiup most of the time, waking to sing an old song; Rob, the fat, benevolent dog; the hens and the roosters. He writes, "But it is all so vital, really common, everyday things, that because they are so common have a beauty that to me doesn't exist elsewhere. You will know exactly what I mean. But though I love it here, yet if possible, I would rather be where I could see you often."

"See you often." How cautious, how shy, how circumspect. Also, I think, how careful. Could this be a preemptive strike against rejection or, for that matter, commitment? Otherwise why not try to sound . . . I don't know . . . a little more reckless? But he was nothing if not cautious.

By early June, you and Grennie are discussing details for the summer. You suggest going to Grand Manan Island off the coast of Maine. He writes: "Is it true that the water is too cold to swim in? I love swimming so please don't go someplace where it is utterly impossible to do it. Haven't had a chance to swim in the sea for twelve years or more. . . do please pick someplace that isn't cold and bleak and fog bound, Jan. We don't have to have that, do we?"

Just the sort of place you love—moody, brooding, mysterious, slightly menacing—not just picturesque, but something to "go against," as you would say. It resonates with your interior landscape and you like to paint places like that. Grand Manan: a lot like Sark, I would think. By the time Grennie is halfway through the letter, he thinks he sounds too negative and devotes a sentence in nearly every paragraph to softening the impression, telling you wherever you want to go is fine—but he just doesn't want this trip "to be spoiled in any way, and also to be able to hear the surf roll up on a beach again and swim."

THE WIND FROM THE SOUTHWEST

The two months flash by. You have been active with friends, you go dancing with a close friend, Louis Shaw, go to the movies, drive to the North Shore with Louis for the day—is he courting you, I wonder?—and then you hurry back.

Then you dash a word or two in your journal: "August 22—return to Brookline, met G., drive Og.—the house on the dunes—the long beach—seals."

Ogunquit, Maine, was where you went to art school and met Anne Stockton, who introduced you to Grennie in 1929 and who married his brother Sage. This is followed by more dashed place-names, sights, impressions, though no mention of Grand Manan. By this time you have a new apartment—at 13 Temple Street.

When my first wife, Jane, and I moved to Boston after graduate school, one of those things happens that makes me understand why some people insist there is no such thing as coincidence. We moved into the ground floor of a four-story townhouse on Beacon Hill: 13 Temple Street. In late 1936 you had a room on the top floor under the cupola, and I never knew it until after we moved in and told you our new address. We were all speechless at first, then recognized this crossing of paths for what it was: a convergence that was somehow meant to be.

Your father writes in his diary on Sunday, October 4: "This afternoon I took Janice and Grennie Goodwin for a two hour sail on the Charles basin. . . . Grennie does not say much."

My grandfather, your father, was an old-fashioned, somewhat provincial, brilliant, literal-minded professor of electrochemistry at MIT. Grennie was a scientist too, though that did not appear to give them much in common. My grandfather's highly circumscribed life was made up of academic routine, conventional pleasures and, being a southerner, certain expectations with regard to social small talk. My grandfather was as stiff and formal as my father was relaxed and reticent.

By October 8, you and Grennie have gone to Connecticut to see his brother Sage and wife Anne, then New York City, then to Huntington, Long Island, where Grennie more or less grew up and his mother lives when she's not in Santa Fe or Colorado Springs. By October 20 you are back in Boston.

On November 3, you write in your journal, "The wind from the Southwest, blowing. . . ."

The rest of the pages of your journal have been cut out. Gone. All I know is what you told me once:

> Grennie then asked me to marry him. I was so confused, I didn't know what to do and said I needed some time to think about it. Grennie said he had to drive back to Arizona in a couple of days and he wanted me to come with him. I needed time. I went and saw Jack Burling, who also wanted to marry me, I think. I don't know—but I trusted him, didn't know who else to trust. Jack and I talked for hours. I didn't know what I wanted. I was scared. I had lost out before and was scared of being trapped forever in Boston. Finally Jack said—Do you love him? I said—Yes. Jack said—What are you waiting for?

You wrote:

Do you suppose
The carrot dangling
Before the donkey's nose
The reason why he goes?
Well
Then
My rose
Of love
I smell my way to heaven

My grandfather's diary records what happened next:

Nov. 7. Tuesday

> I voted for Landon with much doubt, but now I am glad I did not increase the landslide for Roosevelt.
>
> Yesterday Janice told me she and Grennie Goodwin were engaged and she was planning to start today for Tucson with him. . . . They are putting off the wedding until he sees what his family can do for him. He came in my office about 10 o'clock and said he hoped I would not think their procedure was irregular. We had a talk for a while . . . and he took leave. He is very handsome and seems very good-natured.
>
> He came out to breakfast after which we all helped pack the automobile. When this was over we kissed good-bye and they backed out waving good byes. I put on my coat and started for Cambridge with rather a choked feeling. Lil [Grandma] started burning leaves and Clare [the youngest daughter] was standing by the fireplace. And so the most important events of our lives take place with casual accompaniments.

There are three photographs taken by Grandpa. In one you look defiant, hurt, closed in—overcoat on, arms crossed. You're staring at something off-camera, or maybe you just won't look at the camera. You look like the daughter that your parents could never understand. You can't wait to leave.

Then you and Grennie: He looks relaxed, forthright. You're still leaning against the house, tilted slightly toward Grennie.

Now your arms are behind you and you still look awkward, almost furtive, but you can taste the open road. It must have been a ragged parting: your bitter mother showing nothing, feeling . . . what? . . . resentment at this flouting of convention—your final triumph? Your sister Clare, stunned and almost certainly hurt by the suddenness, and your father, nearly overcome, in his own way, with emotions he barely recognizes.

Basically you eloped. That's no judgment on my part. I'm sure you had to do it this way.

Grennie spent the night before at 13 Temple St. and you were on the road the next day. You spent the first night in upstate New York. In his Ford coupe you drove across the country, going first to Colorado Springs where his mother lived. Your journal says nothing about her—

perhaps she was not in residence, but she was a formidable lady and would have made a formidable impression. You left for Arizona and Apache country and were married by a justice of the peace in Holbrook, Arizona. You got a guy off the street for a witness.

I know you didn't exactly climb out of the window on a ladder in the night, but this probably qualifies as an elopement and they are supposed to be like this: impetuous, willful, romantic. But, to me, without knowing the details, it seems slapdash. But then I know you were both rebels.

What were you thinking, I wonder? What did you talk about? You were heading into the unknown, Grennie was going home. You, feeling an unknown freedom I'm sure, had left your family, essentially open-mouthed, at the other end of 2,000 miles of two-lane blacktop and dusty ruts. In the Southwest Grennie was surrounded by family. He had brothers and his mother occasionally in Santa Fe, plenty of friends and colleagues. I don't know. It seems somehow inarticulate. I know just why you did not want your family to be part of it, but I have always wondered why Grennie's was so clearly left out. His favorite brother Sage was back East, and you had already paid him a visit, certainly telling him your plans. Marriage in Santa Fe or Colorado Springs, managed by Grennie's mother, possibly surrounded by the literati, intelligentsia, and artistic aristocracy of the community held little appeal for him. Better, maybe, to get on with it and make a statement of independence at the same time. I often wonder: did it also make a statement about your marriage?

TUCSON

Reading my father's 1936 letters, I try to imagine what his life was like and what you were in for and how he could share it with you. You must have been wondering yourself as you wrote in your diary:

Nov. 25, 1936

> Arrive in Tucson—Begin another life—a challenge and a test
> That I may rise and be what I must be.
> That I may bring all I have to give
> That I may be strong

That I may grow
That I may overcome
That I may not lose myself
That we may grow and grow together always.

You said the Knowleses, with whom Grennie lived whenever he was working on the reservation, treated him like one of the family. Still, Geronimo, Arizona, was a depression-era truck stop, where no one stayed: "a port for missing ships," as my father said. It had nothing like the rich culture—full of life, children, stories, and adventures—that lay just a few miles away on the reservation; but that life could no more be yours than it could be his, as much as he might have wanted it to be.

Morris Opler, a distinguished colleague of Grennie's, used to tell me that when he went to do his fieldwork at the Mescalero Apache reservation he would have to "come up for air" every few months or so. For my father, it may have been just the opposite. When he was away from the Apaches, he may have had to hold his breath. You both were coping with profound changes: married life was only one of them. The reservation was no longer to be part of Grennie's daily life. You were plunged into a landscape for which you were utterly unprepared visually. As you talk about the untouchable country, I wonder how much of what you write is a metaphor for your marriage:

> This land will be hard to live in at first, but it is something to go against and conquer and become part of.
>
> I have come to this far off-standing land of desert and mountains empty handed and I must find the tools to hew out a life in it. My work must grow and go on for without it I cease to be.

Grennie never went back to the reservation for extended fieldwork—he was rushing to finish it before going East to meet you in August 1936. He spent the next three years organizing his material to be published as *The Social Organization of the Western Apache*. You bought some land east of town where you planned to build a house. It was going to be in the old Spanish colonial style, and you went around together looking at the old adobe buildings, making a study of architectural details, building methods, and materials.

I can picture you doing this. My father already full of knowledge about this kind of architecture, you eager to learn, writing it all down as you went around the old Spanish section of Tucson. I think you enjoyed that because you could imagine the house—it was something creative that you could share, and after Grennie's death you went back to Tucson and built the ranch just as you had planned it together, as if it were a reminder of the best of your marriage, and a promise worth keeping—not only for Grennie's sake, but for mine, by rooting my childhood in the desert.

Tucson had the university and colleagues and was fairly near the reservation, but it was a hot and dusty desert town that baked in the summers. The heat is like a hammer. It can take your breath away. It was a rough half-year; you were unhappy, but you were beginning to see the structure of the landscape:

> I have just begun to perceive the underlying force of things—in the design of a mountainside, in the grace of an Indian girl carrying a water jar, in a gray burro or in an Indian on a pony.
>
> The cactus springs from the earth with sculptural vitality.

SANTA FE

You moved to Santa Fe after six months in Tucson. Santa Fe was very different, more hopeful. It had an ideal climate and was one of the centers of artistic and intellectual life in the Southwest. It had a vibrant combination of Spanish and Indian culture. These things you both loved. You were seeing a completely new landscape and palette and way of life. Your sketchbooks are full of figures, faces, burros, horses, landscapes—all powerful, evocative images. Your journals are lush with descriptions of what you see and of how you will get it down. More important, there is a new confidence and the kind of excitement that comes only when, as an artist, you really feel you are onto something no one else is seeing: "to wring the pattern from—to see the assigned arrangement of the markings—the perfect shapes—to create out of the natural form, if such be the limitations—to intensify and carry farther than any other—being based on a more pure form and color—the elemental to be arranged and sublimated. The possibility of a great, a wild and earthy art."

Of Grennie and the marriage, however, nothing direct, only the signs of relentless inner struggle with your painting: alternating episodes of triumph and defeat. You probably don't want to see on the page what is in your heart.

What I like best about your diaries are the descriptions of the trips you took. One of the first visits he made upon arrival in Tucson with you was to one of the most important, most honored of his Apache friends. It was then that you met his Apache family. You wrote to me about it in a letter: "Old Anna Price, the daughter of the great White Mountain Chief, Diablo, was over 90 and called G. her grandson. Soon after we were married, G. took me to Bylas and to her wickiup where he told me to sit on the ground on her right side so she could read my face with her hands, as she was completely blind. It was like being in the presence of a royal personage."

I'm sure Grennie had tried to describe her to you, feeling certain at the same time that he was unequal to the task. She was among the most treasured of his friends, and he had recorded her life story verbatim—an extraordinary narrative that you later included in the posthumously published *Apache Raiding and Warfare*. As you once told me, her memory went back to a time before there were any white people in her country.

Grennie then took you on extended camping trips to the Papago country west of Tucson and the Navajo country in the Four Corners area. He had spent several months on the Navajo reservation and knew it well, knew that you would understand it visually and hoped you would be able to see it as he did. You wrote a long description of the two-week Navajo trip as if it were a letter to Grennie, as if you were talking to him, wanting to make sure he knew how you remembered it. When you came to Canyon de Chelly, you wrote:

> There you led me blindfolded to the edge and we looked down into an immense pink cleft in the earth—the size of which was impossible to judge...The bottom of white sand winding like a river—and close up under the cliffs—starry green patches of Indian corn and their camps—a moving speck across the sand was a lone horse—rounded a cliff and out of sight...this most superb of all places—it was like nothing else.

And later after Grennie and you asked an old Navajo to join you for a meal: "he dismounted and sat down and we gave him some coffee. He ate silently, but when he left he called you his grandson."

The memories of your trips in Navajo country were powerful and indelible, and they compelled you to paint masterfully, creating a monumental work, a tableau that captured the colors, the symbolism, the scale, and the majesty of what you were seeing. But before you did the painting, you seized the memories of these trips with language:

> The monuments became loaves of amethyst almost floating on desert. We waited and waited for the first sign of the Navajos coming—and then silently, almost imperceptibly around the corner of the butte came the women on horseback carrying their babies. After them came some old men, and [they] stopped close by us and spoke—like ancient kings. They sat in their saddles under broad hats—and always they seemed to be looking far off to horizons we could never see and to speak in broad simple terms with biblical grandeur. A white horse, a buckskin and dark horses—soon a mass always moving. A wagon came over the ridge and now they were silhouetted in the sky. Horses and riders moving along the edge of the hill toward the camping place—not a sound from the crowd.

And then a fierce resolve, a vision of a painting: "I must make a dark-rich painting of Navajos built up with blanket patterns—shirts borders, heads, bands—an expressive design—being all the essence of the people—their dignity—their color—their form, their grace and movement."

You were developing a style all your own and a technique that was almost like fresco—borrowed perhaps from the nameless painters who decorated the old Spanish colonial churches of the Southwest that you had come to love so much. In fact you wrote a poem about the Mission San Xavier del Bac.

San Xavier

Saint of the desert
White dove with folded wings
And tilted breast sits patiently
On centuries of sand,
Guarding the treasure of her nest,
Brown, blue, and mottled rose
And brittle gold.
Her painted eyes
Are waiting for the sign
To set her free
And lift her plaster wings
Toward Paradise.

Grennie took you to an Apache girl's puberty ceremony at Bylas—one of the most beautiful, sensual, and affecting of all. You watched it for two days, writing near the end:

> One girl is still dancing. The gá·n enter the circle with forward-tipping headdresses, raised arms. In the daylight their buckskin kilts are ochre—red streamers hang from their elbows—the rattles around their waists shake as they dance. The girl dances continually, and then on her knees she sways from side to side with her hands half-raised looking at the sun. Her hair is long and straight. On her forehead is the abalone shell and eagle plume in her hair. Then face down she lies on a blanket and the older woman molds her, shaping her for life.
>
> We crave a bit of shade to be cool. We cross the baked desert and descend to a lake. The sparse mesquite bushes have hardly any shade. We strip and sink into the cool water. We are the only living creatures. It is hot and still. It is good to be naked in the heat.

Together you shared the long, dusty miles, paced by Grennie's easy, relaxed ways with the Indians and the traders among whom he was accepted. He showed you how to choose a campsite, make a fire, and cook over it; and you came to like doing it well, and you liked the tough, leathery feel of your own skin after a couple of weeks of sun and dust. There was a measure of harmony to your lives: "We walk on the pink earth—up and down arroyos—G goes before and his moccasined feet seem to be tasting the earth—the balls of his feet—springing with neat precise steps."

And you were painting with words—easier, more natural for you than with paints or pen and ink: "The girls move like slow swinging bells in their bright banded skirts. All day up and down the road—some with babies strapped to their foreheads—their heads bent foreward and their long black hair lying smooth behind. The skirt kicking out behind with each step, dipping down in front."

You were taken by the humor and wisdom of the Apache fables called Coyote stories and were moved to begin a series of illustrations. I know you were never pleased with them, but among my own earliest and most cherished memories are those of gazing at them and hearing you tell me the stories.

They must have been good times, those long trips—camping, visiting with Grennie's Indian friends, experiencing the visual spectacle of the Southwest. But you also felt pinioned by the power of the landscape: the heat, the brilliance of the sun, the numbing distance. Your diaries are full of your struggle to understand it, to process it, and to find a voice with which to speak to Grennie about it—to let him know you loved it. Yet you were struck nearly dumb by the Southwest that he had made his home, and you wrote:

June 18, 1938, for G.

Times I have not spoken you must know
It was the rocks too great, the distance lying low.
Know it was the earth when I've withdrawn
And shut away the white and blinding dawn,
The midday sand or sky too full of sun.

But hear the little voice that fills the night—
The cricket in the grass, small armored one,
And know he nearly breaks in praise of light.

And there was too much light. Your painting always took you into the shadows, but you were finding another way: you could close your weary eyes and write. You could paint with words. Your diary has landscapes and a new, brilliant palette that you never tried to create with paint: "Across a yellow sea of sulfur wheat—intense hot yellow that stings—the road is pink that cuts through and the green-mauve hills bulge up. The air is dusty so that all is whitened and mountain ranges lying film on film over the spotted desert are inactual peaks—the shape of fantasy."

But it wasn't long before you were feeling that your brief visual grasp of the western landscape was slipping out of reach, that your talent had in some way betrayed you:

Jan. 1938

The fruit tree, only seen one lovely season,
Thus held in mind as stilled against the years.

Returning to the frozen ground, think not
To find her still extend her golden pears.

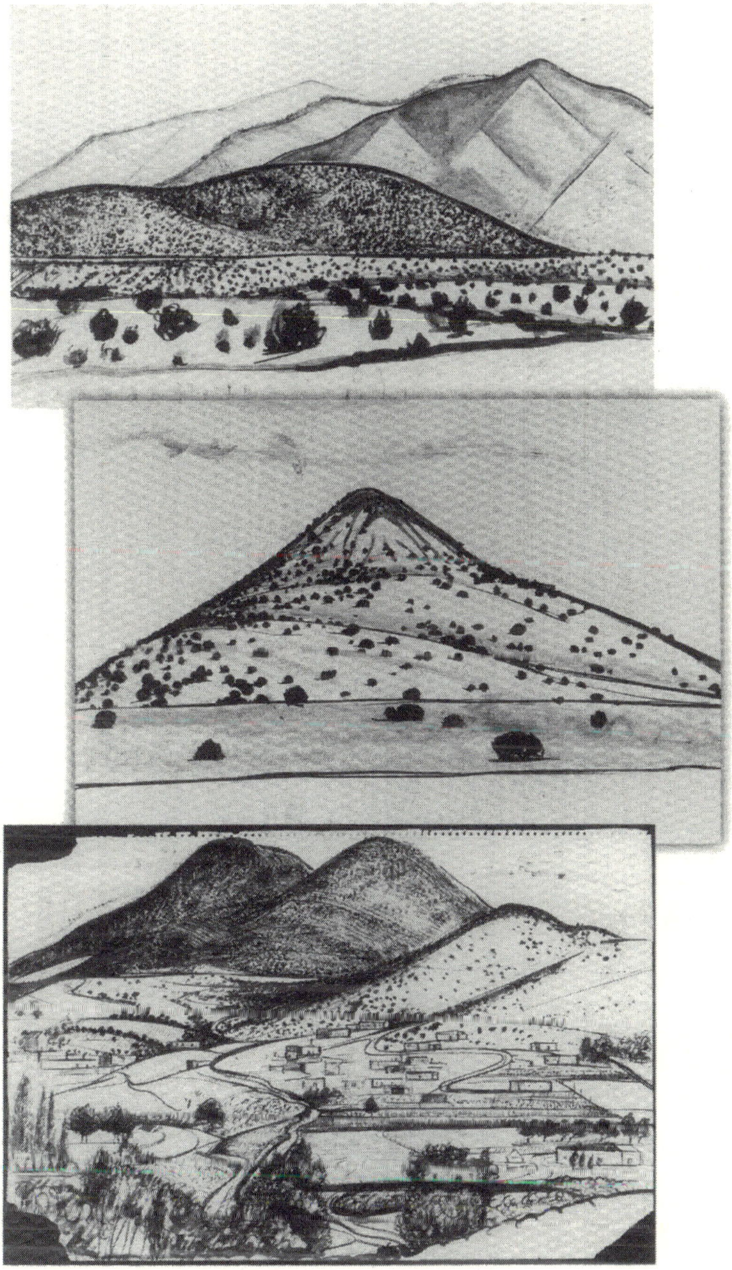

(Top to bottom) Janice T. Goodwin, landscape near Santa Fe, New Mexico, India ink; mountain near Santa Fe, New Mexico, India ink, and landscape near Santa Fe, New Mexico, India ink.

(Top to bottom) Janice T. Goodwin, landscape near Santa Fe, New Mexico, India ink; barrel cactus, India ink; and portrait of a girl in Santa Fe, India ink.

(Top to bottom) Janice T. Goodwin, burro, India ink; Apache women and children, Bylas, Arizona, pencil; Apache social dance, Bylas, Arizona, India ink.

(Top to bottom) Janice T. Goodwin, Apache women, Bylas, Arizona, pencil; Apache women, Bylas, Arizona, pencil; Apache woman and child, Bylas, Arizona, pencil; Woman with pitchfork, Bylas, Arizona, pencil; Apache women and children, Bylas, Arizona, pencil.

(Top to bottom) Janice T. Goodwin, gá·n *dancers, Bylas, Arizona, pencil;* gá·n *dancer, Bylas, Arizona, pencil; and Apache women and children, Bylas, Arizona, India ink.*

(Top to bottom) Janice T. Goodwin, coyote tales: Coyote steals the sun's tobacco, India ink; Coyote steals Abert Squirrel's fire, India ink.

(Top to bottom) Janice T. Goodwin, Coyote tales: Coyote and Bobcat trick each other, India ink; Coyote opens sack containing darkness, India ink, Coyote with Badger carrying darkness on his back, India ink.

Janice T. Goodwin, dancers at Santo Domingo Pueblo, New Mexico, egg tempera on gesso.

Janice T. Goodwin, Navajos in Monument Valley, egg tempera over gesso on wood.

Janice T. Goodwin, Beulah and Ollie Buck, Santa Fe, egg tempera on gesso.

Janice T. Goodwin, Monument Valley scene, Navajo reservation, egg tempera on gesso.

Janice T. Goodwin, Apache social dance, Bylas, Arizona, egg tempera on gesso.

Janice T. Goodwin, two Apache women and child, Bylas, Arizona, egg tempera on gesso.

It was soon after this that you decided to abandon painting. You have been married for almost two years, and the powerful experiences of those two years have only underlined the raggedness of your inner life. You called it a vicious cycle: your painting and your marriage were devouring each other. The many missing pages from your diary probably chronicle in detail the inner conflicts, marital tensions, and impossibly high self-set standards that led to your final discouragement. What's more, your painting, your work, had become something you could no longer share with Grennie. As you told me, he seemed to resent it as time went by, and your relationship became strained: "I think the solution has about been reached to renounce the whole business of painting. Since it is destroying my life. Since I cannot do it and anything else besides. Since I cannot paint without having the fullness of a normal married life."

There is a terse note in the margin, which you wrote in 1954 upon rereading and editing your journals: "I never did any painting after this." Maybe not, but your paintings and drawings were full of self-confidence and self-knowledge, full of maturity and originality. You were on the verge of a "wild and earthy art," and though you may have known it at some level, you did not really believe in yourself. What's more, there was irreconcilable conflict between your painting and your married life. You have said that you got no encouragement from the one whose support you needed most.

On September 23, 1938, you wrote:

> I am so afraid of emptiness. How to integrate these various paths—painting, poetry, life—for they all are separate. I wonder if after all poetry is what I should devote myself to. It seems to go hand in hand with my life. It is a refuge and a joy.

Poet's Game

I am playing with castles and queens and kings,
But I have never learned about these things,

Nor how to start—
Eliminate the little pawns?
How do I part with my most lovely queen?

I do not know
The simplest thing
In this great game—
Oh, how to save my king!

I know that this inner struggle mirrored another struggle being played out in daily life during these first two years of marriage. You talk about the painting, the poetry, and the landscape, but the real trouble, perhaps, was between you and Grennie. I believe you loved each other but didn't know what to do next.

> ***Colorado Springs, July 28, 1938***
>
> *Where we have walked in beauty towards the sun*
> *Where we have stood and listened for a sound*
> *I have planted wooden crosses in the stones,*
> *The resting places of my load of love.*

POETRY

The Apaches had dominated my father's life and consciousness for so long that they had completed him. He must have seemed monolithic. There must have seemed little left for you to do or to give—and you yourself felt so incomplete. But even as you despaired of finding balance and fulfillment, you discovered in yourself a source of energy and renewal:

> When a wakening emotion comes to me suddenly—like love-fear-joy and yet on the verge of tears, I know it is the waking of a poem—that may not come for some time—nor knowing what it might be—nor the cause—except that some unconscious forces were at work. This strange emotion may last a second or a whole day—an exhilaration or unbearable sadness—disquieting until it has been resolved into a poem.

You found your poet's voice, and at your best you were every bit as good in your own way as my father was in his. I only wish you knew how good. Among the most powerful of your poems were your own metaphors for the creative process, for your inward conversion from a painter to a writer, for the finding of your own true voice.

> ***Going East, Feb. 1938***
>
> *Come dark, come quiet, come solitude*
> *Cover a while these light-full eyes. My skein,*
> *So long let loosened over untold space*
> *Now I must sit and wind you up again.*

Recapture you where blown about the desert
Caught in a thousand flowers.
Draw you from the bright mountains
And rocky rooms, un-netting their blue stars.

Untangle you from dust of stamping feet
And drums and singing
Now my quest is not in the far-flinging
But to wind a shining ball in dark retreat.

So, I wonder whether you are talking about your newfound voice, the sense of who you are when you write this and then a series of poems that are tight and wry and crystalline and not about yourself: "with a new happiness I feel these things as if reborn, for the land is mine now."

Javelina

The javelina is a poem,
Or as a poem should be;
In shape compact,
The heft condensed in tailored coat
And none to spare.

The body's burden of the song
Borne lightly
As the pygmy hooves
Go pricking through mirages'
Quivering air.

Desert Tortoise

Bearing his ponderous house of horn
On arthritic legs
The tortoise makes his way,
A saurian eye surveying
With primeval gloom
The path of his protracted stay.

Timepiece from earth's grey beginning
Set for the inheritor,
With measured pendulum
He lumbers on
Between the first sea-scum
And flowering of a star.

You never did go back to painting in a serious way, though you wrote poetry for the rest of your life. Though it was a more or less private enterprise, you did it with passion and commitment and, as a creative endeavor, I think it saw you through. It was something you could do that did not need Grennie's support. Painting was more public, more demanding of you, and, in a way of Grennie, just because of the way it has to be done—the time and space it takes. You were clear in your letter to me that he seemed to resent it. Was it competition? Was it a reminder of his mother's circle of artists that he would have nothing to do with—notwithstanding the fact that all his brothers were involved in visual arts? Was it that he didn't think painting was something to be taken seriously?

There was one important thing you could share: the spectacle of the Southwest. The power of Indian traditions and the beauty of their country have a universal immediacy and a humanity. But that was never enough by itself to form an enduring common ground, and his work was too specialized, too arcane for you to share. The technical language of linguistics and anthropology must have seemed nearly impenetrable to you. These were the tools of my father's trade, and I wonder if, and how, Grennie shared it with you and what you made of it. Although you had your own powerful reservation experiences, there was much of his own experience that he never talked about to you, perhaps never talked to anyone about.

While you felt your own work as a painter was disintegrating, his was on a grand trajectory. More surely mastering his material every day, Grennie must have been totally absorbed in his intellectual enterprise. He found time, in the midst of writing his big book in 1937, '38 and '39, to write several papers and a shorter book, and to prepare a report for the BIA on conditions at San Carlos and Fort Apache.

Whether or not my father's work was a part of your life while he lived, following his death you became a collaborator. You took the manuscript for *The Social Organization of the Western Apache* and prepared it for publication. The manuscript is full of your deft editorial grace notes. Grennie's spelling was never reliable, but you contended with that as well as hundreds of exotic, incomprehensible Apache words with their multiple diacritical marks. There were place-names and technical anthropological locutions as unfamiliar to you as the names of rocks in the Asteroid Belt; then there were acknowledgments, an introduction, chapter headings, subtitles, appendices, and an index. You had to handle business and legal correspondence with the University of Chicago Press and you had to ask Grennie's colleagues for their critical reviews of the text and then, of course, there were the galley proofs.

Whatever in Grennie that was incomprehensible because of his total immersion in Apache culture became clearer to you. He shared with you what he could while he lived. The rest you found out for yourself by your own experience of total immersion in the editorial trenches—in a way that you might never have done otherwise.

And that had an unexpected windfall, for among Grennie's thousands of pages of field notes and other papers, you found the letters.

Letters

chapter five

"Letters" was originally a chapter in *The Apache Diaries* but was eventually dropped during the editing process. It begins by comparing the two mysteries with which I begin the quest of *The Apache Diaries*: the Sierra Madre Apaches and Grenville Goodwin himself—how both mysteries can be explored only through how they are reflected in the minds and eyes of others. Once I started to write this chapter, I found I could not stop. The material was wonderfully rich; and it was leading me in a direction I knew I had to go for personal reasons, even if it became a digression with no place in the book I was trying to write. I eventually dropped all but the last few pages of "Letters," and those pages are used to conclude *The Apache Diaries*. But I am resurrecting the entire chapter in its original form because it adds so much strength to the enterprise undertaken in this volume.

After writing "Jan and Grennie," I found, as I thought I might, that I had come to know my mother, instead of my father, a great deal better. After all, she was her own raw material. In the process she had partially coaxed Grennie from the shadows for me, but able to go no farther herself, she showed me the way to do it: listen to the Apaches. They knew him best.

This section is based largely on the letters Grennie received from his Apache friends over a period of seven years, but as I wrote it I began incorporating other material. The things about which Grennie's Apache friends wrote to him also turned up as references in his daily diary, so I have quoted from it, at first simply to fill in gaps. But the more I used this material the more I found I was beginning to hear Grennie's voice, sense his point of view about things as diverse as sacred knowledge and BIA red tape. In his 1936 letters to my mother are the clearest statements of his own daily life and why he was so powerfully drawn to Apache culture.

In the last year of Grennie's life, my maternal grandfather's daily diary tracks the relentless and rapid decline of Grennie's health against a backdrop of the onset of WWII and the election of FDR to a third term. In an exchange of letters between my father's mother and my mother's mother, the two women struggle for some perspective on Grennie's senseless death. And a letter from my mother to me guides me back to the Apaches for one last letter and an Apache prayer.

The Apaches of the Sierra Madre were in a sense invisible. They are reflected in the many lives they affected, and with the exception of their abandoned camps, a view of that reflection may be as close as I will ever get to them.

So it is with my father—he is visible to me almost entirely through the way he is reflected in others. Because he practiced such determined self-effacement, he might have taken much satisfaction in this finding. In this way, without really trying, he became more like the Apaches than the Apaches themselves. For me he still is a ghost even before his own death. I conjure him up, even after all this, with effort.

Grennie's major work, *The Social Organization of the Western Apache,* is a remarkable achievement of fieldwork and scholarship, though when I read it, I do not sense the individual men, women, and children whom he knew so well. The six hundred–page book is highly technical, a detailed and accurate description of the culture, and for this reason the Apaches themselves treasure it. They love the way their own language flows through the book, naming places, people, practices, articles, plants, animals, and a thousand other things.

But the place where the Apaches, and by reflection my father, come most vividly to life for me is in the pages of letters they wrote to him. They are so rich with life and humor and simple dignity that every time he received one, it must have powerfully recalled his experience in Apache country: the faces, the voices, the profound friendships, the loyalties, the giving, the enmities, the gritty, precarious life, the sound of the Apache language, the heat, the dust, the kids, the daily yin and yang of the sacred and the mundane, the battered pickups and the rank, sweet smell of animals.

The earliest letters were written in 1933 while my father spent a year in Colorado recovering from tuberculosis. Whenever he was away from the reservation for even a few days, letters followed him. As far as I know none of the letters he wrote survive. After Grennie's death in 1940, Neil Buck, Grennie's closest Apache friend, faithfully wrote to my mother and then to me until the mid-1950s. Eighty-four letters remain, though there may have been many more. It's a remarkable number, especially for the Apaches, who frequently had to find someone who could write while they dictated in fractured, yet lyrical and powerfully expressive English. They must have instructed the scribe to write down exactly what they said, so there would be no mistakes, and most important, so my father would read the same words that were spoken—so that while reading the letters he would hear their voices.

I can picture their daily lives through the joys and the far more frequent tragedies they wrote about. I can picture him listening. Every letter affirms that Grennie occupied a special place among these people—a place that I still strain to understand fully. There is a letter written in 1954 by an anthropologist working at San Carlos to my mother's sister that hints at my father's place in the Apache world. He says, "Grennie is almost a god to some of these people. They will quote what he said here, or what he did there. Neil [Buck] (Grennie's closest friend) is completely devoted. Grennie's collection of their folk tales has become a sort of Bible for the Indians."[24]

As I read the letters, I feel the Apaches talking to me as they would have talked to him. But I sense something else as well that leads me to pore over page after page of his daily diaries, his raw field notes, and his letters to my mother, and to go through all the letters from Apaches with a fine-toothed comb. I am looking at a written record that is at once a kaleidoscope and a jigsaw puzzle. Encrypted in these hundreds of pages is the essence of Grennie's reservation experience—something he may have reflected upon but never recorded consciously. Portraits of individual Apaches and of Grennie himself begin to emerge, creating a broad landscape of people and terrain and the place within it that Grennie occupied for so many years. ✣

Anna Price was one of Grennie's first Apache friends. They would spend hours talking about the old times, and by March 1932 Grennie had written down her life story. Anna referred to Grennie as *Shi-cho*, Apache for "grandson," and she once told him that when he came to visit her, it was "as if the world were made new again and that things began over."[25]

Dear Shi-cho,

I am going to write to you because I was very glad when I received your letter. Once I got a letter from you with a three dollar bill in and another time $5. . . . We were very glad when we saw you picture and a good house. We can't hardly see you. We all wish for that house. . . . I am very old now and can't hardly see now. . . . This is the first time I have written to you.

My daughter still says that she thinks you are her brother because you been helping her along.

Your friends,
Anna Price
Susie Preston

Susie Preston wrote this letter for her grandmother, Anna. The daughter that Anna refers to is Susie's mother, Mrs. Jewett Wright. Over time, Grennie became very close to the members of Anna's family. Anna acknowledges the small presents Grennie frequently sent to her and other Apache friends. The house she mentions is probably Grennie's mother's house in Colorado Springs, where he is convalescing. Throughout this year of correspondence he never speaks of his tuberculosis.

About one hundred years old, Anna was one of Grennie's most valued advisors. She remembered what her culture and her country were like before there were any Anglos in the region. Her father, Haskedasila, one of the greatest of all White Mountain Apache leaders, was widely remembered in the 1930s, even by neighboring tribes. When Grennie made a trip to the Zuni pueblo north of the Apache reservations, he delivered a message from Anna to a family her father had known and came back with messages for Anna and stories still told about her father among the Zuni people, as well as a present of Zuni flat bread made of blue cornmeal.

Grennie wrote, "Anna cried when she saw it. Her children made fun of her and said, 'What are you crying over those tortillas for?' Anna Price was much moved by the old times coming back this way. I am very glad I did it for her."

Grennie gradually was accepted almost as a member of Anna's family, and after he and Jan were married in November 1936, he made a point of visiting her daughters, but one of them, Susie Wright, was not at home.

I heard you came to my camp while you was on your way to White-river, Ariz. I would have went with you if I weren't after wood. Also I didn't get to see you wife.

Today I think maybe you would never be here again and maybe left us forever. I thought of you as my brother left me.

Even if you are a whiteman but in my mind you are like an Indian.

I will ask you something and what would you think about it, that is will you sent me a big coffee pot and one for sugar.

All my children are well except my mother is still sick.

During these long nights I have to keep fire going for her.

I sure was very glad when your letter was here and heard all what you said.

Not only that but you have also help me out.

So good-bye my brother and my sister-in-law and Hello to you both.

Yours truly,
Mrs. Jewett Wright (Susie)

Jan and Grennie missed Susie but managed to find Anna. My mother remembers the meeting vividly and told me that she felt as if she were in the presence of royalty. Indeed Anna was one of the great authorities on old Apache culture, much of it learned from her father. She told Grennie that when she spoke, the words came literally from her heart (the Apache seat of emotion) and that it was as if her father were speaking through her. But she was playful too; she and Grennie had a special friendship called a "joking relationship" in which certain familiarities are permitted that would otherwise be considered presumptuous by Apache standards of courtesy. Grennie wrote that once when he sneezed, she teased him that his girlfriend must be thinking of him. "You must have a girl, don't you?"

When she met Jan, she joked that Grennie looked different, then told Jan that, among the Apaches, when people first get married, that's what happens—they just look different. Others reminded him that when a young man first gets married he acts crazy and forgets everything because he's thinking about his girl.

Anna and her daughter, like most of the other people on the reservation, still lived in the traditional wickiup, a domed or conical brush shelter from twelve to twenty feet in diameter. Anna shared hers with the family of one of her married daughters, who slept in one bed to the right of the door. On the other side of the central fire was Anna's bed. Along the back was another place for one of her daughter's grown sons to sleep. A bed consisted of canvas laid on the ground, covered with bedding. There was a bench and a chest for pots and pans and other things. Anna cooked over the fire in the center of the dwelling. It was the middle of the Depression and the Apaches had to make do with almost nothing. Grennie wrote to Jan about Anna and her family: "The old woman is practically the main supporter of her daughter, four grandsons, one granddaughter, and two great-grandchildren. I don't know how they will make out. Imagine trying to support that number of people on $30 a month, but they do it somehow and often on less than that."

There was little employment, and many Apaches relied on what they could grow or what stock they could raise for subsistence, but it was never easy. Neil Buck writes:

> I work on my farm all time and see I can raised better crops this coming summer. I didn't raised much corn, not much water melon not much pumpkin and sugar cane so I got to get busy with my farm mostly every day. We Indian living at Calva didn't raised much crops. I think we put corns in too late that's the trouble we didn't raised much crops. I only make five sacks of corns. Ought to be over 20 sacks.

Constitutional self-government was not to be granted until 1938, so San Carlos was still under the rigid control of a BIA agent, a man named John Kitch. Farm plots on the reservation were capable of producing bumper crops, as they had in the nineteenth century during the U.S. Army administration of the reservation, when the entire military establishment and its livestock were fed from reservation farms. Productivity was dependent on water, and water was regulated by the government. While Grennie was at San Carlos, the welfare of the Apaches was neglected at all levels by the government, and everything the Apaches did was tightly controlled by the agent. The result was typical of Indian reservations across the country: a paternalistic system that treated the Indians as if they were incapable of managing their own affairs. After several generations, the Indians had begun to believe it themselves and felt defeated before undertaking even the most modest enterprise. As much as they resented government control, they had become dependent on it for aid and were afraid of being abandoned if they showed too much initiative. In his San Carlos report, Grennie quoted a widespread Apache sentiment: "Well, if a few of us get together and make a ranch where we can have our cattle and try to organize our roundups, the agent will say, 'Well as long as you have decided to do this, you can look out for yourselves and I will help these people who remain here with me.'"[26]

My mother said Grennie could not bear to see injustice, and he was assaulted with it every day on the reservation. As tempted as he may have been to right the many wrongs he saw, he must have felt it important to remain circumspect, to preserve a visibly neutral standing. In a hundred small ways he became the Apaches' friend, became perhaps the only white man in whom they could place trust. At the same time, if the white power structure on the reservation was even aware of his presence, they saw it as benign to their interests. In fact, Grennie was introduced and recommended to Agent Kitch in a 1931 letter from the curator of the Arizona State Museum as a "young man of few words and reticent habits who will cause no trouble on the reservation."[27]

Grennie believed that the greatest service he could perform for the Apaches was to record what they said and let them speak for themselves to the world in the ways they chose. Neil Buck was a pivotal figure in this enterprise. Of the eighty-four letters that survive, fully a third were written by Neil, the closest friend Grennie ever had and the man after whom I was named. Neil was at first Grennie's interpreter, then his advisor, then his constant companion. They worked together as a team, talking with the old-timers hour after hour. As they did so, Grennie came to know all of the members of the Bylas and Calva communities. Neil's letters tell about life in these Apache settlements and are often long, running to several pages. He usually lists all the things that have happened since his previous letter, knowing that Grennie would want to know it all, guessing that even the smallest details of daily life would contribute to Grennie's picture of the Apache world.

> We all of us Calva Indians are getting along fine but one woman was very sick and she just about go. Say, you know Davie Don work in store? He was in jail about seven days. Because he got *tulipai* in his house.[28] Well the flowers is kind of back now. Oh yes all of my children said to you hello, and little Katie she just laugh.
>
> Neil Buck

As Grennie read these letters while away from the reservation, his mind's eye could summon up the scene as Neil sat down with pencil and paper at his camp. It was a scene described often enough by Grennie in conversations and correspondence with my mother when he was in the field at San Carlos:

> It is nice to be at work again. It is lovely and warm and the family life goes on all about you. Neil's little girl, my friend Katie, is funny, half-bold half-shy, four years old and loves to dance. You would like her. Neil's wife goes and comes about camp, getting wood, cooking. Her father, who must be well over 100, lives close by. Sometimes, he gets to reminiscing about his youth and his prowess then. He may launch into a song of long ago, singing in a high quavering voice. Then there is Rob, a very fat and slow moving old dog, who has the most benevolent expression of any dog I ever saw. Besides he, a lot of roosters and a few hens, and you have a sketchy picture of the surroundings. It is all so vital, really common, everyday things that because they are so common have a beauty that to me doesn't exist elsewhere. You will know exactly what I mean.

Beneath this deceptively prosaic surface was a way of life full of cultural riches. But as closely as he scrutinized it, he did not try to live it himself. As close as his friendship was to become with many Apaches, he never lived among them. He lived just off the reservation in a truck stop called Geronimo, from which he commuted to Bylas every day either by car or by bus. Just as Bylas was a microcosm of the Apache world, Geronimo was a microcosm of the gritty, uprooted Depression-era West. Grennie wrote to my mother:

> Geronimo is on one of the main highways to California. Mr. Knowles runs one of the filling stations. Mr. Knowles is Missourian born, but takes great pride in telling all strangers that he has been here for over fifty years. He is a good old man and as honest as they come, short and almost round, with bushy eyebrows, perpetual overalls and a twinkle in his eye.
>
> Mr. Knowles' store is the general meeting place of the town, regular country store, stove and all. The cafe is run by Mrs. Knowles with whom I board and room. There isn't much to do

in the evenings so I usually go over and sit outside Mr. Knowles' filling station and just listen for gossip.

For months at a time his life was composed of these polar opposites: his evenings spent hearing the small talk, watching dustbowl refugees barreling to California; his days spent among the Apaches, speaking their language, recording their complex, exotic culture, hearing their stories and songs. Charles Kaut, an anthropologist who worked among the Apaches in the 1950s, spent time with Neil Buck and heard much about Grennie's routine of days in Bylas and nights in Geronimo. Neil said, "He worked all the time. He would come each morning with questions about the stuff from last time, then get new stuff, go away then come back the next day to start over. It was like a machine in operation." Neil took great pride in the work he and Grennie did together, loved to talk about their "books" and about the new "book" that would come from Kaut's continuing work with Grennie's field notes.

As rich as Grennie's daily experience among the Apaches must have been, his life at Geronimo, though pale in comparison, may have been a needed respite. Grennie had to have long stretches of time many evenings to go over the day's work and prepare for the next day. Charles Kaut suggests that, had he been living at Bylas, he would not have had much private time at all; he would have been expected to attend the frequent sings and ceremonies that lasted well into the night. Living as he did, retiring to Geronimo after a day's work would have been seen as dedication to his work rather than an impolite withdrawal.

Grennie was drawn so powerfully to the Apaches and their way of life that he was determined to maintain contact even when he was far away. So when he traveled, he distributed his forwarding address to as many as a dozen close Apache friends, and they kept up a constant correspondence. Away from Bylas, Grennie must have received and written letters nearly every day.

Grennie made a very brief trip back East in February 1936, during which he paid a visit to Boston and to Jan. They had met casually twice before but this time was different. A fire had been kindled and Grennie planned to come back later in the year. When he drove East that fall to spend two months with Jan, the Apache correspondence continued even though Jan and Grennie were constantly on the move up and down the coast of New England.

I was very glad to get that letter which you been wrote it to me. We had a horses dance two days. that dance is for everybody. It just pray for life for crops and for rain too. I told old man Joe Salto look after my horses while I gone he said all right. but when I come back home all of my horses is gone. you see I got go after horses every day but haven't found it yet. that's the reason I didn't answer you sooner. I was very glad to had that picture which you been send it to me. Well all my children said to you Hello Mr. Goodwin where ever you are today. I glad you got a new car now.

Neil Buck

Since you left me we have had many good times we had four dances which lasted until midnight and four sunrise dances. One of these dances was on the flat south of my camp. There were more people than I have ever seen together in one place before.

Tom Riley

Old man Huson gone home for dinner but just when he got his home his wife she eat water melon and so he cut about three slices and eat it. And about half an hour after that old Jim Pike bring one gallon beer and old man Huson drink all this up. the Indians said that beer too sweet yet. You see this sweet beer mix up with water melon that poison him and kill him. that night he didn't sleep and next morning he die.

Neil Buck

Writing in his diary, Grennie says that news of sickness and death is always important and is a subject of intense discussion. It is to the curing of sickness that much of Apache sacred knowledge is devoted. Sickness is a sign of disharmony with the world of supernatural power. Old man Huson's death might have been seen not as bad luck or bad judgment alone, but perhaps as a sign of having committed a serious transgression. As we shall see, the powers were not yet through with the Huson family, and soon people would be discussing omens—such as recent lightning strikes, owl appearances, or strange winds—as ways of understanding the visitation of misfortune upon them.

When bad things happen, harmony, balance, and health can be restored by the performance of a curing ceremonial. John Robertson, mentioned in the next letter, was one of the most influential medicine men at San Carlos. An essential part of certain curing ceremonies is the making of a sand painting. Neil Buck reminds Grennie of one of the many such ceremonials they had attended together and of the drawing "on the sand" they saw.[29] And then he continues with an Apache obituary column—an essential part of the news from San Carlos.

> You know one time we went up to see John Robson [*sic*] draw on the sand for sick woman just one mile above Bylas. She died. You know I been ask John Robson for you and if it all right for you to watch that [sand painting], and John Robson said that be all right you watch all you want say you know Mark Twine. he died to and know Old Smily use to live down Camp Vedo he died Oct. 8. Say do you know old Henry Huson his son use to be police at Bylas with Ralph Ruston? His wife died to. you know short man. And you know old man you friend C.F.3 making story to us, that old one died last Sunday 25.[30] This is all about died people. Well I found all my horses except one.
>
> Neil Buck

Grennie would have known all these people intimately. He knew most of the elders in the communities of Bylas and Calva along the southeastern border of San Carlos where he concentrated his work, and he would have sorely missed these old men and women. His network was wide and included the other big Arizona reservation, Fort Apache. He had spent about two weeks there during the summer of 1936 with an Apache named Tom Riley. Also known as Friday, he was Grennie's constant companion and interpreter while at Fort Apache.

While with Tom Riley Grennie noted: "The other day Friday took up his little grandson and teased him by showing him that I was *'inda·* [a white man]. He said that the little fellow had never seen a white man close to before. Then he set him down and told him to run, that if he didn't the *'inda·* would chase him. He ran alright. This is a fairly common way of scaring and teasing children."

Still, the kids must have grown attached to Grennie:

> My two grand children ask about you all the time. They say, "Where is that tall white man? Where that white man go to? When is he coming back?"
>
> Tom Riley

The abyss that yawns between the Apache world and the world of white people is one of the main themes throughout Grennie's writings. In time the things that separated Grennie from the Apaches were overcome by those that joined them, and deep bonds of trust were formed. But there was always an awareness that these friendships formed in spite of the fundamental differences between whites and Apaches. That there was deep trust between Grennie and his Apache friends is made even more apparent by the fact they could joke about their differences and discuss them openly.

Riley had served as a scout with the U.S. Army in the 1890s, as had his father before him. But his father was one of those scouts who turned against the army during a fight at the Fort Apache settlement of Cibecue in defense of the Apache medicine man Nock-ay-del-klinne in 1881. Known also, I believe, as "Dead Shot," Riley's father was hanged for his part in the encounter, and it was said that his wife hanged herself the same day.[31] Riley told my father that after the death of his mother, none of his relatives would take him but that a white man in Holbrook, a town north of the reservation, raised him until 1889, when he came back to Cedar Creek at Fort Apache and married. Riley had seen more of the world than many other Apaches, and perhaps had gained a heightened awareness of the things that separated Apaches from whites.

Grennie wrote, "Friday asked me for two more downy eagle feathers the other day." Riley told Grennie that when he went around with white people or interpreted for them, his Apache neighbors would hold it against him and accuse him of making lots of money. Riley continued:

> You see, I am just an Apache, just the same as the other people here. My mother was of the same people and so was my father, so I am nothing more than an Apache. No matter how much I associate with whites, talk with them, travel around with them, I am nothing but an Apache at heart. I can't help that. But here I have worked with you for three weeks and these people will talk about me and say, "Oh he is nothing but a white man. He goes about with white men all the time. He belongs to the white people. He is theirs." I don't want them to talk this way about me. So, if you give me those feathers, I'm going to tie them on the front of my shirt and wear them out among the people for about two weeks. Everyone will see me with them on and they will begin to think again that I am one of them, that I will hold to their

ways. Then I will take them off after a while and put them away. Everything will be alright for me again.

This sort of social criticism is taken very seriously among the Apaches. Any effort to appear better than or different from one's people could lead to public ridicule or even ostracism—terrible for the gregarious Apaches. Riley introduced Grennie to a friend who spoke of the importance of the community: "You know, your people are different, for some of you white people like to live far off by yourself, where no one else is. But that is not the way with us, for we cannot live like that, it is too lonely. We always like to be around where there are lots of other people and camps all about."

It seemed to some that the differences between the whites and the Apaches were so fundamental as to be on the order of a natural law. Gila Moses, a San Carlos medicine man with whom Grennie spent a great deal of time, said: "The God of my people and that of the whites must be different because the whites had everything given to them to live with and my people had hardly anything."

All the Apaches had to do was to look around them to see the truth in that. The picture of poverty, powerlessness, and prejudice on the reservation was grim. Neil Buck wrote:

> We stop at Goat ranch over night and in next morning that white man who had a goat there he send us away from his ranch. he said he dont want no Indians in his ranch. And so we come back this way about two miles and stay there over again.
>
> Neil Buck

Grennie saw exploitation in almost all contact the Apaches had with whites. This was just one example:

> Shi-cho and Andrew Stanley had gone to work picking cotton for old man Joe Hinton. They had picked cotton all day, but at the end of it, old Joe came out and gave them each a quarter. Andrew Stanley told the others, "How much did you get?" and they all told him a quarter. He stuck them under Joe's nose and said. "You mean to say this is all we get for a day's work?" When he saw that Andrew Stanley did not think much of the way he had done, he said, "shit," and then Andrew said "shit" also right back to him. Then Joe started for him, but Shi-cho got in between them. She did not want any fight

In his report on the San Carlos reservation Grennie has much to say about the tension between whites and Apaches. There are "white bullies on at least one border of the reservation who have run rough-shod over the Indians when they had the chance. The color line is an ever-present barrier to the inclusion of the Indian into the white culture and the Apache knows it."[32] Grennie vividly describes the scene one day at the white-owned and-operated Bylas store, the only place for Apaches to buy anything for miles around.

> I went to Osborne's store this noon after dinner. There were lots of the people in cars outside, and some were sitting in front of the store. Inside were about 20 men, some buying with their cattle money. Most of them had been given their checks this morning. Behind the counter stood Osborne and his clerks, anxious to get them to spend their money there and all pale faced from indoor work. Behind the counter also sat on a box Pasco.[33] He joked with the clerks. The people talked in their own language. There were hardly any women in the store at all and no children, though there were some youths there looking at the postcard stand. By the candy counter with his elbow leaning on it, half way behind it, stood Sam Hinton, red-faced and red-necked and fat, the typical white bully and boss.[34] He was standing there like a red-necked buzzard ready to get his hand on any of the people's money that he could, and there also to collect his debts and drum up his trade, I think. He had been there all day with his blue car parked outside. Later I saw him squatted outside talking with a bunch of the men about things. They sitting there allowing him to talk to them and politely listening, he talking as a boss. When they started to talk in their own tongue, he looked away as if he didn't care what they said. The whole thing left a bad taste in one's mouth.

This is the only subject on which Grennie expresses himself with real partisanship—albeit privately. The Apaches were trapped as second-class citizens in their own world. They were at the mercy of cattle buyers, the BIA, the reservation administration, and the police. In his report on San Carlos he writes: "Any relation between whites and these Indians is tainted by antagonism on both sides. It is hard for the Apache to forget that he has been dominated by whites contrary to his own culture and thought for almost sixty years, that he has been forced to observe and undertake rulings which are not his own."[35]

One of the small pleasures the Apaches enjoy is brewing and drinking a mild beer called *tułipai*. The San Carlos reservation was dry then, as it is now. Even the suspicion of making *tułipai* gave the police an excuse to make a raid. Neil Buck writes:

> Well friend, I am very sorry just because I did not answer you two letters yet. Well I just got back from jail last Monday. I stay in jail 22 days for I had one can of tulpie, this tulpie wasn't my but I got in Jail for it. So this is all for this morning. So Good Bye from you truly friend.
>
> Neil Buck

The reservation enforcers moved in on Christmas Day, 1936, and Grennie wrote:

> It seems to me as though the police and Pasco might let the people alone on Christmas day. They like to have good times on that day as anyone else. I hear they went out among the camps on Christmas day and raided for *tułipai*. They arrested John Rope and the son of Emory Starr and John Rope's daughter and gave them all ten days in jail. Pasco said they tried to fight him but that is not true.[36]
>
> I heard some more the other day about poor old John Rope's Christmas day. They had a can or two in the house there and Pasco came along to the door. He forced himself in and took the can and started to carry it outside. John Rope caught hold of him and tried to talk to him. He dropped the can and grabbed John Rope about the waist and threw him outside the house on the ground. Irene Rope went for Pasco and took hold of each of his ears and shook his head. She was mad at what he had done to her old father. She told him what she would do to him if she could. I don't blame her.

John Rope was one of the most highly respected men at Bylas. He had been a seasoned warrior in his youth before there were any reservations, and then he had served as an army scout under General George Crook in the 1880s during the final years of the Geronimo campaigns in the Sierra Madre. His life story, a remarkable epic, was recorded by Grennie in 1932 and published in *Apache Raiding and Warfare*. His encounter with Pasco must have reminded Grennie, as it reminds me, of a similar encounter in 1885 between a green young army officer,

Britton Davis and the Chiricahua warriors Chihuahua, Mangus, Geronimo, and others at Fort Apache. Tensions were high because of the army's overbearing meddling in Apache affairs. Sick of the prohibition on *tulipai,* the Apaches got reeling drunk, confronted the young officer, told him they had the right to drink anytime they wanted and challenged him to do anything about it. They reminded him that they had been killing their enemies in battle with their bare hands long before Davis was even born. The next day they bolted in defiance for Mexico.

But by 1936 the Apaches were beset by the dominant culture and must have felt powerless to understand and confront its ways. There must have seemed no way out of the white world and its impenetrable, Kafka-esque bureaucracy. There were times when Grennie must have seemed the only reliable go-between.

> Say Mr. Goodwin I going to tell you about what Albert Nellson want me to tell you. he said his son got in jail down at Globe last April and judge give him three months and Albert Nellson said he haven't got any letter from his son yet. he said Sheriff told him that you son is down Tucson. and so he went down there with his wife to see they son. but they son was not there. this boy his name is Fran Nellson. And Albert Nellson come down to Calva last Saturday with his wife to ask me about you, about where you at now. I told them that Mr. Goodwin is up at Santa Fe now. and they said they son might be up to San Antonio Texas. and they want you to found out for him about where his son is if you found out about where he is answer soon as you can please.
>
> Neil Buck

Grennie tried to be of some help because Neil Buck's next letter, written September 7, says: "I told him [Albert Nellson] the way you want me to tell him. Well I been ask Albert Nellson about where his son is. He said he know where his son is now. He said his son be back about 28 of August but he haven't show up yet."

There is no more said about Fran, but the Fates were not through with the Nellson family yet. The same letter continues:

> We heard one boy got kill by lighting over Cedar Creek. Got kill with his horse. Him and horse both of them died. This boy who got kill is Mike Nellson his grandson. You know old man Mike

Nellson we meet him one time down at San Carlos under the first point.

Neil Buck

In fact it must have seemed that there was no end to Apache misfortune:

Sure I glad I got your letter here few weeks ago. Well I'll tell you that I am alright also my family. And over here sometime Apache Indian men and women get kill everyday.

Walter Hooke

Say you know a man name G.1O he died last Sunday night at Rice Hospital about 11 o'clock. He was sitting on the run board on the right side while K. Robertson fixing his tire. and after a while he get up and walk on the other side the car and sit on running board again on the left side that's where he got hit by car. his feet all smash on the right side. Doctor been cut G.1O leg off right way. and he was died Sunday night about 11 o'clock.

Charley Sago

G.10 was a tag-band number used by the U.S. Army to identify Apaches when the reservation was first established, and the Apaches themselves often used these numbers as a convenience (see note 30). G.10's luck ran out this day in 1937, but there was at least one time when his luck was better and it saved his life. In late 1890 G.10 had an encounter with the infamous and widely feared outlaw, the Apache Kid. Grennie wrote in his diary:

One time, when the Kid was around here, before he went to Mexico, he shot G.10. It was on a ration day and all the people from Bylas used to go up to San Carlos on horses or in wagons. G.10 was the last one to go and was himself behind all the others. When he got to that point just west of Bylas, there was a lot of thick brush there and the Kid was in it. He crept up behind the brush and shot G.10 right through the chest and out his back, and knocked him off his horse. Then he came up and pulled off his moccasins and took them. He was going to put another bullet into G.10, but G.10 said, "You are just as well to leave me alone as you have already killed me." So he did. G.10's horse ran

> off then but came back in a little while and nudged him with his nose and woke him up. He got on his horse and rode slowly back to camp and got there in the evening.[37]

In a description of what is probably this attack in the October 18, 1890, issue of the Globe *Silver Belt*, it is claimed that the Kid said he was going to "kill every one of you I meet. I am going to stay here in your country." This threat could have been an extension of the blood feud the Kid had begun three years earlier to avenge the murder of his father.[38] This feud precipitated a series of events that led to the Kid's being arrested, convicted, and sentenced to hang in 1889. Instead of hanging, he escaped to Mexico and took up the outlaw life. The Apache Kid was and still is a favorite subject of folklore and gossip at San Carlos. It was widely known that the Kid moved back and forth between Arizona and Mexico. He would come to the reservation to kidnap women, steal horses, and visit his family. Because of his reputation for kidnapping women, he was given the Apache nickname of Bizhan Nantan—literally "Chief of Unmarried Women"—a term used jokingly to denote a womanizer.[39] It is said that he used to lurk at Geronimo Pass near the Fort Apache community of Canyon Day, waiting to seize women who camped there while traveling between the various settlements of the Fort Apache reservation.

A favorite topic of speculation among Grennie's friends at Bylas was the location of the Kid's many hideouts. Charley Sago, who wrote the letter about the death of G.10, took Grennie and Neil Buck to a series of caves in the mountains on the San Carlos reservation said to have been one of the Kid's boltholes. Grennie recorded in his diary: "Quite a few of the caves, they said, must have been used by the Kid as a hideout, but there was one little pocket in particular that had a lot of dry bushes and grass laid on the bottom of it they said the Kid must have used, and that he must have put the brush in here to sleep on so he could watch from here in all directions of approach."

In one of these caves the three men discovered human bones and a bag containing a skull, much to the alarm of Charley Sago, along with abundant signs of prehistoric occupation: masonry walls, petroglyphs, and one real treasure, a perfect flint knife, five inches long. Charley studied it carefully, regarded it covetously, and finally asked for it. Grennie gave it to him, knowing of the Apache belief that such things are made not by people, but by bolts of lightning. As such it would be a potent possession. Charley, a deeply traditional man, was shaken by his proximity to death in the cave. They reached home late that night, and Charley said he would not walk home from Neil's house and insisted on being driven to the door of his house. He was deathly afraid of encountering a ghost, and Grennie noted that the flint knife from the burial chamber may have been "burning a hole in his pocket."

Grennie was keenly aware of the role played by objects such as this knife in Apache daily life. He brought abalone shells to Charley Sago and Gila Moses from a trip to California. He brought seashells and plant specimens to Neil Buck from the coast of Maine. Charley Sago's mother told him that in the old days, when the men went on the warpath all the way to the Gulf of California, they would gather shells, always leaving something behind in exchange, such as beads or glass. Turquoise and eagle feathers were the most precious gifts Grennie could give.

> I've been so happy as can be when I have read your letter. Time after time, I stuck my nose to read it over again. So the "ring blue stone," which you sent me was marvelous, as to put you in a quick thumping of your heart. For as you told me that you and I will come together again and I hope will go on for so many days this time last time we went only for two days and it was not enough for me.
>
> Jackson Mocasque

> I lost the two turquoise you gave me. I'm sorry. If you can will you please give me some more?
>
> Tom Riley

> Say I forgot to tell you about what I want to ask you, say please send me some of that eagle feather which you found it. also I want some that medicine for ear. this all I want. please.
>
> Neil Buck

> If you have some blue stone and eagle feathers send it to me.
>
> Richard Bylas

> I received the feathers and the blue stone. My wife received the ring from your wife and she likes it very much and it fits on her finger all right.
>
> Richard Bylas

By October 1937 Grennie and Jan had been married for a year. He had finished his intensive fieldwork and they had settled in Santa Fe. He was working on *The Social Organization of the Western Apache* and Jan was busy with her painting. Earlier that year they had received two letters with heartbreaking news from Neil Buck about his son, Loney: "Loney Buck is sick. Now he can't eat much now. He said something wrong with his throat. He hardly talk too. He can hardly walk too. He don't go nowhere now he stay home all the time. Sometime we will be up there to see you and you wife when Loney gets well."

Ten days later:

> I got you letter last Saturday morning while I come up to get some milk for sick boy. I found ten dollars in that letter I am sure glad. I am very sorry for poor boy is died two days ago. Bad luck for me, all of my folks was very glad for that ten dollars which you been send it me. I told my boy about that money which you send it to me, and he said well Mr. Goodwin is good man. I give him one dollar out of that money you send it me. But he did not spent it for anything he still have it when he died I find one dollar in his pocket.

As was the Apache custom, Neil and his family moved their camp from the place where Loney died, and they probably burned their wickiup to the ground. Grennie had written him on hearing of Loney's death and sent some more money:

> Thanks for the money you send it to me. We been move to where old man Salto live. We stay in Joe his teepee yet. We just start to build our teepee two days ago. I feel sorry whenever I go alone, but sometime I go round some Indian I feel alright. I was feel sorry when I ride on my horse down Dewey Flat where I use to go for wood with my boy.

Grennie was urging him to come for a visit to Santa Fe, saying he would come and get him and the whole family anytime. After a visit with Susie Wright, the daughter of Anna Price (Grennie's Shi-cho, or grandmother), Neil writes:

> I went up to Bylas last Friday and stop at old woman her daughter camp. I mean old woman that used to call you her grandson. and that woman ask me about where you was now. I said to her I got a letter this morning and then I been read the letter to her. I show the picture of you wife too. she said looks pretty good. she said she always talking about you and remember you. I been told her about that you want me to come up there with my children sometime.

Then Neil continues about two of his nieces attending the Indian boarding school in Santa Fe: "Two of my uncle his daughters up there at Santa Fe school. They name is Beulah Buck and one Ollie Buck. This two girls is from Bylas."

Jan and Grennie did go to the school and must have seen a good deal of the two girls because eventually Jan persuaded them to pose for a painting, a double portrait. The painting shows the girls just as they must have been, unaccustomed to the artist's scrutiny, their eyes cast down, their faces even more expressive for the mute, averted gaze.[40]

Susie Preston, Anna Price's granddaughter had been keeping in touch, telling Grennie of Anna's health, thanking Grennie for his offer to visit her husband and another relative upon their release from jail a month hence.

> I am still thinking about you two, when you two were here, talking about everything. We are very sorry because my grandmother she still sick yet. She just getting very old now and why the reason for she get sick. That's why one of our school boy is closed from school. And this boy is going to work, for there is no one to support the family. Well I say thank to you because you visit my husband and George Bylas when is they come out of jail maybe in May. Shi-cho said good-bye and hello to you wife and she say she want some calico so she remember of you for that.
>
> Susie Preston

While Jan and Grennie lived in Santa Fe, the human landscape of Bylas was changing fast, and almost every letter came with the news of another loss:

> You know old man Bob Knowles he got run over by meat truck just in front of his house last November 10, 1937. this been happened just about seven o'clock in the evening and he die at 11 o'clock. This old man been buried down at Globe Saturday afternoon, November 14, 1937.

And then, in the same letter, the death they must have been expecting at any time. Anna Price was gone:

> I going to tell you about what old Ci-tco [Shi-cho] her daughter [Susie Wright] want me to tell you. she said her mother been send a note to you for calico to send it down to her but she died after few days. she been ask for calico. she said she don't want to be lost her mother's words. she said what her mother said got to be done not be lost her words. she mean she want some calico for herself. Well Christmas be here soon. I think I go kill chicken for dinner.
>
> All of my children and my woman said to you Hello there Mr. Goodwin and Mrs. Goodwin.
>
> Neil Buck

Grennie sent the calico.

> I sure was very glad when I received the cloth that you have sent to me. All I can say is thank you. You know I can't do anything for you.
>
> Today I went out on the mesa to see if I can find some flower to send it to you with this letter.
>
> I like to hear from you often and help me too. It remind me if I were hearing from my brother. . . .
>
> So good-bye and answer soon.
>
> Your friend
> Susie Wright

In the summer of 1938, as promised, Grennie drove to San Carlos from Santa Fe and picked up Neil Buck and his wife, Ollie, and three children, Bobby, Katie, and Vera. He brought them back to Santa Fe, where they spent two weeks, and then Grennie drove them back to Bylas. Neil and his family in all likelihood had never been so far from home. If Santa Fe was comfort, variety, and adventure, Bylas was heat, dust, poverty, oppression, and thwarted hopes—reminders of all the ways in which the reservation system had failed the Apache people. Never bitter about his lot, Neil remains stoic and writes soon after his return:

> I didn't sold much cattles this year. I only sold five heads and didn't catch up on my grocers bill and so, behind on what you loan me when we was up there at Santa Fe with you. Yes all my folk talking about you and your wife. We all said that Mrs. Goodwin she was lonesome when we left her alone. We always remember you and your wife because you been good to us and take us long way and lots things which we never see before.
>
> Neil Buck

Neil's wife and my mother had become fast friends:

> I was so glad to get the picture of your house. I see that dog and see your mother sitting on the chair. We see you standing by the chair with your husband Goodwin. we see the picture of you house is pretty good. its good house you got we was very glad to see you mother, you dog, you house and you with you husband . . . you know that when we was up there at Santa Fe you and you husband took us every places where we never been before. we always remember that about where we been and where we eating our dinners my children always remember you, Mrs. Goodwin.
>
> Mrs. Buck

A few months later, not having heard from Grennie, Neil writes:

> I am going to write a short letter to you this morning to wants to know where you are. I been write to you one month ago and haven't heard from you yet. so I just want to know where you at now. My children always remember and talking about you and you wife. Answer soon please.
>
> Neil Buck

For perhaps the first time in years, Neil Buck did not know where Grennie was. There is a footnote in my mother's hand, at the bottom of her typed copy of the above letter: "G. may have gone to Colorado Springs to see a neurologist [first signs of brain trouble] while I was in Carmel, California." In 1987 she wrote to me as I was beginning to try to piece together parts of my father's life: "It was in 1938 that he began to worry about strange feelings in his head, as if, he said, 'The top of my head was coming off.' He went to a neurologist in Colorado Springs who was not much help and did not know the cause."

My mother remembers certain signs—mood changes, temperament: "I think about this time his brain tumor might have been starting, as I remember now, certain little things, taking it out on me."

Jan and Grennie made a trip to Carmel, California, to visit a favorite cousin and close friends. My mother remembers this trip well—picnics on the rocks, watching sea otters, the dramatic, moody coastline, fog-bound and rocky. Neil Buck did not know about Grennie's trip to the Colorado doctor, as he had not known about his tuberculosis in 1933, but Grennie finally wrote to Neil, sending abalone shells so precious to the Apaches because of their use in the girls' puberty ceremony. Neil reminds him of two things: how much superior they are to the shells from the coast of New England and that he has not forgotten the money that Grennie loaned to him one time:

> And now last Saturday I got some shells from you and now I know where you was. We was very glad to get that shells which you been send it to us. this shells is better than got from east. this Bylas Indians need this shells pretty bad. they like it. I haven't got any money to send it to you. I didn't sold much cattles this year. my bill in store high yet. we might sell some this spring then we have some money to send it to you.
>
> Neil Buck

The rest of 1938 and part of 1939 Jan and Grennie spent in Santa Fe, but they saw their future in Tucson, where they had been planning to build a house. They may have been planning more than that, and it took a trip on my part to San Carlos and a visit with Barbara, one of Neil Buck's daughters, to find it out.

Barbara is sedate and quiet, but moved by my unexpected visit.

"I had always hoped," she says, "that you would come to visit me. I remember holding you when you were just a baby."

Her whole family must have come for a visit while we were living in Tucson—just as they had come for a visit to Santa Fe. If my father had lived, she would have been my Apache sister—our fathers were that close. I feel the residual power of the tie that bound Grennie and Neil to one another and through that, our two families across space and time.

"You look like your father. He could talk Apache real well," she says.

The Apaches had a name for him: "White Man Talks," because he was always visiting and talking with the people. She remembers my mother well. Fragments come to the surface of her memory: the two-week trip they made to Santa Fe, and a funny joke about Navajos that my father made, the dress her mother made for mine.

Then she tells me something I have never heard before. Before my father died, Neil Buck and his family were planning to move to Tucson. Grennie had found a piece of land, and the Bucks were going to live there. I don't know if the land was near the land he and Jan had already bought east of Tucson or who was going to buy it, but for Barbara and her family it was a reality.

Another plan made, but soon undone, that might have determined the trajectory of my life. Would I have grown up in some way among this Apache family, and become from birth what my father may always have wished for himself? I can only imagine that the plan was that the Bucks were to live near or even with us, and that we would have made a life together.

As close as my father was to Neil Buck, and as close as I might have become to Barbara, my Apache sister, I know that she and I have come a great distance since our fathers planned a life around their friendship and that now we are worlds apart.

What did our fathers have in mind? Did Grennie want to have Neil nearby? Did Neil want to be near my father? They were more than friends, they were like brothers. What, I wonder, would life for the Bucks have been like on East Speedway? That must have been where their land would have been—near our ranch. They were so used to the rhythms of community life at Bylas: the neighbors, the friends, the cousins, the animals, the land, the serendipity of the Apache day with chance visits and gossip. Without those things they would have been isolated in Tucson. Grennie must have known this, so what was the larger plan behind this perplexing piece of information? Since Neil and Grennie were such complete collaborators in the fieldwork on the reservations, perhaps this proximity had to do with Grennie's long-range plans for the publication of a series of monographs on Apache culture based on the encyclopedic volume of raw field notes.

By late 1938, *Myths and Tales of the White Mountain Apache* had been published. The manuscript for *Social Organization of the Western Apache* was finished, though it was not yet ready to be published as a

Left to right: Ollie Buck, Katie Buck, Barbara Buck, Neil Buck, unidentified mounted man; Calva, San Carlos Reservation, 1935. (Courtesy Arizona State Museum, negative #18274)

Left to right: Vera Buck, Ollie Buck, Barbara Buck, Katie Buck, Neil Buck, Jan Goodwin; Santa Fe, 1938.

Barbara Buck King, the daughter of Neil Buck; San Carlos, 1997.

Left to right: Katie Buck, Vera Buck, Barbara Buck; Santa Fe, 1938.

Tom "Friday" Riley at his camp, Fort Apache reservation, unidentified man by car, 1936. (Courtesy Arizona State Museum, negative #18197)

Inset: Neil Buck, my father's best friend; Calva, San Carlos, about 1951. (Photo by Charles Kaut)

Anna Price, White Mountain Apache elder, Grennie's Apache grandmother. (Courtesy Arizona State Museum, negative #18265)

Left to right: Ollie Buck, Katie Buck, Vera Buck, Grenville Goodwin, Barbara Buck, Neil Buck; Santa Fe, 1938.

Tom "Friday" Riley with unidentified children at his camp, Fort Apache reservation, 1936. (Courtesy Arizona State Museum, negative #18150)

Richard Bylas, his wife Susie Jose, and her son, San Carlos reservation, 1932. (Courtesy Arizona State Museum, negative #18245)

John Rope, White Mountain Apache elder, Grennie's close friend and advisor. (Courtesy Arizona State Museum, negative #18257)

book. Jan and Grennie moved back to Tucson for the summer of 1939 when he was given an appointment at the University of Arizona as a research associate.

During that summer, my mother's father came for an extended visit. He had not seen Grennie or Jan at all since the day of their abrupt departure from Brookline late in 1936. My mother was by now pregnant and perhaps she felt it was time to reach out to her folks. She knew her father had been hurt and that he didn't really understand what had happened.

Grandfather was a life-long diarist. Everything he ever did, from the most momentous to the utterly mundane, went into his daily diary. He methodically recorded the details of his visit with Jan and Grennie and the ways in which he and his son-in-law came to know each other. Nearly every day, starting before dawn the two of them, sometimes with my mother, set out for long horseback rides into the Rincon and Santa Catalina Mountains east of Tucson. My father took his solemn electrochemist father-in-law through these foothills, where my grandfather marveled in his diary over the giant cactus, the rattlesnakes, the Gila monsters (they saw two this summer), and the other fauna and flora that must have been utterly exotic to him.

I have no idea what they talked about. I can't imagine my father had much interest in Trollope, Dickens, Thackeray, Bach, Schubert or electroplating—or that my grandfather knew what to make of Grennie's life among the Apaches.

My grandfather was fascinated when Grennie made a fire with two pieces of wood, describing in his careful scientist's way exactly how it was done. Throughout this month they explored the mountains together, and through this mostly silent process, the two settled into familiarity. And my grandfather came to understand how different the life my mother had fashioned for herself was from the one she had left back home in Brookline, Massachusetts.

After my grandfather left for the East, he and my father did not see each other again. Even though my father's headaches were worsening and there was still no diagnosis, he had decided it was time for a new and demanding undertaking.

My mother wrote to me in 1987:

> Having had no formal training in the techniques of ethnology, G. was anxious to learn more and decided to go to the University of

Chicago and take some postgraduate courses. We spent the winter there while his head condition grew worse and began to affect his eyesight and to cause headaches. He carried on with his studies just the same and did remarkably well.

And he never lost touch with his Apache friends. In fact at the end of the summer, Grennie had made the time to take Neil Buck and another Apache named Tony Nasby to San Francisco for a visit, where he had taken pictures of them framed by the Golden Gate Bridge and posed next to a whale skeleton:

> I been told Charley Sago all about what we saw down at the World Fair in San Francisco and the way back too. Well we sure glad to know that you getting along fine with you wife, but we Indian had a whooping cough about two months and a half now. Richard Bylas ask me about you. Charley Sago said him and me will go to see you when you come back to your farm [land that Grennie and Jan had bought east of Tucson].
>
> Katie she is not going to school yet. I been told her about that you going to school up at Chicago.
>
> Neil Buck

I was born in Chicago on March 29, 1940. Things were going well, but a nightmare would soon take control of our lives. My grandfather's diary chronicles the sequence of events throughout April and May:

> ***Sunday, April 14, 1940***
>
> This morning Janice called up from Chicago to ask Lil [my mother's mother] to go to Chicago as Grennie has to go to the hospital for an operation on the brain. So we are considerably worried.
>
> ***Monday, April 15***
>
> This morning, Mrs. Hare [my father's mother] telephoned to say she was flying to Chicago on the surgeon's advice. The operation is to be tomorrow morning.

Jan, Neil, and Grenville Goodwin; Chicago, May 1940.

Tuesday, April 16

This evening Janice called up from Chicago to say Grennie's operation was successful and that it was a tumor on the brain. I was so overcome with relief that I could hardly talk.

Sunday, April 21

Janice called up to say that Grennie was getting on well, the second time she has telephoned since the operation.

Sunday, May 12

I have been expecting Lil since last night. She must have stopped off in Buffalo. The war news takes up a good deal of time and is very depressing.

Sunday, May 26

The war news is getting worse and worse. It makes me feel as though I had failed in something myself.

My mother's 1987 letter to me: "He then had to take to his bed, getting so much worse. When Dr. Fay-Cooper Cole, the head of the Department of Anthropology, came to tell him that the University of Chicago Press was going to publish his epic work, *Social Organization of the Western Apache*, and he would be entitled to a Ph.D., G. smiled, but did not speak."

My mother said to her own mother: "Grennie also has the satisfaction of hearing from more than one person that his material was the finest of its kind that has come out of America."

And then to me in 1987: "We had planned to go to Laguna Beach in California for the summer, and the doctors said we might as well go, knowing G. had not long to live, but I was never told this."

My mother is gone. I know that she died, but I still just think of her as gone. I wasn't there when she took her own life at the age of eighty-six in a final defiant, desperate act of independence. Just as she held the key to her own life and took it with her, so she may have held and kept a key to Grennie's life.

I can only imagine why she was never told that Grennie would not recover, and nothing makes any sense. Perhaps my father persuaded his own mother and the doctors to keep it from her. His mother was autocratic and accustomed to taking control; perhaps she decided that with a newborn, my mother was in no condition to absorb such news, and that for her own good, or my good, Jan was not to know. My mother was tougher than any of them imagined, but she was also intimidated by Grennie's formidable mother and family, and must have felt she had no choice but to trust them and the doctors, though in fact they were depriving her of the one crucial piece of information she needed in order to decide what to do next.

Jan and Grennie had been looking forward to a summer in California. The doctors, knowing now that there would be no recovery, blandly advised my mother to take the train to California, and what . . . "convalesce in the healing sun?"

It all seems such a pointless lie. Did Grennie in his stoicism imagine that he was protecting my mother and me? Was he at all in collusion, or had his mother taken over, cowing the doctors, Grennie, and Jan alike, imagining that by controlling the truth, she could somehow control the outcome of events? Did she believe that if Jan weren't told Grennie was dying, somehow she wouldn't be aware of it until it was mercifully over? Was it all just well-meaning but poor judgment? The outcome of this deception was a descent into hell: "We had a terrible trip to Los Angeles on the Super Chief, and he suffered agonies, begging for more painkillers, but I could not make his trained nurse give him any more."

There were now three of us. Somehow my father must have appeared to be well enough for us all to board the Los Angeles train in Chicago. My mother had no idea what was in store for the next three days. There was a trained nurse traveling with us. En route my father's condition quickly deteriorated and his post-operative pain became unbearable. Inexplicably, the trained nurse with us refused to administer more painkillers, though my father and mother begged her to do so. By the time his condition had become extremely serious, there was nowhere to get off the train. There were no adequate medical facilities en route. When we got to Los Angeles he was taken by ambulance to a hospital. His mother and older brother, Sage, arrived by airplane.

My grandfather's diary:

Tuesday, June 25

> A frightful letter from Mrs. Hare [Grennie's mother] this morning from Los Angeles saying that Grennie has had a relapse and that he cannot recover. So everything that looked so bright a moment before changed completely. Apparently Janice does not know it, but I cannot help thinking his going back to the hospital must worry her.

My mother's 1987 letter to me: "When we arrived in Los Angeles, G. was taken off the train by stretcher, driven in an ambulance to the hospital where he died a few days later at the age of thirty-three."

My grandmother cabled to her son Sage in Connecticut, who had just made the transcontinental roundtrip to see his brother in the hospital: "Grennie died peacefully last night. Uncle Joe, John, and Wally will be there. Do not try to come. Mother."

My grandfather's diary:

> ***Wednesday, July 3***
>
> I have been thinking of Janice at Tucson this evening; the service for Grennie is to be at 7 P.M. there, in an hour and a half. How well I remember it with the heat, the brown desert, the enormous giant cactus, the doleful song of the doves and the smell of the creosote bushes before a rain. . . . Evie [Evelyn Riesman, my mother's sister] telephoned she tried to get airplane reservations to reach Tucson, but it was impossible.

My mother's 1987 letter to me:

> The ceremony was held on the ranch . . . on the highest piece of land facing west and opened to both mountain ranges—with mesquite trees and a giant cactus. . . . Those present were John and Walter Goodwin, Mrs. Hare, Betty Holter [Grennie's first cousin], Jack Burling [a Boston friend of Jan's], and some of the Department. Ned Spicer stood up and said a few words, beautifully simple and moving.
>
> My own great loss is subordinated by the relief that his suffering is over. . . . Afterwards we had a fire and a little picnic supper and the sky was full of stars.

And this letter from Elizabeth, my paternal grandmother, to Lillian, my maternal grandmother:

> It is so hard not to picture all the joys that might have been, but Jan is so right in her attitude; she has shown great character and fortitude. She and Grennie had a very extraordinary relationship. She, as far as I can see, has no self-pity. The ranch was all settled and Jan has found everything in such order that it almost seemed as if fate had shared in the planning. There was no thing unfinished except their life together.

And in a letter to me from my mother: "Among the letters, there is one Neil Buck wrote me after G's death mentioning a ceremonial dance held at Bylas in his honor. I don't believe that any other white man had ever had such a tribute paid to him by the Apaches."

> Your letter of July 8 received about my brother G. Goodwin was died in Los Angeles. A man hand the letter to me while we was eating our supper in evening. So I open it up right away and see my brother has died, and so we just drop our supper and cry with all of my family. I got no more friend than he. I been told all his friend whom a living at Bylas. They said they thinking that Mr. Goodwin was never going to die because he is a good man to everyone down here at Bylas and down at San Carlos. I didn't answer sooner because I got to go around Indians and tell them about their friend Goodwin.
>
> I heard the Indians said that some dance going to start next Friday night up about one mile above Bylas. You know where the dance ground is. they going to dance two night. Big eat, kill about 12 or 13 head steers. We going to have lots meat to eat.
>
> Say, Jan Goodwin, where did you buried him I like to know about where that is so I might go there see sometime.
>
> This is all today so good bye from your truly friend Neil Buck.

After Grennie's death, Jan wrote down these words, and I found them many years later—the only record I have of what Grennie actually said to me:

> The things that Daddy used to say to Neil in Chicago when Neil was a little boy about two months old.
>
> Yes, son, you and I are going places together. I'm going to teach you everything I know. I'll teach you all about the animals and the plants. I'll teach you all about how to camp, and ride, so you will be able to take care of yourself when you are off by yourself—know how to shoot and how to look out for the wild animals.
>
> Yes, son, we'll do all those things. We'll let Mummie come too, because she's all right. We like her and we'll let her come, won't we, son? All those things we will do, boy, you and I.
>
> He would sing high squeaky Apache songs that Neil loved, and would look at Neil and talk Spanish to him: "*Es muy coyote—sí—es muy coyote.*"

The San Carlos Experience

chapter six

This section was not written as part of *The Apache Diaries;* it would have been too much of a digression, but the journey attempted in "The San Carlos Experience" was very much on my mind as I wrote the last part of *The Apache Diaries.* I knew this journey was one I had to attempt, though I had avoided it for two years. I did not know how to begin. I did not know how far to go.

This is about Grennie's total immersion in Apache sacred knowledge. I wanted to explore his experience on the reservation, and I wanted to explore his experience of sacred knowledge, evoking the power with which it spoke to him without ever betraying its secrets. Not that I know any of the secrets of Apache sacred knowledge, at least not in the sense that he did, in the sense that an Apache does. All I have are thousands of pages of Grennie's field notes, transcribed by my mother over a period of many years. I can read what he wrote, but there is much that I do not understand. Copies of these notes are in the archives of the Arizona State Museum, and because of the sensitive nature of much of what they contain, access to them is restricted. Consistent with the spirit of these restrictions, I have been careful not to divulge specific ceremonial or personal details contained in his notes and diaries that would offend the Apaches. All the same I have some uneasiness, as I am throughout faced with the dilemma of what and what not to say. To a certain extent I have been guided by others, but most especially by Grennie himself, who salted his field notes with parenthetical caveats, as if to remind himself of the pitfalls in what he was recording.

"The San Carlos Experience" is about more than ceremonial knowledge; it tries to reconstruct Grennie's reservation experience from the early days of 1928 through his last fieldwork in 1936. He began by simply getting to know people, asking them about their life stories, using those epic narratives as points of departure into the details of everyday life and into the Apache language, which he knew he had to learn if he were to make any real progress. Apache was unwritten, so he had to pick it up by ear. He had a gift for languages and he was young when he started, so by 1931 he was speaking the language fairly well.

Grennie's education continued at the hands of the Apache elders, and the richness of his experience deepened. There are times when an entirely new voice emerges from his writing—one that is personal, subjective, immediate. It is so rich in detail, and the verbal pictures are so clear and vivid, that the Apaches and their culture come brilliantly to life. Although he does not often write like this, when he does I am certain that it is quite deliberate and that he has been moved beyond science.

At every turn, he encountered Apache spirituality and, knowing its vital importance, Grennie allowed himself to be guided through the intricacies of the culture by friends whose advice on sacred knowledge would prove essential to his enterprise. Even so, they could not protect him from what they saw as the dangers in the knowledge of supernatural power. His closest friends felt he may have been told too much. To this day, there are those who feel that the powers about which he wrote may have turned on him, causing his early death. I have been told that it is an Apache tenet that this supernatural power cannot hurt you unless you believe in it, so I take it that the Apaches may feel that Grennie believed. Grennie himself is mute on the subject, but I look for clues between the lines of what he writes. I am told that I do not know enough about these powers (and therefore am not in a position to believe) to be in any jeopardy; nevertheless, it is with some trepidation that I undertake this journey myself. ✣

GETTING STARTED

Grenville Goodwin began his work like a nineteenth-century ethnographer, with one important exception. Although the Apache reservations of the 1930s were administered in a virtually colonial fashion, and many ethnographers of the time had colonial attitudes toward Native Americans, Grennie did not see the Apaches as lesser beings. He was not handicapped with preconceptions or academic constructs. He went straight into the field seeking an experience of total immersion equipped with only his own curiosity, common sense, confidence, and perhaps most important of all, ingenuity. He absorbed Apache culture with a measured but capacious appetite and set it down in thousands of pages of field notes. In all those pages there is hardly a single direct hint of what the experience was like for him. But, somewhat like a star whose orbit is influenced by a hidden gravitational force, there is at the very core of Grennie's years among the Apaches, a deep well of unexpressed experience. I think it came gradually from years of exposure to Apache spirituality through both the simple rhythms of everyday life and his ever-widening grasp of ceremonial and sacred knowledge.

Underlying Apache religion is a belief in certain supernatural powers that govern the course of events in the world and in the lives of all its living beings. The potency of these powers is such that they must be treated with extreme caution, and only by deeply experienced people, such as medicine men. Otherwise there is great risk.

Whether or not the Apaches felt that Grennie should have been researching sacred knowledge so deeply, there appears to be agreement on one thing at least: to do so was potentially dangerous in the extreme, though his friends and advisors protected him and themselves as best they could in their own way.

When an Apache asked me three years ago what it was he died of, and I told her it was a brain tumor, she nodded and said, "Oh. Of course." And she explained to me that there are certain powers that are known to cause such illnesses. She said that my father got too close to the sources of sacred knowledge, that the power turned on him, that she had seen it happen before, that such misfortune is well known.

No one had ever spoken to me of my father's death in this way. I was utterly unprepared for it, and at first it felt like an invasion of privacy, the revision of a history entirely mine: the circumstances of my father's death. Was it also a judgment, a criticism, even a political position growing from the repatriation movement? Worst of all, was his death in any sense seen as a sort of retribution for deliberate trespass? I did not know how to confront these immediate, visceral reactions: the landscape had irreversibly shifted. I could no longer think of my father's reservation experience in terms of the tidy package I had always imagined. It was far more complex and nuanced than I had imagined, and the key to it was in a kind of spiritual experience—something he would not have written directly about, because he may not even have consciously sensed it. It had become the water in which he swam: life-giving as well as life-endangering.

Then, in later discussions with Charles Kaut, I learned that Neil Buck himself had said that people at the time felt Grennie had died because he had gone too deeply into Apache religion. In order to understand it, Grennie had come into contact with the powerful forces of the universe through a series of religious and philosophical dialogues with the high priests of Apache spirituality.

I realized for the first time what truly alien territory he had entered, and what follows is an attempt to understand his journey.

> This I am telling you was told to me by my grandmother, and before she told it to me, she heard it from her grandmother and before that her grandmother heard it from another old person. That is the way it is with our people. You white people have books and written records, but everything we know about our people is written in our heads.[41]

The elders of the San Carlos and Fort Apache reservations were to become my father's university. It is not hard to imagine why he was so drawn to the Apache way of life and to the keepers of the culture. I think he recognized its elemental beauties and fundamental truths as kindred values long before he recorded and mastered their complexities. Far less easy to understand is why the Apaches were so willing to tell a young white man what was written in their heads and allow, indeed encourage, him to write it on paper for the first time. To do so went counter to Apache tradition, to say the least. The linguist, Harry Hoijer, having observed Grennie at work, wrote:

> Grenville Goodwin was one of the few ethnologists I have known who came to the people he was studying with a genuine interest in them as human beings. He became their friend, he learned to speak their language, and lived with them for long periods, entering into as close association with them as is possible for a person of a different social group. The Apache accepted him as one of them; they spoke to him in their native tongue, unhampered by the presence of interpreters and other impedimenta of ethnological research. To them he was not another curious white who came to pry into their lives; he was simply a young man who asked to be taught in the life ways of the Apache. They taught him, much in the same way as they taught the young men of their own race

> and he sat with them with a patience and interest equal to theirs, listening to their artless tales and descriptions and carefully sifting from this wealth of detail the recurrent patternings of their culture.[42]

In 1997 I went to visit Thelma Kindelay, the granddaughter of the great medicine man, Francis Drake, and found that she remembered Grennie's visits. She and the other kids were sent away because her grandfather and my father had important things to talk about. She said that my father always wore a sacred Apache charm, saying that because the charm was sacred its exact nature should remain private—it could be spoken of between us but should not be written down or made public. It would have been given to him only because he had earned it, because he had been deemed worthy. Such a thing cannot be bought nor given casually. What's more, Grennie always carried a medicinal root in his pocket, given to him by Francis Drake for protection. Thelma then gave me some of this root—the last of a batch collected years ago by the grandson of Anna Price, the respected elder who was such a close friend of my father's in the 1930s.

This experience, as affecting as it was brief, was in a way a very small sample of Grennie's own experience—at once intimate and circumscribed. This glimpse has given me a new way of understanding what it was like for my father to live and work among the Apaches. He may have been drawn to them at first because of the intellectual challenge of understanding an exotic culture. What in time bound Grennie and his Apache friends to each other was the simple humanity that they found they had in common.

Although he may have seen something of the Apache people while at the Mesa Ranch School between 1923 and 1925, his first exposure to an Apache community was in the fall of 1927, when he worked at a logging camp in McNary on the northern edge of the Fort Apache reservation. Whether he might have had any contact with Apache culture at this time is purely speculative, but he might well have made Apache friends, picked up a few words, visited people at home. Earlier that summer he had had a chance encounter with one John Hoffman on the Navajo reservation in which he heard something so vivid and remarkable that it may well have determined the course of his life. Hoffman, a white BIA policeman, told Grennie about a 1910 encounter with the legendary Bronco Apaches who lived in the wild in Mexico's Sierra Madre. They were dressed in the old time way—G-string, headband, moccasins. They still lived by hunting, gathering, and raiding local ranches. Mexicans were terrified of them, but these Apaches welcomed Hoffman and he was their guest for three days. When he left, they gave him a message for the Apaches at San Carlos.

Grennie tucked this compelling information away, perhaps wondering how he could find his own purchase on this story. In the meantime he was trying on various professions for size. He spent the winter of 1927–28 as a fire warden manning a watchtower in the forest southwest of Los Alamos, New Mexico. In the spring of 1928 he made what appears to have been a serious historical and scholarly trip through old Spanish colonial settlements from Texas to California, producing a meticulously written and illustrated personal monograph with a focus on missionary settlements and architecture. He and a cousin then spent the summer as resident superintendents at the Frijoles Canyon (now Bandelier) National Monument, an archaeological site in northern New Mexico full of ancestral Pueblo cliff dwellings.

TUCSON

Following a brief August 1928 trip to Mexico, Grennie moved to Tucson. He had maintained contact with Dean Byron Cummings, the noted archaeologist at the University of Arizona, and in the coming months, Cummings's mentoring would become a decisive factor in the course of Grennie's life. Details are sketchy. He had a university student card, but there's no transcript for this year, so he wasn't officially enrolled. In a letter to his mother, he says his landlady keeps a vase of fresh flowers on his dresser "which is nice." So I know he had an apartment or a rented room and, though not exactly homesick, he at least wanted his mother to know that, though he had abandoned the world in which he was raised, he had not coarsened beyond recognition. Whatever he may have been doing at the university, he was already spending time on the San Carlos Apache reservation. It was in the fall of 1928 that he first met the respected White Mountain elder John Rope, the equivalent of a chief, in Bylas, a settlement at the southeastern corner of the reservation. But Grennie was leading a far from settled life and was not one to miss a chance at real adventure.

In December 1928 or January 1929 Grennie packed his bags and headed for Canada to join a distant cousin, Douglas Burden, in the making of an epic motion picture called *The Silent Enemy.* It was filmed on location in a north woods deep winter. The cast was made up almost entirely of the Ojibwe people of Lake Temiscamingue, Ontario, and the film, a more or less scripted drama, depicted the all-too-real struggle of the people to survive the northern winter when food ran low and life depended on finding the elusive caribou herds for the tribe's hunters.

Years later, Grennie told my mother that his job was to be in charge of the caribou for the hunt sequences. That may well have been the case, but what he seemed to have spent most of his time doing was learning to speak Ojibwe and making meticulous pencil drawings and watercolors of the things the Ojibwe made by hand: snowshoes, animal snares, hide stretchers, birch-bark containers, birch-bark canoes, moccasins, crooked knives, and dozens of other things. He took pictures of the Ojibwe people he met and made long lists of Ojibwe words. I can tell just by looking at the notebooks from this winter how much he loved the work. It was done with a skill, confidence, and passion that leave no doubt he knew perfectly well how accomplished he was. He spent most of the winter there, and in due course came back to Tucson having done his first real piece of original ethnography.

Continuing a sort of apprenticeship with Cummings, Grennie spent the summer of 1929 in the University of Arizona summer school working on the archaeological excavation of a prehistoric pueblo at Turkey Hill near Flagstaff. He returned to Tucson in the fall as a full-time undergraduate, but he had been busy making contacts at San Carlos. He spent Christmas that year at Bert Rupkey's trading post in the reservation settlement of Coolidge. He remembered these months as the beginning of his long study of the Apaches.[43]

The escalating warfare between the Sierra Madre Apaches and Mexican ranchers in Sonora and Chihuahua was beginning to make headlines in American newspapers. In February 1930, Grennie went to the Arizona border town of Douglas to find out more, and he began to keep a written record of all he heard about these people. Entries became more and more frequent during the course of the year, and by November he was back in Douglas about to begin his search for the Sierra Madre Apaches.

If going to Mexico had been all he did in 1930, it would have been a remarkably productive year. By the time he came back, he was the first ethnographer to have taken an interest in the Sierra Madre Apaches and one of the few white men at the time not bent on their destruction. Going to Mexico was only one of the many enterprises he undertook in this pivotal year, however. Grennie finished out the semester at the University of Arizona and headed directly back into the field—not to Apache country, but this time to the Navajo reservation and a job at Goulding's Trading Post in Monument Valley. Encouraged by Cummings, he had tentatively decided to make a study of the Navajos. He had already spent time on the Navajo reservation and would have been familiar with their weaving, jewelry, and dramatic ceremonials.

He took my mother back to Goulding's in 1938 and told her about his summer there, cleaning up an enormous pile of trash behind the post, leaving his footprints in wet cement in a storeroom they were building, spitting pumpkin seeds for distance with the trader's brother, Paul Goulding. Whatever else he may have done there, he appeared to have done precious little ethnography, but he did learn an invaluable lesson. Working at the trading post gave him a "real" reason to be on the Navajo reservation among the Indians. That is to say, he was not there as an anthropologist, he was just "the new kid behind the counter at the post." He could learn the ways of the people by just watching. He told his older brother, Sage, that he learned the most by just listening and saying nothing.

Grennie was at Goulding's off and on until January 1931; I know that from his dated notes, but it was clear that his interest was already shifting to the Apaches. One of the things he found out at Goulding's was that the Navajo reservation was already thick with anthropologists. He spent much of August at places he already knew on the Apache reservations, partly at Coolidge Dam, where he worked behind the counter at Rupkey's Trading Post, as he had at Goulding's—meeting people and asking them the Apache words for everyday things. He got around though. He spent at least a week on the Fort Apache reservation—at Carrizo and Cibecue. With connections made at Rupkey's, he could easily have hitched a ride to Fort Apache, but my guess is that he had his own car and he made his way to Fort Apache by giving rides to people who needed them. Between August 9 and 16, he went to two separate puberty ceremonies at Fort Apache, and there would have been people at San Carlos who needed a way to get to these all-important coming-of-age ceremonials held for relatives on the neighboring reservation. Grennie's record of the ceremonials contains a brief but vivid description of an image that, seen for the first time, has unforgettable power, timelessness, and beauty:

> They started at about nine o'clock in the evening. The singers with four drums sat in two lines facing each other. Girls selected their men partners by touching them on the back. The girl for whom the ceremony was being given chose hers by touching them with the cane. Part of the time she danced with a girl partner who had had a dance held for her the night before. They had abalone shell disks in the hair over their foreheads and a downy eagle feather in the hair at the back of their heads.

Perhaps he had seen such a ceremony before, but the description dated August 9–10, 1930, is his earliest recorded observation among the Apaches that I have found. Before leaving Fort Apache, he had a conversation with an Apache policeman at Cibecue who told him a story that hooked Grennie for good on the Apaches in general, and the Sierra Madre Apaches in particular. He was told that "Geronimo's people" sometimes came up from Old Mexico—as recently as the previous year—to steal horses and young women. They were, of course, talking about the Apaches who remained in Mexico following the surrender of Geronimo in 1886. Not only were the Sierra Madre making headlines in the newspapers, but the people of Fort Apache and San Carlos had known of them from the very beginning.

Grennie was unable to sit still once he heard this, and began at once to make plans to find a way to go to Mexico and find out about these people for himself. Before he did he went to another puberty ceremony at Victor's Bluffs at San Carlos. Then, it seems, he returned to the Navajo reservation, and on November 10, asked a Navajo friend in Kayenta to go with him to Mexico in search of the Sierra Madre Apaches. By November 14 he was back in Douglas; he left briefly for urgent business in Gallup, returning by the 18th to meet up with Bill Curtis, a Mormon rancher whose acquaintance he had made and who had agreed to guide him in Mexico. There was no further word of the Navajo friend from Kayenta.

Grennie returned from Mexico and the Sierra Madre at the end of December and, when he learned that an immediate return with Bill Curtis was not to be, he headed back to Fort Apache—exactly what for he did not say, but his output speaks for itself. To judge by his notebooks from early 1931, he was laying the groundwork for full-time field ethnography while finishing out the spring semester at the University of Arizona.

Once finished with that semester Grennie did not go back, though he went to the San Carlos reservation with the blessing of the University of Arizona in the form of a letter of introduction, probably from his mentor, Byron Cummings.[44] He was at this stage intending an ambitious study of both the Apache and Navajo languages and cultures that would prepare him for a subsequent series of studies comparing these southern Athabascans with the northern Athabascan tribes of British Columbia.

LIVING WITH THE APACHES

It was among the Apaches that Grennie discovered his true university. He attended a puberty ceremony on July 4 at Whiteriver on the Fort Apache reservation, and while there, he must have discovered that he was not the only ethnographer on the reservation. Columbia University was sponsoring a broad program of ethnography among various Southwestern tribes, and graduate students were being sent into the field that summer to conduct research. A young woman named Christine Schmerler, who had not been accepted into the program, decided to go as a self-supported freelancer over the objections of her advisors. She went to the Fort Apache reservation and took up residence in a cabin a half-mile from the East Fork Mission. Apache witnesses claim that she was indiscreet, that she became overly familiar with more than one young Apache man. The indiscretions of white people were often tolerated by Apaches, but at a horse dance on July 18, she was friendly with the wrong man. He raped her and then, as she fled, he killed her. Grennie had been at Whiteriver only two weeks before. If he ever met her, he never said so, though he referred to the matter obliquely in a letter to Morris Opler a year later: "There has been quite a lot of talk about that murder trial, and I'm afraid Columbia is pretty unpopular out in the Southwest now, although I don't know just how much they [Columbia] are to blame for all this."[45] The young man accused of the murder was convicted and sentenced to life in prison.

The tragedy of the young woman's death may have been lost in the controversy over the circumstances of the killing. It surely set back relations between Indians and anthropologists, and it must have been a harsh object lesson for both—a lesson not lost on Grennie, I'm sure. The event made it dramatically clear how easily an irreversible misunderstanding could arise and escalate out of control. Good Apache manners were often a matter of mere common sense and discretion, but there was much to be learned as well; and my sense is that Grennie had made learning social etiquette his first order of business. If he hadn't, he could not have learned as much as he did by the end of the summer of 1931.

The brief written record Grennie left for this summer suggests more than it actually reveals. He must have been extremely busy. There is a brief mention in his introduction to *Myths and Tales of the White Mountain Apache* of travels he made with Charley Sago in the hills north of Bylas in August of that year. My mother told me of the lengthy trip on horseback that Grennie made with two Apache cowboys for which the ground rule was that only Apache be spoken. It was on this trip, camping, cooking, handling horses, listening to traditional stories at night, that he came to know Charley Sago so well. Similarly, Charley came to know Grennie as a companion; bonds of trust and shared experience were beginning to form. Whatever Charley and other Apaches may have thought of Grennie at this point, the last thing he must have looked like to them was an anthropologist.

He had begun a notebook that eventually contained thousands of Apache words and linguistic constructions using the Sapir system of phonetics. The traditional stories he heard from Charley were all written down in Grennie's immaculate, minuscule hand, filling ledger after ledger. He must have told his companions of his recent trip to Mexico and of his interest in the Sierra Madre Apaches, and he was rewarded with a wealth of stories about these people as well. There were dramatic tales of raids for women and horses on San Carlos and Fort Apache made by the Apache Kid and other Mexico-based "renegades" in recent years. These tales must have sharpened his already keen appetite for the Sierra Madre Apaches. He must have been planning all summer to go back to Mexico, for by September 22 he noted that he was "through at Bylas for the time being." He headed south to Douglas and a rendezvous with Bill Curtis. Seven days later the two arrived at Bill's ranch in Pulpit Canyon about forty miles south of the border.

Grennie returned from Mexico in early November. The last entry in his diary says that he was going to Tucson, then home by way of San

Carlos. I'm not altogether sure where "home" was, but it must have been either his mother's New York City apartment or perhaps her country place in Southampton on Long Island. Grennie drove East for the fall. He stopped off in Chicago for a visit with Morris Opler, and Opler's remarks in *Grenville Goodwin Among the Western Apache* reveal just how much Grennie had accomplished more or less on his own. Opler was impressed and intrigued by Grennie's notebook filled with hundreds of watercolors of Apache artifacts, but he was most impressed with the fact that "Goodwin could speak Apache surprisingly well."

Except for the myths and tales, most of Grennie's extended conversations with Apaches had been about Apache material culture: articles, food, hunting, dwellings—all carefully and voluminously recorded. Most important, Grennie had learned the language by asking questions and by listening. It was a simple, commonsense way to begin: learning how the Apaches said things and how they did things. Except for the myths and tales Charley Sago had been telling him, Grennie had apparently carefully avoided any questions about sacred knowledge and power—at least so far as it is possible to judge from his dated field notes. But the very fact that Charley Sago was telling him stories in the summer, when the snakes, insects, and lightning people would be listening and might be angered to hear themselves talked about, indicates that certain allowances were made for him—as Grennie indicates himself in his introduction to *Myths and Tales.*

By the end of 1931, Grennie had covered a lot of ground on the reservations. He had been to Cibecue, Carrizo Creek, and Whiteriver on the Fort Apache reservation, where he had met people and watched ceremonies. He had been to all the communities along the southern border of the San Carlos reservation—Calva, Bylas, Coolidge Dam, Peridot, and Rice—and he'd gone camping with Charley Sago and others. He wrote to Morris Opler that he was going back to San Carlos for several months, perhaps the whole year, under the auspices of the University of Arizona to do a complete study of the Coyotero Apaches, whom he later referred to as the White Mountain Apaches.[45] He could have found plenty of White Mountain people at Fort Apache, but the communities along the Gila River on the San Carlos reservation had mild winters and the hot summers he loved. Because of his boyhood brush with tuberculosis, doctors advised life in the outdoors—which was possible nearly year-round at San Carlos and out of the question at Fort Apache, where winters could be brutal. For what it was worth, San Carlos was much closer to Tucson and the University of Arizona,

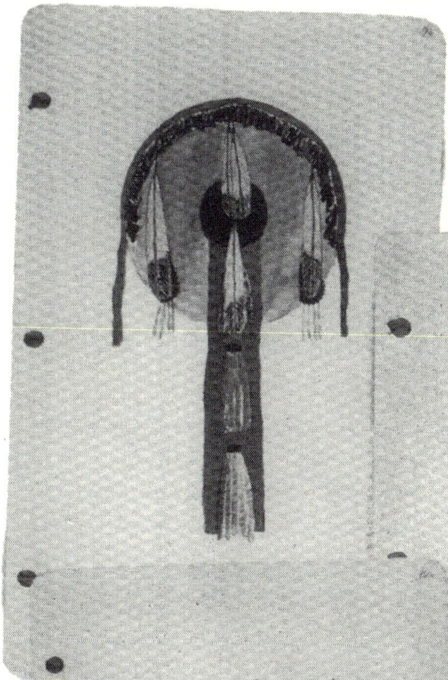

Western Apache shield, Peabody Museum, Cambridge, Massachusetts. Watercolor by Grenville Goodwin. (Courtesy Arizona State Museum, negative #c21364)

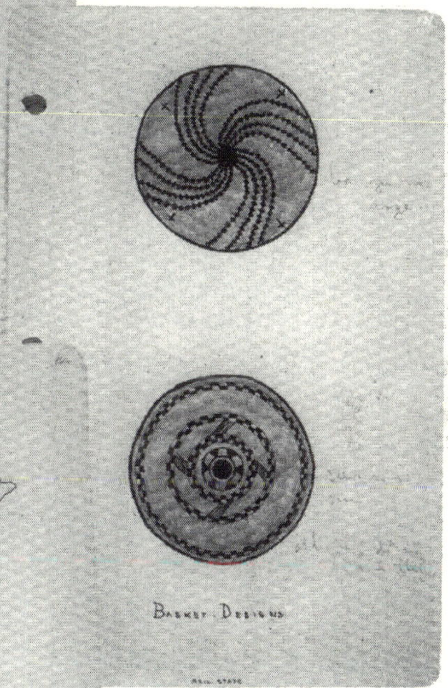

Western Apache basket designs, Arizona State Museum. Watercolor by Grenville Goodwin. (Courtesy Arizona State Museum, negative #c21399)

Western Apache medicine buckskin, The Smithsonian Institution, Washington, D.C., catalog #9392. Watercolor by Grenville Goodwin. (Courtesy Arizona State Museum, negative #c21435)

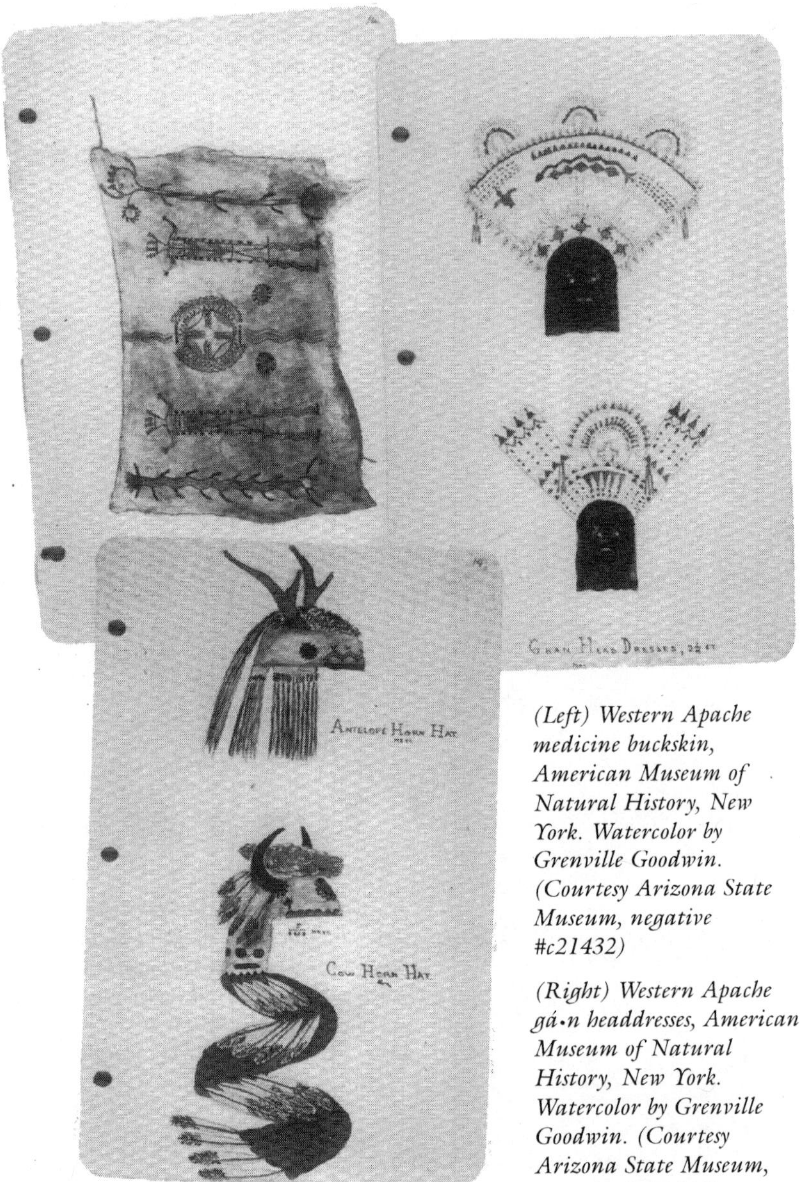

(Left) Western Apache medicine buckskin, American Museum of Natural History, New York. Watercolor by Grenville Goodwin. (Courtesy Arizona State Museum, negative #c21432)

(Right) Western Apache gá·n headdresses, American Museum of Natural History, New York. Watercolor by Grenville Goodwin. (Courtesy Arizona State Museum, negative #c21444)

Antelope horn hat and cow horn hat, The Museum of the American Indian, Heye Foundation, New York. Watercolor by Grenville Goodwin. (Courtesy Arizona State Museum, negative #c21418)

Western Apache medicine buckskin, Chicago Field Museum. Watercolor by Grenville Goodwin. (Courtesy Arizona State Museum, negative #21433)

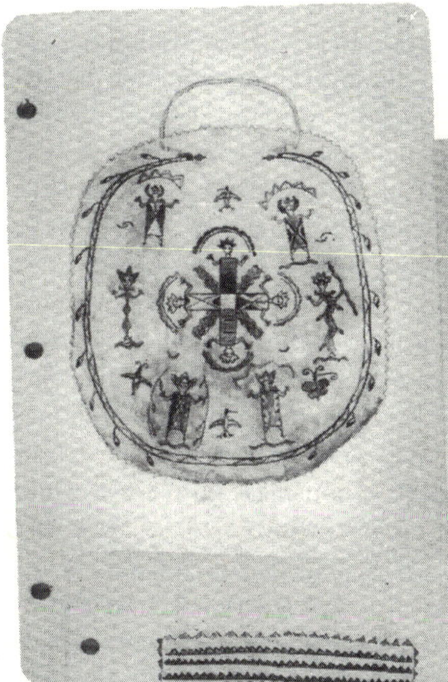

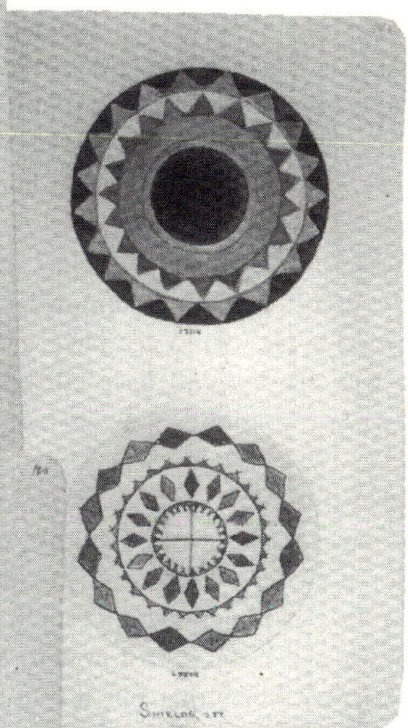

Western Apache shields, Chicago Field Museum. Watercolor by Grenville Goodwin. (Courtesy Arizona State Museum, negative #c21370)

Western Apache medicine shirt, Smithsonian Institution, Washington, D.C. Watercolor by Grenville Goodwin. (Courtesy Arizona State Museum, negative #c21437)

where he now had an appointment as a research associate so he could carry out work with some sort of academic affiliation.

If Grennie were to have chosen to work full time at Fort Apache, he would have had to live on the reservation in an Apache community, as had the late graduate student from Columbia. He knew better than to violate taboos, but he also understood the value of keeping his distance. In spite of the close friendships he had already formed, he sensed it would be important to live apart from the Apaches—impossible at Fort Apache without appearing unfriendly, but easy if he were to work at the border communities of Calva and Bylas, only a few miles from the gritty little settlement of Geronimo, just outside the reservation to the east. Living alone on the reservation would have posed other problems too. There simply is no place for a single man in an Apache community: it is considered unnatural for a young man to live alone, unmarried.[47] He would not have wanted to live among the Apaches in a way that they would have considered abnormal—even for a white man, whose ways the Apaches had long recognized to be extremely strange.

Perhaps most important, he had discovered a very high concentration of vital, well-informed, highly respected elders in Calva and Bylas. As Morris Opler remarked in his introduction to *Grenville Goodwin among the Western Apache,* Grennie lacked an anthropologist's technical vocabulary and sense of how to organize abstract cultural information. Grennie knew that but it did not bother him at all, so he simply did what came naturally: he worked on getting to know people. He had made a good friend in Charley Sago, and made a promise to him that one day he would take him to Washington, D.C., as he was later to take other Apache friends to California. In Grennie's will he directed that if this promise had not been kept, Charley was to receive $300—enough, perhaps, for Charley to buy himself a ticket to Washington one day.

Charley Sago, also known as Charley Moccasin because that's what he wore all the time, knew the old culture intimately. In time he would help Grennie learn the language; he would tell Grennie about games, plant medicines, mythology, and religion. He had sacred powers and practiced healing ceremonials. Charley was intelligent, politically powerful, and a leading cattleman. His father, a Yaqui Indian ("Sago" in Apache), had been captured in Sonora by Apaches raiding deep into Mexico in the 1870s—hence Charley's last name.[47]

Although Grennie understood the Apache language, having an interpreter was crucial to capturing shades of meaning in making verbatim transcriptions of interviews. Grennie's first interpreter was Charley's brother-in-law, Richard Bylas—educated, influential, son of a respected chief, bilingual, and literate. Interpreting for Grennie became one of Richard's jobs, along with working part time for the BIA and for the local white doctor at the Bylas clinic. In the years to come, Richard would become one of Grennie's frequent correspondents, keeping up a flow of news by letter when Grennie was away from his Apache friends.

Route 70 was a main east-west route. It passed through Geronimo and Bylas, through the reservation to Globe, and on to California. Alberta Rope, the granddaughter of John Rope remembers that Grennie sometimes used to take a bus from Geronimo to Bylas. Only a child in the 1930s, she remembers the visits my father paid to John Rope and that they used to sit and talk for hours in the shade, shooing the children away when they made too much noise.

John Rope, the son of a clan chief himself, was the equivalent of a chief at Bylas. He possessed certain sacred powers, which endowed him with the ability to perform ceremonials and other traditional rituals and in turn established him as someone of unusual stature.

Rope had a large family, and was politically influential and widely traveled. He was to impart a great deal of his knowledge to Grennie, but Grennie's first order of business in, I think, a shrewd act of respect, timing, and curiosity, was to ask John Rope to tell his life story.

Not only was John Rope living history, he was living *Apache* history. His life story, if recorded, could begin to fill the void in public knowledge about the Apache experience from the Apache point of view. His was an epic life, full of danger, adventure, excitement, and tragedy; full of the ordinary, vivid details of Apache daily life, including his own memory of what white people looked like when they were first encountered. As a child in about 1865, John Rope saw white men for the first time as he watched some soldiers from a hiding place. He remembered the increasing presence of the army, the establishment of the reservations, and the slow erosion of the traditional Apache way of life. In the 1880s he, like many other Western Apaches, joined the U.S. Army as a scout to help round up the most resistant of all—the Chiricahua Apaches led by warriors such as Juh, Victorio, Chihuahua, Loco, Nana, Chato, Mangus, Naiche, and Geronimo.

THE ELDERS

During the course of 1932 Grennie filled at least ten bound notebooks with the life histories and cultural knowledge of thirty-five elders of the communities of Bylas and Calva. Like John Rope's, their narratives contained a wealth of knowledge, wisdom, memory, and compelling descriptions. Among the most powerful and poignant was the life story of the oldest man in Bylas, Palmer Valor, which began with these words:

> I was born a long time ago at Canyon Day. Then the earth was like new and there were lots of animals and plants. There was red grass, yellow grass, blue grass, and white grass. When the wind blew through these grasses as it is blowing now, the air smelled sweet. Now it is different.[49]

In an early introduction to *Social Organization of the Western Apache,* Grennie wrote, "The material comes largely from stories told me by 34 different old Apaches. . . . Any value in this paper is largely due to the infinite patience with which these Apaches of whom I speak told me their stories."

It was a time-consuming, rambling process in which old timers told him every detail of their lives that they remembered. Grennie was getting to know them personally; and he was showing an interest in who they were, what their experience had been like. He was also constructing an oral history of the people: a factual record from the Apache point of view. The oldest people, some born as early as 1840, remembered what it was like before the white man came into Apachería—before the Mexican War.

The oldest people were children when white Americans entered the Southwest, and although at first there were examples of peaceful contact, those were not the scenes seared into the childhood memories of the elders of San Carlos:

> One day the soldiers came and set up their camp below us. They put up a white flag. Some of the older people told us that this white flag meant they were friendly. A woman who was married and had lots of children had gone down to the soldiers' camp. She never came back. They never found her body or any sign of her and no one knew what became of her. The soldiers had their white flag up and so three men went down to see their camp.

When they got there the soldiers caught two of them. The two they caught they hung to a sycamore tree and killed them.

At the San Pedro Agency the white people had a slaughter house. There was a white man in charge of this. He treated some of the Indians bad, and for this reason one of our men grabbed an ax and struck down on that white man's shoulder and killed him.

Now some of the soldiers went over to our camps. When my uncle saw them coming, he took his bow and arrow and shot at them and killed one off, I think. The soldiers ran after him and shot him dead. Then one of them cut all the scalp off his whole head. This one brought the scalp back with him to where we were, carrying it up on the end of a stick. Our camps and everything in them they burned.[50]

Anna Price told a story that happened up by Black Rock a long time ago. A lot of *dził-a* [a Western Apache clan name] were camped up there. A party of white soldiers surprised them and captured most of them. They took away a lot of the women with them. They took four of the men and tied them up to a tree, and while they were still alive they spread their arms out and drove a nail through the wrists of each, crucified them. Then they shot them and left them.

With time, the old people took Grennie beyond these accounts of violence to a detailed picture of an all-but-vanished way of life. And, of course, the humanity thus revealed made the violence seem all the more horrendous.

These people were, metaphorically, the flint-knappers Grennie had tried to imagine as a boy following the farmer's plow on his mother's Long Island place, picking up wondrous, magical arrowheads as they gleamed dully in the freshly turned earth, their shapes at once beautiful, durable, and deadly. It must have been thrilling, almost overwhelming, to strike a vein of human remembrance and experience so rich.

Grennie wrote short, pithy descriptions of them in his field notes:

Francis Drake: 68 years old; served in U.S. Army, Savannah, Pensacola, 1893–1895 with company of 50 White Mountain men; knew old culture, mythology; had strong snake power, some hawk power, some deer power; called Dr. Drake because famous medicine man; was hired to sing at Fort Apache and San Carlos.

Silas John: son of Yo an, an old White Mountain scout; lived at Fort Apache; was put in jail for killing his wife (on circumstantial evidence); had snake power; was founder of Silas John religion; had great influence; disliked by the government for his religious activities.

In fact Silas John may have been framed by the authorities, who feared a religious uprising. The lawyer and prolific writer of Perry Mason mystery novels, Erle Stanley Gardner, became interested in Silas's case and was largely responsible for his release from prison after having served many years for murder.

David Longstreet: old man; wore long hair; some transvestite traits; made beautiful buckskin dresses and men's buckskin shirts; had skunk power; had girl's puberty ceremony; served in police and as scout.

Gila Moses: old man; blind; was a feared medicine man at one time; had wind power; knew about old times and culture; had snake power; claimed to know all powers; was often hired to sing [in ceremonials] at Rice.

Harvey Nashkine: both parents were Mexican captives; was an old man; wore long hair; served as scout; knew old culture; sometimes ridiculed.

Peaches: old man; lived at Cibecue; married a Chiricahua woman and went with her people to Mexico in 1882 [with Geronimo when he broke out of the reservation. Peaches later led General George Crook to Geronimo's stronghold in the Sierra Madre]; knew old culture, myths.

Anna Price: daughter of great chief Diablo; was captured and taken to Washington, D.C.; sister to Old Lady Grey; was equivalent of head woman; was very fine and highly respected; very keen sense of humor, a joker; knew all about old times; had medicine power, coyote power, bear power, toothache power; had fire power; knew plant medicine; very old—probably over 95.

John Robertson: lived at Bylas; spoke some English; stuttered; one of the best gá·n medicine men there were, as was his father; power acquired by dreaming; sang a pollen dance at Bylas in 1932.

David Longstreet, White Mountain Apache elder, Grennie's close friend and advisor . (Courtesy Arizona State Museum, negative #24868)

John Sippy: elderly man; wore long hair; often ridiculed at Bylas; claimed that he had the power to cure people struck by lightning with four rifles; claimed to be a great medicine man and know about old times; made good hide saddle bags and buckskin capes; liked to dress in G-string.

The thirty-odd other thumbnail biographies list the respective expertise each of the old Apaches had. From these descriptions emerges a picture of the broad spectrum of knowledge upon which Grennie was able to draw. He was learning about Apache culture from A to Z without pursuing any subject in particular. The interviews combined autobiographies with long sidetracks into raiding and warfare practices, hunting, basketry, medicinal herbs, local gossip, witchcraft, and religion, to name only a few topics.

POWER AND SACRED KNOWLEDGE

Grennie was also keeping a record of his own observations of daily life. The following is part of a description of a pollen-giving dance held at Bylas on July 25, 1932. His simple, documentary approach gives the event respect and dignity that a more artful account might have eclipsed:

> This dance is usually held about this time every year. The object of it is to distribute pollen[52] among the people so that they will have good luck on their way.
>
> That afternoon down on the river bottom, by a grove of cottonwoods, they piled the wood up for the big fire in an open place. That same day the men went down to the river to make a sweat-bath and talk about the ceremony to decide if it should be held today or tomorrow. They decided on this day, so that by evening people started to move over from their camps to the dance ground.
>
> As soon as it got dark the fire was lighted and they started to sing. When I arrived, about half an hour after they had started, the singers were seated in two lines facing each other in the usual way, on the west side of the fire. They had about four drums. The small girls were dancing back and forth by themselves in couples, or threes or fours, just a few, on the east side of the fire. After several songs these little girls started picking small boys to dance with them from the group around the singers.

> After a few more songs a medicine-man got up and made the announcement that all were to pray. John Rope was also going around, telling the people what to do. Almost everyone lined up in a great circle about the singers and the fire, the men all on the west and northwest side, the women on the east and southeast side.
>
> The medicine-man led several songs and then made a prayer for all the people. During this prayer everyone kept absolutely still.[53]

By this time Grennie had spent a part of each of the last four years on Apache reservations and he had seen dozens of dances. These ancient rituals, at once sacred and social, expressed two of the bedrock values of Apache life: community and religion. In a report to the BIA about the San Carlos reservation written years later, he tried to make the case that to be effective and humane, BIA administration policy should mirror traditional Apache lifeways:

> Due to the Apache mode of life now, distribution of the population of the reservation to conform with white men's ideals is quite impossible; that is, the spreading out of families, each family owning or using a ranch, and all families living separate. The population must be concentrated in communities where families are in close contact. For a single family or even two to live permanently apart from others is absolutely foreign to the culture. Apart from the social side, families are unwilling to separate themselves from communities through fear, a fear which goes back over centuries. Myriad imaginary dangers and evil influences, ghosts, evil animals, malevolent forces of nature which fill the Apache mind are sufficient reason to prevent his putting himself or his family in any lonely and vulnerable position.[54]

The traditional Apache's world was ordered by supernatural powers that are potent in the extreme. Knowledge of how to contact these powers was vital to the spirituality at the center of the Apache way of life. Sacred knowledge governed rites of passage, the gathering of medicinal plants, warfare, hunting, agriculture, healing; it governed the ways in which people spoke and thought of the plants and the animals, the wind, the lightning, the rain, the sun, the moon, and the stars. Grennie was coming to understand how compelling and even workable a worldview this was for the Apaches, and he wrote:

> There are a few old men who claim emancipation from the "old superstitions" as they bravely term them. Some younger persons, particularly young men, feign disbelief and ridicule the old customs. However, this is not as deep as it may seem and is mainly done for the benefit of whites. With their own people and under stress, such an attitude may quickly disappear and the individual accedes to the old custom. The permanent bond of race, color, and speech is of prime value to the average Apache.
>
> Ritual is still used in connection with agricultural and wild crops, in the handling of horses, in hunting, and other ways. It is vital in reservation life and gives the Apache something he feels to be his own and by which he attains results, both spiritual and practical. To try to stamp this out would indeed be disastrous.[55]

Grennie's thumbnail sketches of the community elders who were to become his friends contain an inventory of the holy powers they possessed because these powers defined, as much as anything did, their stature in the community. Grennie observed:

> The possession of holy power and knowledge of certain rituals were believed absolutely necessary to attain various ends. Thus a man's prowess in hunting, in war, his bravery, his leadership were all vitally aided by it. Possession of good ritual knowledge may almost be compared to possession of property, for a man having it was considered a rich and influential person. The belief was deep rooted in the culture that to live and make a success of life, one must have at least a little knowledge of holy power.[56]

Though many of the people Grennie came to know possessed holy powers and practiced them in ceremonials, only a few were considered true medicine men. As he wrote:

> To be a great medicine man is to be a great public figure, much respected and valued. A community feels far safer when it has living within it medicine men who are known to have strong power and ability to cure. Families have sometimes moved partly because they wish to be close to such men.[57]
>
> The status of the Apache medicine man is based on the number of cures he has been able to make and the more miraculous these cures seem to be the more his clientele increases.[58]

Grennie sat with the elders, several of them important medicine men, and listened. They did not tell him all they knew, for they said certain things were dangerous and could not be discussed. Sacred knowledge could be used to bring about great good, but handled improperly, unwisely, or carelessly, this knowledge could cause misfortune, illness, death, and disaster. Although Grennie shared his knowledge about the Apaches with Morris Opler, he wrote that he would have to make an exception in the case of "material which I have been asked to keep to myself by the men who told it to me."[59]

As much as Grennie depended on men and women with possession of sacred knowledge, I don't believe at this time he made a point of asking them about it. Based on the notes he kept, in late 1932 he was interested primarily in social organization and material culture. Nevertheless, he must have been privy to all kinds of information that he was expected to keep secret—from sacred knowledge to loose gossip to stories of prohibited activities that could get his Apache friends into serious trouble with the authorities. For example, the relatives of the Apache Kid were still nervous about the possibility that they might have to pay for crimes he had committed in the 1890s, especially if it were thought that he had been secretly in touch with them, having survived the many attempts on his life. The elders might have talked about clandestine contact with other Apaches remaining in Mexico or with those who had broken out in the 1890s.

Grennie would not have forcefully pursued a line of questioning on any of these subjects, though his friends might well have volunteered information, especially after hearing of his recent trips to the Sierra Madre and of the sensational nature of the manhunts and escalating violence there.

Nor was he ready to pursue an inquiry into sacred knowledge, beyond what he had learned by attending ceremonials and recording the traditional stories that were to become the substance of *Myths and Tales of the White Mountain Apache*.

By the end of 1932, what was probably the first phase of Grennie's research was nearly complete. From Whiteriver, he wrote his mother a letter in November saying that his work was "shaping itself, which is always encouraging."[60] Grennie at some point had taken his mother through parts of Apache country. He had once introduced her to "Old Laban James" with whom he told her he had just spent ten days over at Cibecue. He then reminded her of Smiley, "just as grouchy as before," the old chief at Camp Verde, the Tonto Apache reservation. Grennie had just returned from an automobile tour of traditional Tonto homelands stretching 120 miles northwest from Globe. He traveled with his friend and interpreter Neil Buck and an old Tonto couple living at the time on the San Carlos reservation. They had grown up in northern Tonto country before white Americans brought reservations to Arizona. Grennie wanted to show them the country and to have them tell him about it as they drove through. As they traveled, more of the pieces of the old culture would have fallen into place in Grennie's widening portrait of the people: old campsites, known game trails, waterholes, and landmarks; but most important, Grennie and the old couple would have shared a journey and all its unexpected events together.

It would not have been a short trip, for the roads were not good and travel would have been slow at best. Moreover, this trip would have been one of constant detours as they tried to find dimly remembered locations. The old Tontos teased the names of these places from their memories and Grennie wrote them all down, filling more notebooks. Place-names were of the greatest importance to the Apaches. Important events and events whose outcomes are object lessons are forever attached to the places in which they happened. In fact, the collective wisdom and history of the Apaches in many ways resides in the landscape, as Keith Basso so vividly illustrates in *Wisdom Sits in Places.*[61] The lessons taught by cautionary tales are recalled simply by mentioning the names of the places to which they are connected. The old Apaches said to Grennie, "Once all these places had names. Now they no longer have names."

"If only these walls could talk, what a story they would tell," we often say. So it is with places in Apache country, and once the names are lost, so is the power to call upon the places to speak. On this trip and on what must have been many others like it, the landscape and the people were speaking to Grennie. He had a thousand fragments, and he must have been itching to begin putting them together.

Based on all he had gathered, he set about writing a paper for the Department of Anthropology, presumably under the direction of Byron Cummings. He settled down with stacks of notebooks—probably in Colorado Springs, though he might have been in Santa Fe—and by May 1933 he had produced a 490-page manuscript that he sent first to the University of Arizona and then to Morris Opler for review and criticism. Soon after it was completed, Grennie was back in Bylas, knowing that as much as he had accomplished, he had only just begun.

TUBERCULOSIS

Grennie was already making a name for himself in anthropology circles. He had given talks to classes at the University of Arizona, and following the completion of his long "Report on the San Carlos Indian Reservation" for the BIA, he delivered a groundbreaking paper at a Las Cruces meeting of the AAAS on the structure of Western Apache clans. It was an original piece of fieldwork and marked him as someone from whom the scientific community would be hearing much more.

None of his dated papers or field notes from the summer of 1933 survive, but if the letters written to Grennie by Apaches are any measure, he had a busy three months at Bylas. Addressed to him at his mother's house in Colorado Springs are letters of thanks for money orders and for packages of cloth and paint; the letters are full of community gossip and hopes for next year's watermelons, corn, and cattle. Neil Buck asked him for a cure for the mysterious illness plaguing his son Loney. In a coincidence that no Apache would ascribe to mere chance, Grennie's own health collapsed late in the summer or early in the fall from what may have been a disease related to Loney's. Neil Buck wrote: "My boy is the one not feel good for two years. He got sore on his neck for two years. He has been down Phoenix and stay two years, but doctor wouldn't do any good for him, so he just got back. I wish you would find something would cure him please. He got sore all around his neck now."

In his daily diary two years later, Grennie speculates that these might have been tubercular sores. He knew about tuberculosis firsthand. Both his mother and his stepfather, Meredith Hare, had had it. Grennie himself had come down with it at the age of fourteen, recovered, then had a relapse at sixteen and recovered again. But, of course, in those days one never recovered from tuberculosis; dormant, it could wait for years to strike again. And strike it did. In the fall of 1933, when Grennie was twenty-six, it came raging back.

The clean air and high altitude of Colorado Springs had made it one of the favorite spots for tuberculosis recovery and convalescence; in fact it had been the reason for his mother's move there in the 1920s when her second husband had come down with it. So, when Grennie was struck anew by tuberculosis, he moved into his mother's place at the foot of the Rockies. The only prescription for the disease at the time was fresh air and bed rest. He was weak, but he still managed to work—"only two hours a day" he wrote to Opler in January 1934—

continuing to write up field notes, reading, and keeping up a voluminous correspondence with his Apache friends. As far as I know, none of the letters written by Grennie survive, but judging from the letters the Apaches wrote to him, Grennie did not appear to have told them that he had come down with tuberculosis, although his other correspondents, such as Opler, knew.[62]

It might have been stoicism; he simply might not have wanted to talk about himself or draw attention to himself, but the real reason is probably more complicated. Grennie was well aware of the Apache attention to sickness and its causes. He knew that news of his extremely serious illness would be a matter of discussion and speculation at Bylas and this, I suspect, he did not want. He would not have wanted the Apaches to believe he had caught the disease from them as a result of simple biological exposure. That is, he would not have wanted them to feel responsible. But much more important, he knew that many Apaches believed that illness did not simply arrive for no good reason. Illness and misfortune may come from transgression of some taboo, from the misuse of sacred knowledge, or from offending one of the supernatural powers. Most unsettling for Apaches, sickness may come from witchcraft. It is quite likely that Grennie did not want his illness to be subjected to interpretation because he knew it might compromise and complicate his relationships with his Apache friends. Together they had spoken of the dead and they had told myths and tales out of season, both taboos. Grennie had already learned how carefully he had to tread; he wrote in his diary:

> The first day I worked with Palmer Valor [in 1932] at Bylas he told me of some of the old chiefs who are dead. The next day when we went back to work with him, he said that he did not want to, as last night he had had a dream and these dead chiefs had come to him and said that if he wasn't careful, they were going to kill him for telling about them and calling them by name.

Grennie's eighteen-month convalescence was a watershed. His third and most serious bout with tuberculosis was a stark encounter with his own mortality. As a hedge against the worst from tuberculosis as well as other potential misfortunes, he learned to read Braille and to write with his left hand. By June 1934 he had moved from Colorado Springs to the house of his brother Walter in Santa Fe. He remained there until the end of November, regaining his strength and structuring the lines of inquiry to follow as soon as he could return to the reservation.

Of the letters the Apaches wrote to him between October 1933 and November 1934, twenty survive; there may have been many more. They thank him for his letters and apologize for not answering sooner for a variety of reasons: because they had been in jail; there was nothing happening; there was no one to write a letter for them; they had been away at summer grazing and gathering areas; or they had been too busy. There were thanks for medicine, for a crate of apples and peaches, for money, for fabric, for paint, for cigarettes, for photographs and, always, explicit and implicit thanks for his friendship.

At the same time, Grennie was busy sharpening his academic ethnographic skills through reading and keeping up with the other scholars in the field. He had also determined to rewrite the 490-page manuscript he had written for Cummings at the University of Arizona. Not only did it need restructuring, but it was clear to Grennie that it was only a first draft of his own understanding of the Western Apaches. He wanted to learn much more.

My father's older brother Sage is ninety-six now. There are still a few old Apaches who remember Grennie, but my Uncle Sage is the only one left who knew him so well and for so long. Sage has a flinty Yankee wit that is as fresh and wry as ever. His memories of my father have survived, vivid and intact, since they last saw each other more than sixty years ago, a few days before my father died in Los Angeles. I asked Sage what Grennie had told him of his time with the Apaches. What he remembered was the basic nature of his brother's technique—which was, in fact, no technique at all: "One of the reasons that Indians gave him tribal information was that he'd sit around with them and whittle a piece of wood or something until they started to talk. And they kind of accepted him as a piece of furniture."

Sage then added another facet—one that must have appealed to the Apaches: "He had definite ideas about everything, and a sense of humor, too. He used to think that some things were awfully funny. And he had a nice laugh. And they used to say that when he laughed, everybody laughed, because he was enjoying himself so much."

Then Sage brought up a simple sentence that had been lodged in his memory for nearly seventy years. It sounded oracular, like a fragment from a Socratic dialogue—perhaps an echo of the way Grennie spoke to him and to others of his work among the Apaches: "I learn the most when I sit and listen and don't say anything."

Grennie was a man of few words. Perhaps it was his style to deliver an epigrammatic, encrypted essence like this, hiding more than it revealed. His statement is not as modest as it sounds, for it conceals a wealth of ingenuity—not to mention a natural and well-mannered Apache taciturnity. He was the most unusual of white men: he could speak and understand the Apache language, and that would have intrigued the elders, many of whom spoke little or no English. They could talk to him in their own tongue, and they could tell him personal things in confidence that would not find their way back into the Apache gossip mill. In fact he might have been the only such listener in the community. Grennie's act of witness as he sat and listened was anything but passive; he had much to master before he could learn from just sitting and listening. But what draws me in is not his mastery of technique but the very thing of which he spoke the least: his view of himself in the Apache world.

BYLAS, THE DIARY, AND TOTAL IMMERSION

When he returned to Bylas in late 1934, Grennie began doing something he had not done before: he began to keep a daily diary—not in order to record his personal feelings or reflections, but to keep track of the places he went, the people he saw and what they said to him, and what he observed. Separate from his voluminous field notes, this diary is full of the details of the daily life of the Apaches—the trivial, the mundane, the tragic, the sacred, the comical. It consists of well more than two hundred typed, single-spaced pages.[63] He would doubtless be pleased to know how little of himself he betrayed even in this private forum but, of course, a writer always reveals himself in time, and it is in the realm of Apache sacred knowledge that the key to Grennie's reservation experience may lie. In pursuit of this knowledge he was given the greatest trust, but he was also at the greatest risk of making missteps and, at least in the eyes of the Apaches, of courting real danger in the form of illness and misfortune or worse.

On the first page of the diary, he writes, "Can it be shown that the culture and religion of the Western Apache conform to the environment which it is in?" He had done most of the heavy work for *Social*

Organization of the Western Apache and was thinking far ahead to other aspects of Apache culture. He knew that spirituality was the key to the culture; he also knew that sacred knowledge was the subject about which the Apaches were the most protective. It was not hard to get a clear picture of the Apaches' environment—physical, climatic, social, historical, and so forth—but to answer the question he had just posed to himself, he would have to gain a knowledge of Apache religion rarely if ever granted to a white man. It is no wonder then, that he had left most of this topic till this point—several years into his research.

Almost as soon as Grennie returned to San Carlos in February 1935, he sat down with Gila Moses, the great old Bylas medicine man, now blind but once feared because of his powers. It was winter and the holy beings were sleeping and would not mind if people talked about them. Grennie and Moses had met two years earlier, in 1933, and cautiously began working together then on myths and ceremonies. These were the most serious topics an Apache could speak of, yet the conversations took place in the most ordinary of surroundings. The setting itself was an eloquent metaphor for the inextricable way in which the sacred is woven into daily life.

> Gila Moses is living in a small wickiup just below that of one of his sons, Johnny Moses. In Johnny Moses's wickiup, where we have been doing most of the story-telling are Johnny Moses and his wife and their little girl and boy, about 4 and 6, and their baby. There are a lot of mice in the walls of the wickiup and you can hear them rustling and squeaking as they run along inside. Gila Moses says that the myths he is telling me, in fact all the myths of his people, are about the times when all the animals were people and acted as such.
>
> While the old man was "telling story" to me yesterday morning, the two small boys in there started making quite a racket in their play, so the old man gave them a scolding and told them that he was busy telling me a story and for them to keep still. They did. [Later] the little girl of Johnny Moses started to cry over something, but her mother told her not to cry. She was doing her best to hold it back.
>
> When nursing, [Johnny Moses's wife] holds the baby lengthwise on her lap as she sits and pulls up her blouse on one side then the other. She nursed it twice this morning. She does not try to conceal it at all.

> Moses says that besides the ceremony for broken bones and injuries from falls, he also knows the wind ceremony and the rain ceremony. That is how he knows the rain ceremony myth and could tell it all so well. During the latter part of the morning the old man stopped for quite a long time to say a prayer, to ward off evil from telling this story to me. He spoke quite rapidly and in a rather low tone. He made it up apparently as he went along.

Day after day for nineteen days Grennie and his friend and interpreter, Neil Buck, came to talk with old Gila Moses, his stature as a medicine man in stark contrast with the family's treatment in a sudden raid by the reservation police, looking for the illicit beer *tułipai*. Grennie writes: "The police came yesterday to Moses's camp, two of them (Indian police) to look for *tułipai*. They had long sticks with which to poke the ground to see if there were any soft places there inside the wickiup" [where cans of the drink would be buried].

They apparently found none, but these surprise raids and the strict prohibition against homebrew were a feature of reservation life. One could even be charged with a crime for possessing sprouted corn, one of the ingredients of *tułipai*, as Gila Moses had been only a few days earlier. Being arrested for something they saw nothing wrong with, for breaking a law made by BIA officials, was rarely a deterrent to the Apaches, and the making of *tułipai* was as regular a practice as the making of white lightning in the hollows of Appalachia.[64]

Grennie was spending all this time with Moses to learn about sacred knowledge, but what he really wanted to see was how that knowledge worked in everyday life, to see what it meant to be a great medicine man. In actual practice, he found, it was like being a country doctor, a parish priest, a political tactician, and a company CEO all in one. He was the first figure people went to when there was trouble:

> Day before yesterday there was an accident up the road. Two cars met head-on after dark. In one car were two men, one of them was instantly killed and the other was thrown out on his head so that his scalp was cut, and also his upper lip had to be sewn. Yesterday two men [came] in a car to get Moses and bring him up to Rice to sing over this man. But he wouldn't go because the man was in the hospital. Then [they said] that it was alright, that they would come after Moses when the man came out of the hospital. They said for Moses to go on telling me the story and they

> went out. Before this Moses said that he would not sing if they only paid him 10 dollars, but if they gave him more than that he might stay and sing for three or four nights. Moses told me that he wasn't going up there to Rice and sing unless they gave him 20 dollars. Neil says that is the way. A man doesn't like to sing very much if he doesn't get paid much for it.[65]

Very much aware of the custom, Grennie did not expect Gila Moses to spend day after day with him for nothing. As was so often the case, involved in the transmission of this knowledge was a ritual exchange in which Grennie's part was to give certain objects with talismanic value. The transaction made, Moses was required to keep his end of the bargain, but not without taking precautions from time to time.

> About the middle of the morning Gila Moses stopped to make a prayer while he was telling the story. There was medicine in the story and he did so that no harm would come. He prayed for about three minutes and during this mentioned about the man who was hurt at Rice in the automobile accident. He was about to go up to Rice to sing over this man.

In an early draft of the introduction to *The Social Organization of the Western Apache,* Grennie wrote, "These Apaches told me their stories and made me understand facts, which at first seemed outlandish [in another version, "incredible"], but which later took on their true form and relation to the culture." Grennie put his faith in rational, Western science, and I suppose when he used the word *outlandish* in the first part of that sentence it was the novice scientist's reflexive posture when faced with another culture's faith in the supernatural. In the second part of the sentence a more seasoned observer is speaking, one who has seen and heard the record of traditional Apache ceremonial practice. He was learning why the Apaches were so often suspicious of the doctors at reservation clinics and why they turned to their own for cures. In his report Grennie wrote: "His [the medicine man's] cures owe much to the faith in him, continually encouraging the patient to set his mind on getting well, to think no more of dying, of illness, and to listen to the words of his song and prayer."[66]

When Moses was asked to sing for the man who was in the car wreck, he started telling Grennie about other cures he had performed. The others present all remembered and affirmed what the old man said:

> Moses says that one time CJ38 broke his leg and that they took him up to San Carlos to the hospital. The doctor there wanted to cut off his leg as the only cure, but the old man's relatives would not give their consent and said, "That old man down there at Bylas [Moses] is the one who can cure him." Then they sent one of his relatives to see Moses. He said that they were going to give him one steer, kill it for him. Moses said all right, and went down there to where the sick man was. . . . This sick man said to one of his relatives: "I have twenty dollars over there. Bring it to me, because I am going to give it to him [Moses] for singing over me." Then he said to Moses: "Besides this money and the steer, I am going to give you one of a team of horses that I have here. This all together makes three things that I'm going to give you."
>
> So then Moses started to sing over him. He sang one night, and the man was a little better. Then he sang a second night, and then a third night. Then he sent a man up onto Turnbull Mt. to get some wood for a medicine hoop. When this was brought back he made it into a hoop and tied buckskin onto it, painted with ceremonial figures.[67] Then he sang the fourth night, and after that the man was completely cured. He says that in curing broken bones he used an iron over the break and sort of irons it out just as you do clothes, making it smooth.

Later that week, Moses told Grennie that it was easy to learn the songs for ceremonies and medicine "if you dream it." Some he came by this way, but others, such as the emergence myth, he learned from his father, "who had learned it from his father, who had learned it from his father, who had learned it from his father, who had learned it from his father before." He explained to Grennie that it had taken six months to learn these stories from his father—three months during one winter and three months the following winter. Moses went on to say:

> When a person tells the story of the Emergence and when Changing Woman remade the world, it makes them young again. Also when you tell this story it means that the world is as if going to be made new again, and new plants grow up and blossom, and Moses said, "You see, the earth will be made as if new again and there will be lots of young plants coming up soon."

Skeptic though Grennie was, these solid weeks with blind, powerful old Gila Moses, hearing his compelling language and his healing powers, must have been a heady experience, especially when Grennie found that he, not the sons of Gila Moses, was the one to whom much of the sacred knowledge was being entrusted. He wrote in his deadpan style:

> Moses says that his sons have not learned his myths or his ceremonies. He says that he wanted to teach them his ceremonies, but that they said it was too much trouble to learn them. He says that lots of men have said to him. "Well, I guess that you have taught your sons your ceremonies, so they are medicine men also," but he tells them, "No, they do not want to learn them."

I don't believe that Grennie was under any illusions at this point that he had been nominated to follow in the footsteps of Gila Moses or any of the other medicine men with whom he talked at such great length. He was not learning how to perform the ceremonies, but he was recording their elements, at least those that Gila Moses and others were willing to tell him.

Why they did even this much has to be a matter of conjecture on my part at this point. In some circles at San Carlos today, Grennie's gathering of sacred material is controversial. Some say that people divulged ceremonial secrets against their will and better judgment, because no Apache would say such things voluntarily to a white man. Grennie's daily diary does not address this issue directly, but its overall candor suggests that he and his Apache friends were engaged in a collaborative enterprise in which they all were endeavoring to record as much of the old culture as they could and as much as they deemed safe. That is not to say that there was not some soul searching among the Apaches when it came to discussing sacred knowledge, but it seems clear that they were willing, even eager, to tell what they knew to someone who was so sincerely interested and dedicated to preserving it. And they always took precautions, as Grennie notes in his diary:

> Yesterday, when Anna Price taught us the four coyote songs, she did [it] this way. She had told me to bring four feathers out of the tail of an eagle, so I did that. She told Neil to tell me to let her see the feathers first. She looked at them and said they would be all right. Then she laid out a piece of cloth on the east side of the fire. She said she was going to sing four songs and that she wanted me to take them down as she sang them, not to wait and take songs down after she had sung the first four, as I suggested. She said that this would be going back over again and would be bad.

> So she spoke the words of the first song, and Neil put the first feather over, and so on till the fourth feather had been laid over. *Shi-cho* [Apache for grandmother, the term by which Grennie always addressed her] said, "Now I am going to sing two songs for you. That is the way they always do." So she sang the two songs. All of them were beautiful ones. She kept the feathers, rolled them up in the cloth, and put them away.

Grennie and Neil Buck returned the next day to Anna Price's camp to continue, and she leveled with them:

> *Shi-cho* said this morning that she had prayed a long time yesterday afternoon in regard to what she had told us about the coyote ceremony. She said that she had done this so that there would be no trouble come out of it. She prayed, "I have told a person some of your power. He is like a relative to me, as if he was my brother. He has been good to me and that is why I have done it. But I have not told him all of it. I have kept most of it to myself. I only gave him a little part of it. That is the way it will be all right."

Not long after that, Grennie and Neil Buck were back, this time to talk about medicinal herbs. Grennie wrote: "When we came to work over the plant medicines the other day I asked Anna if it would be all right to ask her about them. She said yes, that it would be with the exception of . . . . . , that she did not want to talk about that at all, as it was dangerous for one who was uninitiated."

Medicine men frequently acquired their powers through dreams. My mother said that Grennie used to refer to these as "big dreams," ones so compelling and so vividly remembered that a person who had one would feel that certain powers were calling to him or her—a call that could not safely be refused. The ceremonial power thus gained was considered one's personal responsibility, as Grennie was to see in one late-March session with the great medicine man John Robertson.[68] He had been telling Grennie about the dream by which he had acquired a certain power. John had said he did not want any men there, though he did not mind the presence of his wife and a couple of women from neighboring camps. As the session proceeded, however, first one man, then another, then another drifted by to listen. Robertson was a powerful and effective healer, and the inner workings of his power would have been a matter of urgent interest to the members of his community. Before long there were five men riveted by Robertson's narrative, among them another medicine man, who in time declared that such things should not be discussed. At that point Robertson said:

> "There are too many people about here and that is not good. I don't mind telling you this stuff myself, but these people here don't want me to tell it. But it is my own, I dreamed it and so it belongs only to me. Therefore I can tell it to you all right. It would be different if it were something like myths, or things that all of us know. But this is something that only I know. Now I have gone and told it to you. It is a good thing and I ought not to have told it. They told me, the ones who gave it to me, that I should not tell it. But I have gone and done it. Now God knows I have done it, and even the stones here, so it will be all right. It is all the truth, every bit of it. I have given away a good thing." The following day when Neil and I went back to his camp, Neil said that yesterday he had been stimulated. When a man is that way, he is not afraid to do and say things that he would be afraid to ordinarily say and tell.

John Rope, though not a medicine man, had holy powers of his own and further explained the taboos surrounding discussion of sacred knowledge:

> This morning, John Rope said, in connection with talking about . . . (a war god of some sort) that it was dangerous to talk of him as the clouds were gathering overhead and that it was not right. They were gathering all right. He also said it was very dangerous for him to talk about powers and supernatural beings that he did not have the power to talk about, that it was better to save them 'till winter. He said it would be all right to talk about some power or ceremony that he knew or owned, even in summer, because he could go off and pray and fix things up all right so that nothing would happen to him, but if he did not have the power he could not fix it up and so remained in danger.

Grennie was by now well known in Bylas, Calva, and the other southern San Carlos settlements, and many of the people knew what he was doing, to whom he was talking, and what he was gathering. Inevitably there was gossip and the good-natured joking that sometimes takes place around things that are deadly serious. Grennie noted: "The people at J. Robertson's camp were kidding I and Neil about being medicine men, because we had worked with so many medicine men. Neil said that he had never picked up any of it [meaning sacred knowledge], and there was a lot of joking about it all."

Another time, while visiting the camp of a prominent medicine man, Grennie wrote, "The other day when we went to his camp, he said in a joking way, 'Come on, give me $20 and I will show you all my power, teach it to you.'" And there were even some who, loosened by drink, sought a relationship with Grennie through the coin of holy power:

> The other night there was a man who was a little tight (very). I took him home to his camp and he was very grateful for it, and all the way kept telling me that he had holy power and that he knew deer power and that he knew where God lived. He kept repeating this and saying that tonight I had helped him and that he was in a position to help me also as he had these holy powers. The idea was I was in his good graces. (An Apache always wants to be in the good graces of a medicine man so he will have good luck and can get help when he needs it.) This is what he was trying to impress on me.

This suggests a gradual evolution in Grennie's role at San Carlos. It suggests that as he gathered more and more material, his attention may have become more and more desirable on the part of Apaches. At its most basic, the transmittal of cultural information was a simple business transaction. Grennie paid at least some Apaches for their time: interpreters, of course, but he also paid his "teachers"—both for the oral traditions and for items of material culture. He paid David Longstreet for the buckskin girl's puberty dress now at the Arizona State Museum. Acting again for the museum, he paid John Robertson for a *gá·n* dancer's outfit, and the payment was enough for Robertson to buy a second-hand Ford, vintage 1930.[69]

But the transmission of this knowledge was rarely straightforward, and it always appeared to be complicated by the events of everyday life. When Anna Price's son-in-law, Jewett Wright, became very ill, she told Grennie and Neil Buck that she wanted to continue to work with them on ceremonial material. She knew Jewett was going to die and wanted to earn some money for new clothes in which to bury him. Grennie wrote: "She cried about it, but I asked Neil and he thought decidedly we should wait, and though he did not say so, I am sure that the reason was that to launch forth on work such as we have been doing with her (ceremonial) with him in such critical condition would be unwise."

As he so often did, Grennie followed Neil's advice and they did not work with Anna Price during the period of Jewett's illness. Anna was torn. She was worried about Jewett but was convinced he would soon die. She even said that Jewett, a medicine man, knew it himself. Medicine men always do. What was more, Jewett had sent for his son who was in school, and both Neil and Anna were convinced that he would not have done so were he not certain of his imminent death. At least part of the problem was solved with a loan of four dollars from Grennie to Anna for the purchase of the clothes.

Jewett had pneumonia, and his illness engaged the whole family and much of the community as well. He may have been in the local hospital for Grennie made a point of talking to the doctor at the local clinic:

> He said one of the things in the way of his getting well was that the family were continually in the room with him and would not let him rest. They thought that he could not breathe, he guessed, so they would work his arms up and down every so often and manipulate him about. "They even had him up and walking about the floor between them," he (the doctor) complained.
>
> I remarked about this to Neil, and he said: "Well that's our way. We believe that when a person is sick that they should not be left lying still and out straight like you white people let them. We think that if you do this a body gets stiff and weak so we never let a sick person lie still."

In addition to this proactive vigil, there may have been prayers said and a curing ceremony performed, though they were not often permitted in the hospital. In any case the pneumonia prevailed, and after Jewett Wright's death, members of his family began to recall unusual things that had happened shortly beforehand that in retrospect were taken as omens. For example, George Bylas and his wife had heard a strange whistling two months before Jewett's death. It had frightened them, and they had rushed back to the safety of their home. They told Grennie about it and said it must have been an omen of Jewett's death.

Grennie himself was by this time seeing things that might be construed as omens. In spite of himself he was beginning to see the world through Apache eyes:

> I told Neil about having the eagle swoop down at me while on the top of a hill the other day, and that it must have mistaken me for a rabbit or something. I asked him if this could be any sort of an omen. He said the eagle had made a mistake and for this rea-

> son it meant nothing. "But, if an eagle did that to you in a level place, then it would not be a mistake and it would be an omen that something bad was going to happen to you."

The death of Jewett Wright was a shock to the people of Bylas. He was more than a much-loved man; he possessed invaluable holy powers that would be sorely missed. John Robertson talked about him with Grennie: "That was a good man who died at Bylas, wasn't he? Lots of the children even cried when he was buried, and women, lots of them. They all felt very bad about him. He was the only one who knew all the *go·jo·shi* songs. He was the best singer. Now he is gone and there is no one left who knows those songs, and can sing them as he did."

Grennie was so moved by the death of Jewett Wright that he wrote to my mother about it:

> It was he who had the cycle of songs used in the girl's puberty ceremony, and he used to always lead the singing which is so vital to the whole thing. You see, that cycle of songs is one of the oldest of Apache cycles and it is passed on from generation to generation. He had never taught anyone the cycle. Now it is gone. He was going to tell me part of it this spring."

I believe that the evolution of Grennie's place in the Bylas community was such that some of the elders may have sought him out as the one most interested in the preservation of the old culture. Official BIA policy did not encourage traditional practices. The Apaches often said to Grennie that there were fewer and fewer powerful medicine men left. And to some of Grennie's devoutly Christian friends that was only as it should be. One man told him that medicine men "would get Hell for practicing ceremonies and the old religion, because it was not right, and that it said in the Bible that all fake doctors and charlatans were to be thrown out of the temple."

Although this man scoffed at Apache religion as superstition, he was eager to hear the old stories told and listened with riveted attention as the elders spoke proudly of their holy power. One elder told Grennie that he had owl power, lizard power, and horse power, but Grennie observed, "It seems deer power is his long suit. He has the most deer power of anyone on either the San Carlos or Fort Apache reservations." Another man knew nearly all the ceremonies and had a wide variety of powers. And another man explained his level of holy achievements in terms of the sacred number 4: "One is not much, two is a little more, three is almost all of it but four is everything. No one ever gets to fourth place. I am the only one who has reached there."

And people continued to tell Grennie of holy powers that they had told to no one else before. One elder confided:

> When my father taught me this ceremony he said to me, "You must never change the words or add to what I have taught you. Keep it exactly like I taught you, no more, no less." I have not told anyone this power though lots have asked me to tell them about it, but I didn't want to. They offered lots of goods for knowing it. But I would not tell them. Now I have told you.

But Grennie appeared always to observe great caution. One of his closest friends and advisors was John Rope. As he prepared for a session with this old man, Grennie outlined the ground he wanted to cover, and asked Rope to indicate what he did not want to talk about ahead of time because it was summer and a dangerous time to speak of certain things. Grennie noted: "The things he cast out were: fire power and ceremony, snake medicine and ceremony, and all of section 14 which has to do with the sun, moon, sky, stars, earth, wind, water, thunder, lightning, rainbow, and rain.[70] These are the things he did not want [to talk about]."

But Rope offered to describe the dream from which his greatest power had derived:

> It was from this one dream that I got all my power for deer. I told you stories before about deer dreams, but it wasn't from them I got my power, but from this dream I told you. It was long ago I dreamed this dream, about thirty years ago.
>
> I didn't want to tell you this dream till winter. But I have. All the people know I have this power. Even San Carlos people know I have this power. Several people have asked me for this power, but I wouldn't show them. This thing I have told you is my own personal power.

This man's very Christian son-in-law, Emory Starr, who scoffed at the old religion, was nevertheless an Apache at heart and confided in Grennie afterwards: "E. Starr said it was good of John Rope to tell us the prayers that he had, and that there were lots of wonderful and beautiful things in them, that other men who knew these things would not want to give them away like that, but would want to keep them only for themselves."

It was early summer 1935. There were taboos against speaking of sacred matters in the summer, but summer was the time for ceremonies to be performed, and Bylas was buzzing with activity having to do with several girls' puberty ceremonies.

> There has been some kind of talk about someone in E. Starr's family who is having a monthly. E. Starr and J. Rope talked about it and J. Rope has asked twice if it has already come. I think this is the next to youngest of E. Starr's daughters, though I am not sure. It is interesting that this girl has been sent after wood several times that I have known of and had to pack a load home on a burro during the last few days. She also has been working on the shade house up at E. Starr's camp. I don't know if this has to do with the monthly or not. Two times I have heard women singing songs up at E. Starr's camp in the morning on different days. She has now gone to the mountains and is staying up there at a work camp with one of her sisters.

Buried in this passage is a hint of Grennie's modus operandi. He has not asked anyone who the girl might be, just notes the talk he has been hearing. He knows something is afoot and is putting pieces together: which girl is performing tasks she did not perform before, preparing herself for the responsibilities of womanhood. John Rope and his skeptical son Emory Starr are discussing the matter, and Grennie is employing his most effective research technique: learning by listening and saying nothing, picking up all the rich detail of daily life. He wrote of what he was hearing:

> There is a man at Calva who knows the fire medicine and he can take up a hot rock from the fire. He carries it slowly with no hurry or pain. It does not burn him at all. He can also take a red hot coal and put it in his mouth and it will not burn him at all. He cures babies this way when they are cutting teeth. He will take a red hot coal like this and put it in his mouth and blow his breath on the baby where its mouth is sore and it will get well again.
>
> Today Chris and John Rope were laughing greatly at John Rope's little granddaughter. She was crying because there were two burros just below the camp and one was trying to climb the other. This upset the little girl as she thought one was trying to hurt the other. She came running up to her family where they

were all sitting and cried out, "There is another burro trying to sit on my grandmother's burro. Go and get him off there. He is sitting on my grandmother's burro. I don't want him to do that." Everyone laughed and thought it was a great joke.

In the meantime people are busy preparing for the upcoming ceremony for another girl, the daughter of a man named George Gray. Several families are out gathering and roasting mescal, one of the traditional staple Apache foods. Smoke is in the air from fires at different locations in the hills around Bylas. Grennie describes the preparations:

> John Robertson came into camp this morning and said he had just come down from Turnbull Mt. where his wife was roasting mescal and he was making a set of *gá·n* hats. He is going back up the same day and will stay until he gets them made. He came after red paint. It will be quite a long time before they are finished. He is coming down next week to meet me about the money.
>
> As we sit in John Rope's camp many mornings we can see down at the river edge smoke coming up from where they are making sweat baths. The men and young men are always going down there to take them, both in morning and afternoon. J. Rope usually goes about noon when we get through work. This smoke you can see in about the same place about four times a week anyway.

THE PUBERTY CEREMONY OF GEORGE GRAY'S DAUGHTER

The puberty ceremony for George Gray's daughter had been planned for a year, since her first menstruation. It was to be an elaborate affair lasting four days, involving huge quantities of food, much social and sacred dancing, and people from both the San Carlos and Fort Apache reservations. Though not an especially wealthy man, George had many relatives who were called upon to contribute to this celebration of his daughter's entry into womanhood.

One of the obligatory stops to be made in planning the dance was a visit to the man who ran the reservation, BIA Agent James B. Kitch. On the agenda was what to do about drunks at the dance. A delegation from the family was sent, among whom was John Rope, the head man at Bylas:

> He told Kitch that if any of the men got drunk at the dance, he thought that they ought just to be put in the little adobe house near the place for the night and be turned loose in the morning, the same thing for drunk drivers. But Kitch said that any man who was drunk at the dance would get thirty days in jail and anyone who drove a car drunk would get sixty days.

Draconian measures perhaps, but appalling car wrecks were frequent. In fact only days before Grennie had documented this accident:

> A car load of San Carlos people were on their way home from Globe. They were drunk. They were going along too fast and a woman said, "Please go slower, my brother." Right then her husband in the front seat said "shit" and reached over and turned the lights off. They were in the dark and ran off the road into the ditch. The men were all thrown free, but the woman had some piece of metal driven into her head and was killed.

It is very important that the ceremony be an orderly affair, with a minimum of drunkenness. George Gray and his family had been saving money for two or three years and had amassed a small fortune of $200 to $300 to be spent on food and as fees for the medicine men. The ceremony was to be directed by a number of influential men. Among them was David Longstreet who was in charge of a segment called the tipi ceremony.

During his years on the reservations, Grennie amassed an immense collection of Apache things—most of them now in the Arizona State Museum. David Longstreet, one of Grennie's key Apache advisors, was renowned for the quality of the buckskin clothing he made, especially the beautiful and elaborate girl's puberty ceremony dresses. Longstreet had made one for Grennie to add to his collection for the Arizona State Museum. Grennie offered it to George Gray for his daughter's ceremonial before taking it to the museum in Tucson. While Grennie was visiting with Anna Price, David Longstreet stopped by to discuss business with Grennie:

> In the afternoon, D. Longstreet stopped in here and told me that if I came to the dance I should take some pictures with my camera. I told him that if I did George Gray and his family might not

like it, so maybe I better not. But he said that he was the one who had the say about it, that if I wanted to take pictures it was up to him. He is the man to whom the tipi ceremony belongs and who conducts it.

As well known as he was to George Gray and the members of his family, Grennie knew all too well how easy it would be to give offense by taking pictures, but a few days later when Grennie brought the dress to Longstreet, the old man said again that he should be sure to take pictures, adding that the girl's mother wanted to have a picture of her daughter in the dress.

She would be wearing the buckskin dress throughout the exhausting four-day ceremony. The dress would be heavy and very hot, but it would be a magnificent garment, symbolic of her coming of age and of the central place women occupied in the matrilineal Apache society.

Grennie had described many puberty ceremonies before, but none so thoroughly or so vividly, nor had he probably ever seen one so lavish and heavily attended. His narrative is sixty pages long, and it is far more than pokerfaced ethnography. As before, I will be weaving together passages from his daily diary and this dance narrative. Although what follows has segments from each of the four days over which the ceremony lasts, it is highly condensed.

The day before the ceremony began, George Gray and his relatives could be seen riding their horses to the dance grounds: "There were about twenty-five of them and I saw them all riding along in bunches on the way to Calva. In the rear rode George Gray on a brown horse. They were talking as they loped along and made a grand sight."

First Day

I arrived at Bylas early in the evening as a new moon was just setting to the north of Mount Turnbull. From the road could be seen the pink glare of the bonfire at the dance ground down by the river bottom in a clearing among the cottonwood trees. The singing and drumming had started and a social dance was going on at one end of the grounds. Four little girls were dancing in a row back and forth towards the singers, and beyond several rows of older girls were moving back and forth opposite some young men. Small boys were playing all about, some with sparklers and others lighting fire-crackers and throwing them in the air or leaving them on the ground and running for dear life. Young men,

> dressed in their best, were sitting about in front of the booths watching the dancing.[71]
>
> Away from the light of the fire little groups of women with babies and children were seated on the ground watching the dancing which was mostly on the east and south sides of the fire. There was very little talk—only an occasional comment in a low voice.
>
> On the south side were rows of older girls about fourteen to seventeen years old dancing in pairs opposite the young men. (The girls remained in the same pairs throughout the night, going everywhere two by two.) They were dressed in their best in bright colored calico dresses, reds, pinks, light greens, purples, blues, yellows—some wearing silk shawls. Those with long hair had it combed straight down the back, but those from school had bobbed hair pinned up with bobby pins. They looked grand.
>
> Standing where everyone could see him, one old man wearing a blue shirt, vest, gray pants, and a big uncreased hat with the brim rolled up in front, made several talks to the crowd about dancing, proper conduct, etc.
>
> There was a line of little girls dancing together in back of some of the older people. A boy sneaked up behind them and dropped a string of fire crackers at their heels. Immediately they started popping and the little girls scattered in confusion. The dance bosses hurried over shouting reprimands on all the boys there, who rushed off in all directions.
>
> George Gray was there supervising and quite excited, going here and there, and being nice to the men. He came up and spoke to me and took off his hat, which was sort of embarrassing as that is a sign of respect.

Although Grennie knows that everyone is welcome at such ceremonials (in fact heavy attendance is considered to make them more effective) he is uncomfortable with this public gesture of esteem from his host. He knew that it would be noticed, and being conspicuous was just the sort of thing he always tried to avoid. Although it would have been difficult for a six-foot-two white man to make himself inconspicuous in such a gathering, he felt his place was out of sight, somewhere on the edge of things. Nevertheless, the sign of respect may have been intentional. As public an affair as the ceremony was, George may have felt pleased, if not actually honored, to have Grennie in attendance.

George Gray was pleased that his daughter was so splendidly attired in the borrowed dress. What's more, Grennie's serious study of the traditions of the puberty ceremony may have given him a measure of stature among the people of Bylas.

> George told me, "My camp is down at the dance ground now. I have moved down there with all my family." They will remain there until the dance is over.
>
> Some of the young men danced as if reluctant, and lagged behind the girls, dragging back and forth in more of a walk than a dance, and the girls had to slow down to keep with them. But others danced freely and easily in perfect time with the girls whose long and full skirts swung gaily like bells. The dragging young men held their heads down sometimes as if embarrassed, but those who danced well held their heads up and looked as if they were really enjoying themselves, some whooping and hollering.
>
> A White River man sitting by me pointed to the dancers and said they were not good, that they were too slow, that they had good dancers up at White River. He gestured with his face to three girls who seemed to dance with the same man all the time and said that they were the only ones who were dancing well. One of the girls was George Gray's daughter, which might explain this good dancing.
>
> Every once in a while a new type of song was introduced. One of these songs had a wonderful rhythm and livened up the dancers. [It] started with the drum beating and then one or two men sang the words in a very low voice that could hardly be heard, then many men joined in with the chorus that rolled out over the heads of the people.
>
> ## Second Day
>
> At seven o'clock the next evening the drumming started somewhere among the trees. The usual groups of small boys were running about with sparklers and firecrackers. As the moon was setting firewood was brought to the dance ground and the men, young and old, began to assemble, one with a drum he tuned up and began beating, and some of the men started to sing. A big crowd was gathering, nearly 1,000 by now.

Four small juniper trees had been set in the ground at the cardinal points about the great fire. There was the glimmer of a cooking fire in George Gray's enclosure, and when I approached I could hear the jingling of the tin dangles on the buckskin dress that I had loaned for the occasion as the girl walked about in it.

In the background vague shapes of tents and here and there a glow of a fire showed where people were eating and sleeping during all that was going on. The sidelines were jammed with young men, many of whom had just come that day. There were so many girls filling the area about the fire that their bright dresses made a solid mass of soft rainbow color in the haze of dust.

Then a man appeared out of the dark from the east holding up a kerosene lantern. The crowd became tense with anticipation. From the trees the vague shapes of the *gá·n* emerged in single file, their bright fan-shaped headdresses above the black cloth masks lit up weirdly in the firelight. The head *gá·n* wore an antler headdress unlike any I have ever seen.

Then Richard Bylas got out in front of the crowd and started to talk. George Gray had asked him to do this. He talked in a loud voice for a long time. He said that he knew about this *gá·n* dance and what it was for and why this celebration was being given by George Gray for his girl. He also admonished the people about drinking and disorderly behavior at the dance. It was a long talk and before he got through the *gá·n* had come in again, but he could hardly bring himself to stop even though the people were not listening to him any more.

They danced out in front of the people and singers—savagely this time—and the people grew very excited. John Robertson was singing and the *gá·n* put everything they had into their dancing and the crowd seemed lifted up with the power of the song. The singers roared out the song and the hide and sticks and the drums slapped and boomed out the rhythm.

On their way out the old man with the owl feather cap danced along with Clown, making fun for the crowd. An old woman who had an American flag wrapped about her waist danced out into the open and tried to get Clown to dance with her, but he would not and refused her in a funny way which made the people laugh. The singing continued after the *gá·n* went out and the old woman danced out towards George Gray's daughter, giving a long wail and bowing low to her several times which brought a laugh from the other women.

About then, Charley Sago's wife and Mrs. Neil Wright danced up to me and David Longstreet told me to go on out and dance with them, which I did.

Henry Telto, a graduate of Carlisle, gave a fourth of July talk about how the fourth had started; how it meant the Americans' independence from England, and about liberty and the Thirteen States. He added that the Indians were the first Americans and the whites were the second Americans. The crowd applauded him well. After this speech came the pie-eating contest.

Third Day

George Gray cleared a lane toward the east through the crowd and at the end stood a man with a small bowl of pollen. First the old men, then the younger men from the sideline went down the left side of the lane, having first removed their hats—took a pinch of pollen and came back on the opposite side and sprinkled the pollen on the heads of the girl and *na-ai-e-es.*[72] After this the women and girls lined up and did the same.

The beads of the girl and *na-ai-e-es* were now caked and yellow with pollen, and the girl was so hot and weary she could hardly stand. Her father was close by her fanning her with his big hat and wiping her face with a handkerchief, helping her so that she could go on. Before this the girl had been wiping the sweat and pollen from her face with her own handkerchief.

Na-ai-e-es next made the girl kneel down on the blanket facing east and for about ten minutes she swayed in time to the songs, holding up her arms with her palms turned outward. From the semicircle of people in front of the girl, old Anna Price walked up and knelt on the ground facing her and swayed back and forth with her until the song ended, when she spoke some words to her. As the girl knelt there she fell over onto the blanket and had to be raised up, but she managed to go on somehow. Her mother was standing close by ready to help if needed.

Then *na-ai-e-es* told the girl to lie face down, head to the east, fully outstretched. As the singing continued *na-ai-e-es* started to mold and knead the girl into shape, starting at the shoulders, pressing them flat, then down each side of her back.

The girl was then told to run out around a man standing by the cane, then around Charley Sago who was standing on the south, then on the west and north with the men running after her.

Two young men and some small boys were beating on the hide that had been laid on the ground and the singing had changed to *gá·n* songs just before the *gá·n* came in. These were older, heavier men and much better dancers than those of the night before. Their bodies were painted black with white designs, their legs white, and the outer parts of their arms were painted with a series of white star-shaped marks. They danced with a splendid sort of fury, puffing with exertion, the sweat pouring off them, and the crowd nearly went wild with excitement. At the end of each song they stopped and trotted off around the fire clockwise and stopped and danced in front of the singers while Clown whirled his bull-roarer.

The girl continued dancing with her partner on the east side of the fire. She was wearing a yellow dress and the weight and heat of the buckskin dress almost exhausted her and might have prevented her from going on with the ceremony.

George Gray's daughter was not dancing now but stood and watched the *gá·n,* smiling a little and not appearing as tired as she had in the morning. When the *gá·n* went out, she and her partner retired to the enclosure for a long while.

Finally the singing and drumming stopped and it was all over. One man in the crowd shouted out in English, "Got it now," meaning that the girl had all the good of the ceremony.

About the central fire, which was now reduced to a heap of glowing coals and ashes, boys and girls were dancing in couples, very slowly. Some of the boys holding their girls or sweethearts close in their arms as if loath to be parted.

Then George Gray went to his enclosure and brought back a sack of store bread which he dumped on a canvas by the ashes of the fire, and set a pot of food on the ground as a sort of feast for the singers and dancers who had been there all night.

Fourth Day

David Longstreet took down from the east pole a bucket of liquid white medicine and the brush which was a green plant about fourteen inches long with two eagle feathers tied to it and mixed some of the medicine in a tin pan. Then he took some pollen from a little basket and made a cross with it over the medicine.

Then number-one *gá·n* danced up to the pan of medicine and peered at it as if wondering what it was, making several motions over it as he danced. John Robertson motioned the *gá·n* to dance about the southeast pole and as they did they almost stepped in the pan so David Longstreet carefully set it out of the way.

The girls came into the tipi and stood in the center facing east. David Longstreet motioned Fred Wesley to come in and handed him the pan of medicine and told him how to paint the girls—mostly on the hair. When this was done David Longstreet told Fred Wesley to take the brush full of the medicine and splatter it on the people. When they saw him coming they all drew back and some ran to get out of the way, or covered their heads so as not to get splashed. The men seemed to mind more than the women, but they were all good natured and joked and laughed about it.

Then David Longstreet took the pan and brush and sprinkled each of the four poles around the bottom and the willow branches, and walked out through the tipi to the east, sprinkling the ground as he went, followed by John Robertson and another man and the *gá·n*, the two girls, and then the singers and drummers. All at once the men from the sidelines rushed after the others and crowded through the tipi, removing their hats as they went inside. Then led by Mrs. George Gray, all the women and girls came, pushing and laughing, some with babies in their arms or on their backs, others leading their children. Among the crowd were some very old women bent with canes and a few old men with canes. Quite a number of the women danced in the procession, but only a few men did—those directly behind the singers and drummers.

> David Longstreet's long black hair flowed in the wind, his wrinkled face impassive as, still sprinkling the ground, he slowly led the happy procession that looped like a great snake back through the tipi again. Just behind him walked John Robertson straight and tall and very dignified, proud and satisfied because of his part in the ceremony and the fine performance of his *gá·n*.
>
> It was now about eight o'clock and the sun well up. Someone started to sing a *gá·n* song and the drum sounded. Two *gá·n* started to dance in front of the people. The girl and her partner stood in back of the crowd for a minute or two and then walked wearily toward George Gray's enclosure. No one noticed them leaving, everyone was intently watching the *gá·n*. They danced with all their skill and were an impressive sight in the daylight. A lot of the men whooped and hollered at them.
>
> Some old women danced out in a semi-circle by themselves. Anna Price went out and danced back and forth, bent over her cane. Mrs. George Gray danced with an old woman carrying a dog, all the way around the outside of the crowd. Everyone was rejoicing and I joined in the dance.
>
> The *gá·n* were through and filed out to the east and disappeared in the brush, gray figures brightly garbed, but belonging more to darkness than the day.
>
> People began packing their belongings into wagons or cars. Mothers were calling their children, almost everyone was in a hurry to get home, but a few still sat about. David Longstreet and I stopped and talked for a while.
>
> The last thing to be seen was George Gray riding his horse eastward to the river with an expression of contentment and tranquility on his face.

When I read this description, I hear a voice I have not heard before—a voice that has, for the moment at least, relaxed its usual scientific rigor to reveal a subjective, personal experience. As it has many times before, Grennie's own inner metronome moves to the syncopated rhythms of the pageant. Time seems almost to vanish, and his experience of the four-day event is one of total immersion. He was not a mere spectator. He expresses his understanding of this human drama by conveying its blend of the spiritual, the comic, the petty, the generous, and the majestic.

APACHE TIME, APACHE POWER

As the summer of 1935 wears on, Grennie's diary continues to record his daily conversations. Anna Price tells a story about her youthful prowess as a runner and how she outran boys by placing a hummingbird feather in her moccasin.

A boy who had set out from the San Carlos community to go to the Gray girl's ceremony at Bylas never showed up and was feared dead. A few days following the ceremony he turned up:

> They found him down near Victor's bluff and he was out of his mind. He said that he had been living on *huc* (a kind of cactus) and he had the stickers all around his mouth. He said it was as if he had been all over. It was as if he had traveled in a trance. He had a dream, he said. Neil says that maybe this young man will become a medicine man now. He says they may hold a dance and ceremony over him to find out what it all means.

By this time, Grennie's reputation had earned him the attention of Alfred Kroeber at Berkeley, and Kroeber asked Grennie if he would help out a student of his by the name of Edward Gifford. Grennie agreed and, as requested, squired him up to the Camp Verde reservation at Payson for six days of interviews with an old Tonto named Henry Irving. Grennie duly noted the usual ground rules for discussion of sensitive topics:

> There were several things that the old man was reluctant to talk about in the work: one was the ceremonial part of birth, one was death, burial and mourning, and all kinds of holy power he declined to talk of. He talked about war medicine all right but did not want to talk about the stars, sun, or moon, or sky, or earth. He said that if I came back in the late fall he would tell me all about those things as he knew how the stars were made. He absolutely refused to talk about lightning or snakes or thunder or rain till the late fall. He pointed to a small juniper tree in the yard that was struck last summer by lightning. Fred [the interpreter] looked at it in awe and with a little apprehension. He was right in the middle of telling us about some medicine, when he stopped dead. He would not go on. "I'd better stop now. I just got a twitch in the leg. That is a sign to stop now before trouble comes to me." So we stopped there.

Grennie did not come back that fall to Payson for further discussion of sacred topics, but at Bylas in October he and Neil Buck planned to pay George Gray a visit to talk about some of his holy powers. Even though Grennie and Neil had paid dozens of similar visits over the years, Neil reiterated his habitual advice: "Neil said that if we asked George Gray about wind power, should he say that he did not know about it, it would mean that he did not want to tell us about it so we would have to drop it there. This is the way they do if a man does not want to talk about something."

And the next day: "George Gray opened the conversation by saying that it was bad and dangerous to tell about wind power if you did not know it very well, as if you got some words wrong in there, or left them out, the wind might pick you up and carry you off someplace to the mts."

Wind power was potent and dangerous. It was used on the warpath to call up a great wind to fill the air with dust for escape from the enemy. But, like so many other powers, it could turn against he who possessed it; it could twist a man's body, make him crazy, carry him off. A man could get sick from the wind, and there was no one who knew how to cure it. The only person who could had died, and the knowledge had been lost. Even so, George Gray felt it was safe to speak of wind power as well as his war charm with Grennie and Neil, and agreed to do so after payment with certain special objects had been negotiated.

> George Gray, after he told his wind dream and about the war charm said, "Lots of men about here have asked me to tell them this that I have told you, but I never would do it even when I was drunk I would never talk about it to them. It is worth a great deal to tell about. I have been offered big payment to tell about it, but I would not. Now I have told you. I don't know why I have told you, except that I must have liked to do it I guess."

It was not only the traditional exchange that prompted George Gray to speak of sacred things, and it was one of many times that Grennie had been told things that not even Apaches had been told. George said simply that he must have liked doing it. What private measure of trust, respect, or unspoken purpose could be contained in this ingenuous declaration? Somehow Grennie was to be trusted where many Apaches were not. Indeed Grennie may have been sought out as a witness, a repository. Is it possible that there was some stature in the Apache community to be gained from such a collaboration? Grennie was spending a great deal of time with the most influential leaders and medicine men of the reservation. To be numbered in this select company might have meant a considerable measure of prestige.

Grennie continued, noting that George Gray had put on a war belt in the afternoon, and he told Neil to put it on too, so that what they had been talking about would not harm them but would do them good instead. When Grennie made such observations, the mask that had lifted while he wrote about the puberty ceremony drops into place again. I can tell nothing from his deadpan prose, but as time goes by he is exposed time and again to the reasons why the Apaches have such faith in their traditions. They seem to work often enough to justify themselves:

> One time a man got *gá·n* sickness. He went to bed all right, and the next morning he could not get up. He had terrible pains in his legs. They brought him down here and J. Robertson gave a ceremony to cure him, a *gá·n* ceremony. Two men had to stand on each side of him and hold him up. I saw it at the ceremony. When it was over he got up right away and was all right. I saw him walking about not long ago.

Grennie wrote about a Mexican family at Solomonville, south of the reservation, who came to hire John Robertson to perform a ceremony over a member of their family who was paralyzed on one side. After agreeing on the fee, he conducted a two-day ceremony the result of which was that the woman could move her hand and arm for the first time. The Mexicans were so impressed that they said they were through with white doctors from then on.

The eyewitness accounts like these that Grennie gathered were small islands of concreteness in a sea of sacred knowledge and ceremonial practice. During the fall and winter months of 1935 and 1936, he gathered hundreds of pages of raw notes on Apache religion, divining powers, cosmology, curing, and rite-of-passage ceremonies. As the fall of 1935 progressed, the pace of the acquisition of sacred knowledge picked up. His notes faithfully recorded the many discussions about the danger in the knowledge. He never pressed for information against the advice of his friends and advisors. Precautions were taken, but there were still risks, and it is possible that Neil Buck was worried that his friend Grennie was getting in over his head, that he was acquiring too much knowledge of too much sacred power too fast, and that he was too inexperienced to possess such knowledge.

Among the Apaches with whom I have spoken there is a divergence of opinion on this score. Some believe that it was important to record as much of this material as possible for the cultural heritage. Others feel that Grennie was exploring realms of knowledge where he had no right to be, that such knowledge should be transmitted only to an Apache apprentice who will use it as a practitioner. They feel that if it is forgotten, it was meant to be forgotten, being perhaps too dangerous to pass on. Traditional elders at San Carlos today are by turns grateful for and dismayed at the information Grennie recorded. On the one hand they are using his material to reconstruct knowledge and practice that might otherwise be lost. In the process they find things written down that are not meant to be written down, that are meant only to be spoken. They recognize that Grennie himself knew this, for occasionally they find the names of sacred and medicinal herbs referred to only obliquely or deliberately misspelled, as if in the privacy of his own record keeping, Grennie was treading with the same caution that his Apache teachers would have used.

It is difficult for non-Apaches like me to understand that knowledge about supernatural power could be dangerous unless, of course, that power is somehow made manifest. In the traditional Apache world, danger was everywhere in the form of enemy peoples, wild animals, starvation, ridicule, exile, exposure to the elements, vendetta, and much more. Rather than seeing these battalions of misfortune as random events, the Apaches identified them as the acts of supernatural beings. If a person could acquire the power to make allies of these beings, he could protect himself—by no means a unique religious paradigm. Perhaps this is what Grennie was getting at when he wondered if Apache religion conformed to its environment. The unspoken subtext in his diary is his witness of the fit between the daily Apache experience of the world and the Apache understanding of the powers that organize that world. Rarely if ever does the evidence suggest that the Apaches had it wrong. That is not to say that Grennie was actively searching for a belief system, though some Apaches have told me that his search may have been impelled by a void in his own spiritual values. Even as he was trying, as a scientist, to know the unknowable, he was being exposed to a deeply compelling religious experience in which he was finding a home of sorts, and as he did so, his Apache friends signposted the dangers along the way—to protect him as well as themselves. The fact that Grennie died as he did, from a brain tumor, only reaffirmed the Apaches' belief that there was danger and power in what Grennie was hearing and recording.

He wrote that witchcraft is not thought to endanger white people, and Apaches today say that the power contained in sacred knowledge cannot harm a person who does not believe in it. That, of course, begs the question: did they feel Grennie believed? More important to me: did Grennie himself at some level believe in or accept the Apache worldview and the supernatural powers by which it is ordered? Though he never spoke directly to this question, it is not as unanswerable as it might appear.

In spite of the complex structures and proscriptions of Apache religion, there seems to be a personal dimension to and individual experience of religion and supernatural power. Time and again Grennie notes the ways in which his Apache friends spoke directly to their powers—for guidance and reassurance or to negotiate an exception to some rule or standard practice. What began for Grennie as an intellectual examination of Apache religion became a compelling personal encounter with a value system having both personal and universal dimensions. The system clearly had a profound appeal to Grennie, especially because he saw these beliefs at work in the context of the environment in which the Apaches lived. And this brings us full circle to the question he posed, which is quoted at the beginning of this chapter, and I believe that Grennie's own experience may have answered his question.

Apache religion derives from a profound, inescapable, and daunting relationship between people and the world around them. Although Grennie personally practiced a few of the Apaches' rituals, such as participating in sweats or carrying a charm and some medicinal herbs, I have no evidence that he went beyond this in private observance. Consciously he was too much the scientist. Nevertheless, I continue to wonder how he could gain such a detailed, firsthand understanding of this vivid, functioning religion without being affected by it. Would he have found it possible to remain forever a witness on the bank, having watched and understood the great river of Apache religion for so long? All his life Grennie had been open to, perhaps even looking for, a spiritual or moral structure for his empirical, instinctive embrace of the natural world, and in the company of his Apache friends, I think he found it.

Spiritual knowledge, secret knowledge, encounters with supernatural power lay at the gravitational center of Grennie's reservation experience, and with it lay the great dilemma he would have faced had he lived longer.

Grennie himself wrote of the profound differences between the Apache world and the white academic world. Having gathered so much privileged knowledge, what would he have done with it? Publish it? Archive it for the future? I think he would have found a way to put it to use for the benefit of the Apaches themselves. I believe he saw himself as a messenger from one world to the other. I believe his years among the Apaches gave him a sense of mission and of his own place in the world.

An Apache Family's Day

chapter seven

"An Apache Family's Day," Grennie's fictionalized but entirely accurate description of a day in the life of a typical Apache family in the 1930s, seems a fitting addition to this volume. When Grennie wrote it, he meant it to embody those things he admired most about the Apaches: the simple dignity, the earthy grace and rhythm of their lives. They were, after all, as far as Grennie was concerned, just people; and he liked to hang out with them. He liked the way they did things. He desperately wished they had drawn a better lot in life. He saw the injustice, the bureaucratic bullying, and the economic dead-end that handicapped the future of so many Apaches.

Grennie admired the Apaches and in his own way felt that his own people had much to learn from them. He told his sister-in-law, Anne Stockton, that the world was changing too fast, that people simply were not meant to adjust to such rapid change, and that he was deeply concerned about the future and about the values by which people would be living their lives in an ever more rapidly changing world.

The names of the people in the following account may sound stereotypical and even clichéd, but in fact they are quite typical of the everyday nicknames used by Apaches. There is a variety of other names, some formal and some so private that they are never spoken. What Grennie writes here is deceptively simple; in fact it is an accurate reflection of traditional relationships, which remain today much as they did in the 1930s.

Grennie takes obvious pleasure in this. He was drawn to the Apaches in the first place by the rhythm of their lives

It is early morning of a November day in the Gila Valley. The place is Calva, an Apache farming community on the Gila River, about which are scattered Apache families in their conical-shaped brush wickiups. The long land to the south slopes gently from the hill's edge along the river, then steeply upwards gaining in its momentum as it nears the summit of sharp-pointed, solitary Mount Turnbull. To the east, up the broad valley, bending as it goes, there is the beginning of an orange light behind the yet dark jaggedness of the Gila Range.

It is still dawn in the valley, sunken in the cold shadow of the earth between the long running ranges edging it in, to north and south. Suddenly the sun's light is on the upper part of Mount Turnbull. It is only a matter of moments while it slips down the mountain's side and into the bottom where the river's water will mirror its light in a long writhing body to the east.

These fall mornings in the valley are cold. In another month there will be frost on the dry grass. From among the mesquite trees on the bench bordering the river comes the sound of an ax being used on dry wood. Red-Woman is using it, and she swings it with experience. Soon, with an armful of the wood, she walks from the woodpile to the entrance of the wickiup, bending slightly as she enters the low entrance door. It is still dark within as she lays some twigs on the white nest of ashes that was last night's fire. Soon there is a blaze.

A large bed is built on the ground on one side against the wall of the wickiup. Tiptoes, Red-Woman's husband, is sitting on its edge, yawning as he laces his shoes. In his pants and undershirt he walks outside and stretches in the cold morning air. He may pray there for a moment, facing the sun in the east, his lips moving slightly with barely audible syllables. He is praying for his life; but most important, for his children's lives.

In no time a blackened coffee pot is shoved against the fire by Tiptoes's wife, and with a few other preparations, the morning's meal is in progress. Two little girls, White-Foot, a cunning youngster with glistening black eyes and a cherubic countenance, the other, She-Turns, some eight years old, with black shiny hair and a face like a beautiful wild thing full of mischief, are still in bed, under the mound of blankets which their parents, till a moment or two ago, had shared with them.

On the opposite side of the fire from where Red-Woman and her husband sleep with the two children, there is a cot against the wall of the wickiup. It has been slept in recently, and soon its occupant enters from the outside where he has been the last few minutes. Squatting beside the fire he warms his hands.

Named Angry-Walking, he is a boy about twenty-four years old, of rather slight stature, with an aquiline and a thin face for an Apache. His blue work shirt, blue jeans, and shoes are like those of his father, Tiptoes, and come from the traders' store at Bylas, five miles distant up the river. There is something intangibly sensitive about this boy, with his sparse dark eyebrows, the delicate mold of his face and his thin finely-shaped hands; intangible, because at the same time all his features are solid and strong under the brown skin of his face.

The mother of Angry-Walking, a *t'i slednt'i dn* clanswoman dead some fifteen years, was Tiptoes's first wife. They were married when they were very young. Now Angry-Walking, not having married, still lives with his father, his [father's] second wife and his two little half-sisters.

Tiptoes had two other daughters by his first wife, one a girl of eighteen now working as a helper in the government hospital at San Carlos, and a second about twenty-seven who is married to a young man, half-Yavapai, half-Apache. The young couple also live at San Carlos, thirty miles down the river. She and her husband may come to visit Tiptoes today, for it is Saturday, and the children won't be in school.

As the father and his son eat their morning meal of coffee and tortillas, Red-Woman sits to one side. She will eat after they are finished this morning, though she sometimes eats with them when company isn't present.

Angry-Walking talks to his father, "The horses are gone."

"Maybe they are down in the mesquite brush," his father suggests.

"No, I looked there in the corner of the fence, and the wires are broken down. They must have gone through that way."

"Long Lost drove his horses over across the river yesterday; maybe ours are in with them now," Red Woman says as she tugs with one hand on the blankets under which the little girls are beginning to stir and mumble.

A sleepy, cherubic face appears from under the edge of the blanket and White-Foot creeps out to her mother, who starts putting her shoes on—all that is necessary, for she has slept in her clothes, as has the rest of her family.

"Hey, my little girl," Red Woman teases as she sees the sleepy look in the child's eyes. "Where is She-Turns?" her father asks her, speaking slowly.

"There," says White-Foot, pointing to a patch of black hair blowing from under the cover. Her father likes to get the little girl to talk; she is just learning, and her childish syllables are appealing to her parents, especially to her father, whose favorite she is. However, there is little else mentioned during the meal, and after all, when people are busy eating, it is not the time to talk.

Tiptoes and his son eat quickly and sparingly, arise, and go outside. The little girls are up by this time and eating with their mother by the fire.

"We better see which way the horses went," Tiptoes says, and he and his son go down in the sandy bottom outside their fence, separating to cover more ground. Soon they join nearer the river. "You better go over after them. You can go to Long-Lost and ask for one of his horses. He has three there at camp," Tiptoes tells the boy.

Long-Lost is Tiptoes's sister's son and so there is no hesitation in asking him for the horse, or almost anything, for that matter. The special relationship that he bears Tiptoes precludes any possibility of refusal of help between them when it is at all possible. Long-Lost is the relative whom Tiptoes counts on most of all. True, he has a brother's son living close by, and a sister and half-brother whom he often visits five miles away at Bylas, but Long-Lost is the one he most often turns to. The two men are almost of the same age, and not only do they help each other, but they are companions on more than one venture.

Angry-Walking starts back to the wickiup without saying anything. Such jobs as wrangling horses often fall to him and he knows, as other boys his age do, that his father expects him to help in such things. It is a grown son's obligation to help his parents while he lives with them. The time would come when he married, and then his efforts would of necessity be directed in aiding his parents-in-law. His parents would not expect his help in everyday things such as these.

Angry-Walking was back soon with the horse from Long-Lost's camp on the opposite side of the field. He took a saddle from its place in the storage-shed beside the ramada.

"You better look near that spring across the river. The feed is good and the horses may be over there. I'm going up to Bylas with the old man. It's pension day today," his father told him.

The boy kept right on saddling as if he had not heard a word, though he took it all in. His father would expect no answer. He finished, mounted, turned his horse, and trotted down off the bench to the sandy river bottom, the *batamote* bushes slapping and scratching against his pant-legs as he rode through them.

Tiptoes's family camp was one of sixteen located about the new farming tract which the government had cleared and allotted—two acres to each man. It was not hard to distinguish demarcations between families about the edges of the brown-striped fields composing the tract, for each little group was separated from the other by a short stretch of brush and unoccupied ground.

Tiptoes's camp was composed of four structures: a large wickiup in which they lived, slept, and ate; about two yards distant a small frame storage-shed in which saddles, bridles, ropes, horse feed, and other odds and ends were stored; and beside it a large ramada or flat-topped shade, which in warm weather was used for sleeping, eating, and working rather than the large family wickiup; and last of all, a small dome-shaped wickiup slightly lower down on the side of the bench than the other structures, and about ten yards from the main dwelling.

In this lived an old man, the reason for Tiptoes's interest in pension day. Old Angry-He-Looks-About was one of the *tsi des gaidn* clan, and the father of Red Woman. He lived here beside his daughter and son-in-law, who took care of him. The old man's wife had died long ago, and he had to have somewhere he could stay. His daughter's home was the logical place, for had he not a good son-in-law in Tiptoes?

But he was getting too old to even think about such things. He was continually complaining about the cold this winter, and though his daughter kept a fire going in the little wickiup, he still shivered, he said. Some days he never came out of his little dwelling at all except to relieve himself, but on sunny warm mornings he liked to totter outside with his staff and up the little incline to sit with his back against the gentle outside curve of the large wickiup and sun himself. He ate in his little wickiup where his daughter, or sometimes her little girls, brought him his food.

Angry-He-Looks-About had been quite a man in his day. He had fought down in Sonora, in Old Mexico, many times on those raids of long ago, and to look at his wrinkled old face—so old that it was neither man nor woman, but a concentration of sexless age—it made one wonder how far back the things he liked to reminisce about occurred. Maybe they happened more years ago than a mortal has a right to remember. He was married and had several children when the white people first came into the country. Later on when the soldiers came and reservations for his people were established, he enlisted as a scout with the United States Army and thus he came by a pension of forty-five dollars a month.

Now, old and bent as he was, deaf and almost blind, he had two consuming interests: his grandchildren and his reminiscences. You could be sure if you heard him prattling to himself, he was either mentioning some exploit of his youth or talking about the two little girls—what they were doing or should do—bringing up some mishap that had befallen them, maybe an ant bite that he had cured with his Ant Ceremony, mumbling that their mother should guard against such things.

Only the other day She-Turns had failed to return from school in the afternoon, and that evening in anxiety her father and Angry-Walking drove their car down to Bylas to find out what had happened to her. The first place they searched was at Tiptoes's older sister's camp where the little girl had often visited with her mother and father. There she was, asleep in her aunt's wickiup, and so cross when woken up that she would not return home with her father, but insisted on remaining with her aunt for the rest of the night.

She-Turns had merely taken it into her head not to come home that afternoon. By doing so she nearly caused her grandfather to break his neck. The old man, on being told of the absence of the little girl, was much exercised, and the next morning, as no one came to tell him what news there was, he started out to find his daughter in the big wickiup. On the way he missed his footing and rolled down the bank, head over heels. Seeing the accident, Tiptoes called to his wife and both of them went to the old man anxiously. Red Woman picked her father up, for it would not do for Tiptoes to help his father-in-law from such an ignominious position. On seeing that no damage had been done, everyone laughed, and his daughter took him back to his fireside.

Red-Woman had brought the bedding out to hang in the sun. She had washed the cooking things and was busy using a broom made out of willow branches to sweep up the yard and interior of her dwelling. Tiptoes was sitting on a stool in the sun and the two little girls were running in and out of the wickiup, playing with each other. White-Foot stumbled and fell; her older sister coming close behind, landed on top of her. The little girl started to cry, "*ye'o*, what are you trying to do? You should not chase her like that," said Red-Woman as She-Turns did not make a move to get off her sobbing playmate. "Go on, get up. You are making her cry," her mother scolded and made a feint to swat her with the broom. She-Turns jumped up and dashed away. The crying White-Foot was lifted to her feet and otherwise left to recover herself without sympathy.

Both little girls had been racing about and getting in their mother's way. She had patiently stood it, as she always did. "Children don't know any better than what they do. Why should you scold them when they don't know they are doing wrong? You have to teach a child what is good and bad," she would have said, like any good Apache mother. But She-Turns was sometimes a difficult child and talked back to her mother. Then, and not until then, did her mother slap her.

"We better start for Bylas. There will be a lot of people at the traders' store this morning and we want to get back here before afternoon. Get ready now," Tiptoes told his wife. They would go in the car, an old Chevrolet truck.

Red-Woman called to the children, and with their blankets to wrap about them, they bundled into the back of the car. Their mother went down to her father's wickiup and, entering, told the old man to come along. He followed her to the car in his old army overcoat. She helped him into the body of the truck while Tiptoes sat at the wheel.

All in, they started off, the old man hanging on to the side-boards with a feeble hand, the top of his staff showing over his bent knee. At the traders' store he would be helped in by his daughter, who would shout into his deaf ears instructions about putting his thumb mark on his pension check, after which the trader would cash it.

They returned from Bylas at noon. The check had been cashed and Red-Woman had done the trading as she usually did. Most purchases were in the way of food, but even with clothes, she did the greater part of the buying, except when Tiptoes or Angry-Walking had to buy clothes for themselves. Sometimes when Tiptoes went to Bylas and Red-Woman did not go with him, she told him what to buy before he left.

The pension money all went into the family purse, and Red-Woman's father had little actual use of it. This time he returned with two sacks of Bull Durham for himself. His daughter had shouted to him in the store, "Father, do you want anything?" and after several attempts to make the old man hear, elicited from him his wish for tobacco.

The government pension in the family is a great asset and makes up the bulk of the yearly income, as it does in many an Apache family of today. But Tiptoes also has his two-acre farm on which he raises some corn, squash, and melons, but the soil being alkaline, sufficient vegetables cannot be obtained for family consumption. The few chickens scratching about the yard only furnish occasional eggs; but though the family, like other Apaches, would not eat their chickens, they sell them to white people at times.

As well as these sources of food and income, Tiptoes has cattle, some thirty-five head running on the range with other Apache stock. Originally amounting to twenty head issued him by the government, through a pay-back percentage plan due during fall and spring when sales after roundups are made to visiting cattle buyers, they are gradually increasing. What he realizes out of his two or three head sold at a roundup is little at present, but in time, with his debt paid off, it will be more, possibly a hundred and fifty dollars.

Tiptoes sometimes goes along on roundups to do his share of the work required of cattle owners, but when he is busy he sends his son in his place. Once he sent Long-Lost to work for him, furnishing his horse as is customary. But he didn't like to ask him to do this again, as the two men are too near the same age. One gets one's younger relatives for such tasks.

Angry-Walking came driving the four horses across the river, splashing in the shallow water as they approached. His father went to open the gate for him and helped to get them into the corral, which he had repaired in the morning before starting to Bylas. "Where did you find them—far off?" he asked his son.

"Yes, they were headed down the river. That new black horse from San Carlos was leading them off," Angry-Walking replied.

Tiptoes walked up to the young horse. It was not long since he was a colt, but now it was almost time to cut him. He was going to talk to his half-brother up at Bylas about it. He would need help in the operation and his half-brother had cut horses before—knew some of the knife power necessary in doing it successfully. Besides, his half-brother would, he thought, be glad to do it for him without payment, though he usually got two or three dollars when he did it for people not his close relatives.

When Angry-Walking unsaddles Long-Lost's horse, he turns him loose in the corral with the others, and Tiptoes throws in a little hay for all.

A car is coming down the sandy road to the gate. It turns in and comes to a stop below the bank on which the camp stands. In it is a young man, and beside him a woman with a baby in its baby-carrier in her arms. They sit there for a minute or two, taking no notice of the various members of the family, who keep on about their duties as before. But Tiptoes has seen the car from a distance and called to his wife that his daughter and her husband were arriving from San Carlos.

The young woman with her baby gets out first and walks slowly up the incline towards the main wickiup. She is small, with the same finely molded face as her father, her chin coming to a little rounded point, and her whole face set in the surrounding curves of her sleek black hair hanging down over her shoulders. She is dressed in maroon, the loose-sleeved blouse hanging over the top of her bell-like skirt, full of shadows where the long pleats run down it to the ground.

Her husband follows closely behind, dressed in the usual work pants, shoes, blue shirt, and cap. Rather tall, he also has a pleasant face, edged by the fine growth of short hair down over his temples.

Before they reach the top of the hill, Red-Woman speaks to them. "You have come from San Carlos today? We thought you might come."

"Yes, we wanted to come down here to visit," the young woman says.

As they talk they do not group themselves together, but stand apart at some distance. Close quarters with others, except at places where crowds are unavoidable, such as dances or meetings, indicates familiarity, and there certainly is no marked familiarity among these people.

Red-Woman was sitting against the wickiup sewing on one of the children's dresses and the young woman sat down near her. They talk together, the visitor describing a mishap, a blow-out on the way over from San Carlos.

Her husband says to Tiptoes, "We had too many chickens over at our camp and so we have brought a crate of them. They are on the back of the car. Where do you want them?" "Over here, under the ramada," is the answer, and Angry-Walking returns with his brother-in-law to the car, where they unload the crate and carry it up. No thanks for the chickens is voiced and none is expected. The gift is taken as a matter of course. It is right for a son-in-law to help his wife's parents. Tiptoes would gladly do the same, though he bears less obligation to the younger man.

Soon the two women enter the wickiup. Red-Woman is getting a meal ready and the younger woman is helping her. The slap, slap, slap of tortilla-making can be heard, and the scrape of the sheet of tin as it is placed over the fire to heat. The tortillas will be spread on it to cook soon. A pot with meat is boiling, and Red-Woman grinds some acorns on the metate to add to the stew.

The men sit outside, conversing of late events at Bylas and San Carlos in slow respectful tones. "I hear that the checks for the cattle will be in soon, maybe next Monday. . . . They say that Black Rope at Bylas sold fifteen head this time. He will get lots of money. He has his debt paid off. . . . The superintendent told the committee at the last meeting he wanted to get new horses to replace those the government killed on the range two years ago. . . . He Kills is on the committee. He is a good talker. He told the superintendent he should have done something about it long ago . . . " and so on, the talk goes.

But it is serious, not insignificant gossip as so often is heard in other Apache conversations. Tiptoes and the young man, bearing the relationship they do to each other, cannot indulge in small talk. They respect each other, are never familiar. That would not be right.

But with Red-Woman, the situation is different from the average mother-in-law. The young man sees her, even addresses her at times, though always respectfully, and eats in the same wickiup. He would not do that were Red-Woman his wife's real mother. Then there would be a respectful avoidance, the two never permitting themselves to see each other or converse except under greatest emergency. Red-Woman, though she could have asked for the respect relationship, had never done so, and so it was not observed.

Red-Woman had been married before to a cross-cousin of Tiptoes. She did not get on well with this man. They fought continually and finally separated. Tiptoes was then a widower. He had known Red-Woman for some time and liked her. One day she came to visit at his sister's camp where he stayed with his children in order that they might have attention. He saw her and decided he would do something. "My relative-in-law, I can't let you go home from here. You will have to stay, now that you have come."

"Yes, I think you are a good man," she answered.

That is the way they were married.

Inside, the conversation was freer, though still slightly constrained. The young woman was in the process of telling Red-Woman some local news.

"Yes, that's right. I heard it the other day. Wolf-Track's wife ran off from him with another man. Wolf-Track was mad. He said to let that woman go where she wanted to; that he was through with her. She just runs about in the brush with men like a coyote. . . . Thin-Girl's baby was sick the other night. It had a sore mouth and they hired an old Tonto man who knew the Fire Power to work over it. Better this morning. . . . The school children do not like one of the teachers at the mission school. The children say that he threatens to switch them sometimes, and that all they do is read the Bible in that house. . . . "

Before very long the meal was ready and Red-Woman called to her husband to come and eat. Tiptoes, his son, and his son-in-law entered the wickiup. They ate together, the two women waiting for them to finish. White-Foot and She-Turns ate with their father this time, sharing a small bowl of food together. They were much interested in the young mother's baby, lying in its carrier on the big bed. Too young yet to be called by a kinship term, it was just a baby to these little girls.

After the men finished they walked outside to sit and talk again. The women ate their meal together and soon came out also. Angry-He-Looks-About had retired to his wickiup shortly after the return from Bylas. He was asleep in there, exhausted from the trip.

The afternoon went swiftly and soon Tiptoes' daughter and her husband left for home, after Tiptoes had said he intended to come to San Carlos on some business before very long and would stop at their camp.

Not long after the visitors departed, a stout man rode up on a bay horse. His round face was all smiles under his broad-brimmed hat, and his belly seemed almost to hang over the saddle horn in a blob of white shirt front as he jogged up to the camp. His blue trouser legs grasping his mount were absurdly small for such a big upper half.

The newcomer shifted his hat to a rakish angle and pulled his horse to a stop in front of the smiling but silent Tiptoes. He had some idea of what was coming, but preferred to see what move the other would make. "Hey, my cross-cousin," said the newcomer, "What are you doing here? Has your wife run away and left you? If that is so, it is too bad, for I have just come to take her home with me."

The fat man was Mountains-Running-Together, a member of Tiptoes' father's clan, and unrelated by blood. These two, being cross-cousins could joke, and as Mountains-Running-Together was such a jolly old man, the two usually exchanged some such ludicrous repartee when they met.

Tiptoes had an answer for him. "Well, if my wife has run off, I will marry you," and they both laughed. The fat man was on his way to his camp a quarter of a mile below, and after telling Tiptoes what he had come for—namely that the cattle checks were to be issued next Monday—he rode on.

It is dusk and the brush in the river bottom is already becoming lost in dark colors. Only the fluttering of the quail jostling for places to roost in the mesquite trees can be heard. In the west the yellow afterglow is almost gone, and in the east the heavy purple of night rises up in a widening band across the sky.

Supper finished, the family is inside and almost ready to go to bed. In fact the little girls are already in bed and falling off to sleep after their busy day, exactly such a one as the family would have many times again.

It is night; the moon has risen, etching out the long curves of the rising land as it arches up to Mount Turnbull.

Such a page might be taken from the life of any simple Apache family. Actually, the family described above is a real one, and the events taking place occurred over the space of time in which I (Grenville Goodwin) was in close contact with it. No two families are exactly the same, and an unending series of accounts could be given about them. But this one is fairly typical and is presented with the aim of making the reader feel and see the workings of at least one such unit.

chapter eight

An Apache Ranchería

This section is the sum total of the surveys and inventories both my father and I have made of the major Apache ranchería in the Sierra las Espuelas mountains in Mexico, some thirty miles south of the New Mexico boot heel.

Grennie was guided there in 1931 by his friend, Bill Curtis, and he entered a thorough description, inventory, and survey of the place in his diary, including photographs, drawings, diagrams, and maps. His description was so thorough that a group of us—my wife Margot, my son Seth, his wife Kathy, Barney Burns, and I—were able to find the place in January 1997. We were able to spend only two days there and saw only some of the camp's features. When we left, we all knew we had to come back for a complete exploration of the place. I wanted to do a comprehensive and accurate cartographic survey, and I wanted to account for all of the features of the ranchería that Grennie had found and mapped in 1931. Our first visit had left us with so many unanswered questions that only a second, exhaustive exploration could begin to unravel the mystery of this place.

Although this was an Apache camp, it contained features so un-Apache that Grennie wondered who really lived in this camp. It should be kept in mind that there is another, similar ranchería about thirty miles south of this one on the Sierra Chita Hueca. Discovered in 1929, the Chita Hueca camp was almost certainly built by the people who had abandoned the Sierra las Espuelas ranchería in 1926. In 1976 and again in 1987, I went to the Chita Hueca site with companions and found some of the same artifacts that Grennie had found and photographed in 1931. Compared with the remains at the Sierra las Espuelas ranchería, there is not much left at the Chita Hueca camp—only a low rock wall and scraps of glass and barbed wire.

View over Sierra las Espuelas ranchería.

Bill Curtis at the Apache camp in the Sierra las Espuelas, 1931.

If the Apaches in the Sierra las Espuelas and the Sierra Chita Hueca sites were in hiding, why did they do so in the backyard of some of the biggest and most prosperous and most fully manned ranches in Mexico?

Were these the same Apaches who were responsible for a decade of violence that began in 1920 with the slaughter of the Molinas family in the Tinaja, some fifty miles to the south?[73] This attack was followed by the ambush, three years later, of Jesús Pedrego and Leonardo Olivas, two men from Bavispe.[74] There were other attacks during the 1920s, then the violence culminated in the 1927 murder of María Fimbres and the kidnapping of her three-year-old son Gerardo, who was murdered some three years later.

Was there any way to tell how long the Apaches had lived in the Sierra las Espuelas ranchería; why they built a permanent, year-round camp; and what they were really doing there? Why weren't they more concerned about discovery, living as close as they did to expanding cattle ranches and a well-used smuggling route across the border through the mountains immediately to the west?

We had to wait three years after our first visit to this site in 1997; but in May of 2000, we returned, in a party of a somewhat different makeup. There were still Seth and Barney and myself, but we were joined this time by Alan Ferg, an Apache specialist from the Arizona State Museum; by Austin Lenhart, an archaeological surveyor, and by

At the concrete dam halfway between the main arroyo camp and the upper camp; left to right: Alan Ferg, Neil Goodwin, Seth Goodwin, Austin Lenhart, Barney Burns; Sierra las Espuelas, May 2000. (Photo by Seth Goodwin)

Diana Hadley. Diana is a historian from the Arizona State Museum with particular expertise in pioneer and ranching history of the region and a friend who has been in on the search for the Sierra Madre Apaches for many years.

What follows is, like in chapter 2, a conversation of sorts between my diaries and the diary that my father kept while in Mexico searching for the Sierra Madre Apaches in 1930 and 1931. In places I have inserted my own comments into my father's diary entries, and these are enclosed in square brackets. Instead of trying to overlay long-gone features onto our survey maps, we simply reproduce our maps and Grennie's side by side, using the same feature numbers that he used. Our experience of the ranchería and our interpretation of it is far more vivid and cogent if understood in light of what Grennie saw there seventy-five years earlier. ✣

NEIL'S DIARY

May 2, 2000, the Carretas Plains

The Apaches had chosen the site for their hidden ranchería well. The Sierra las Espuelas is an impenetrable range of mountains at the northern end of the Sierra Madre, beginning just south of the international border. For centuries the Espuelas had been a labyrinthine high ground from which the Apaches attacked Spanish, then later, Mexican and American settlements. This range is located at the approximate north-south center of the original homelands and raiding territory of the Chiricahua Apaches and the Western Apaches. These homelands stretched from central Arizona and west-central New Mexico well over two hundred miles south of the border into the Mexican states of Sonora and Chihuahua—much of it in the Sierra Madre.

Raiding parties going south from homelands in Arizona and New Mexico could disappear into the Sierra las Espuelas when pressed by either Mexican or American armies. No one knew these mountains as the Apaches did. The Sierra las Espuelas was where the Apaches had always felt safe; the place into which people did not pursue them, did not try to find them, and it remained thus until the late 1920s.

The Apaches had the mountains to themselves largely because of their notorious reputation as warriors, persisting well into the twentieth century. But there was another reason: the Sierra las Espuelas range was owned by the Palomas Land and Cattle Company, a ranch of immense proportions that comprised all the land in Mexico along the international border from El Paso west to the Sonora state line, a swath of geography of some 175 miles long east to west, and some 30 miles wide north to south. It had been assembled through separate purchases of thirteen adjacent ranches in 1902 by a consortium of American investors. At two-and-one-half million acres, it was at the time the largest ranch in North America. Its headquarters was the Nogales Ranch, just at the north end of the Sierra el Medio. From there you could look directly west across the Carretas Plains at the Sierra las Espuelas.

The assembling of this property was not the first time that title to Apache country had passed from the hands of one uninvited landlord to another. In 1848, the United States gained possession of half of its present trans-Mississippi West as an outcome of war with Mexico, and with this land, what amounted to half of Apachería and several thousand resident Apaches.

When the Apache Wars of the nineteenth century were concluded in 1886 with the surrender of Geronimo, it was thought that all of the Apaches were accounted for—either as prisoners of war or as reservation residents. In fact there were some that never surrendered, and when the founders of the Palomas Ranch picked up the Sierra las Espuelas in 1902, they became unwitting hosts to an undetermined number of Apaches who were the last of their kind: free-roaming semi-nomads still living in the old way—hunting, gathering, raiding—and answerable to no one. Though the Palomas Ranch may have had legal title to the Sierra las Espuelas at the western end of its property, the mountains were, in fact, essentially under the control of the Apaches who never surrendered.

They lived there, a presence unknown to all but a few, until discovered by accident by two American Mormons raised in Mexico, Bill Curtis and Moroni Fenn, who were prospecting for gold in 1926. Bill was to become my father's guide in his search for the Sierra Madre Apaches in 1930 and 1931.

Long a shadowy presence unknown to the outside world, the Sierra Madre Apaches began making headlines in Southwestern newspapers in 1929 and 1930 following a sensational 1927 murder and kidnapping some 120 miles south of the border. While traveling on a remote trail between Nácori Chico and the mountain mining town of Pinos Altos, a Mexican family by the name of Fimbres had been ambushed by a group of Apaches. María Dolores Fimbres was killed—her throat slit—and her three-year-old son Gerardo was kidnapped. Her husband, Francisco Fimbres, witnessed the attack but was too far behind her on the trail to come to her aid. The Apaches disappeared in a flash. Francisco Fimbres and a heavily armed posse made up of friends and relatives spent the next three years on a near-perpetual manhunt, combing the Sierra Madre hoping to rescue young Gerardo and avenge María's murder.

The headlines generated by this event attracted Grennie's attention while a freshman at the University of Arizona. He resolved to find out firsthand all he could about these Apaches, knowing that it might not be long before they were all killed. Mexican ranchers at the time were shooting them on sight. He slipped away from school in Tucson in the fall of 1930 and went to Douglas, where he knew he would find a number of people who had had personal experience with these Apaches. His first stop was with Leslie Gatliff, the Douglas chief of police. I'll let Grennie tell it.

GRENVILLE'S DIARY

Nov. 14, 1930, Douglas, Arizona

Now went to Mr. Gatliff's house and told him what I wanted to know. It would be almost impossible to come in contact with these Apaches, he says, they being so wild. But there would be a chance to see their camps. However, it would not be safe for one to go alone, either because of danger of accident or from harm by Indians or Mexicans. He admitted that a good deal of false information had come out in the papers, but that the reports of the wildness of the country and the plentiful game were true, and that the Apaches were really there, and actually in a wild state. He told me of a Mr. Bill Curtis who had found an Apache storage cave in the Sierra Espuela, southeast of Douglas. He advised me to go see him to get further information, as he had brought some of the material found out with him.

Mr. Bill Curtis turned out to be a Mormon, one who had come south from Utah in the '90s to the new Mormon Mexican settlements. I told him what my errand was, and he gave me a lot of valuable information. He has a ranch down in the Sierra Madre, southeast of Douglas, which has brought him in close contact with these Sierra Madre Apaches. Fimbres and other parties concerned in these affairs are well acquainted with him. About the storage cave they found, he related the following:

About 4 years ago, he and another man [Moroni Fenn] were up in the S. Espuela, when they ran into one of the Apache men. This fellow was by himself, and mounted, being dressed in the old-time way. He ran for it and would not stop to parley. On riding a little further up a canyon, blue birds commenced to fly up out of the brush in its bottom somewhat further. Taking this as a sign that other members of the band were the cause of the birds' being disturbed, Curtis and his party got out of the mts. in a hurry.

NEIL'S DIARY

At the time Bill and Moroni discovered this ranchería, they had no idea how extensive a complex it was. The bluebirds told them they were not alone, and they hurried out of the area before they encountered any more of the camp's inhabitants. Although Grennie writes next that Bill found five camps, I believe what Bill meant was that within the ranchería there were five widely separated dwelling sites that may have taken them several days to find, explore, and ultimately loot and partially burn.

GRENVILLE'S DIARY

Later on, gathering up 15 men, and arming themselves, they came back and picked up the trail of the Apaches, following them for several days, and coming on 5 successive camps, just recently evacuated. Right at the crest of the S. Espuela they came on several caves used for storage by the Apaches.

One or two of these were sealed with mud and rock, which they tore out, finding much Apache material stored. Inside were some moccasins; a pair of buckskin breeches; women's dresses of cloth; several four strand, twisted, rawhide riatos of various sizes; a good many tanned cowhides; some big balls of tallow, a burden basket, a dish basket, and a pitched water bottle; a buckskin saddle bag; several saddles, one of which bore the brands of all the local ranches cut into it; two cowhide shirts; arrows of two kinds, one of mt. willow, and of cane with separate hardwood point, sometimes tipped with a nail; one or two bows of mt. willow hardened by fire, backed with sinew, shaped in 2 demi arcs, and strung with sinew; and finally a flat stick about 12 in. long which had on it paintings of horses, cattle, deer, etc., done with great skill.

In one of the houses of this Apache camp by the caves was found a sort of rawhide shot or powder bottle, sewn with heavy yellow thread. He showed me this bottle, one of the rawhide ropes, a saddle bag sewn with sinew, several pieces of tanned cowhide which had much the same texture as buffalo skin, and a calf hide bag. This last had been skinned over the head, the tail and legs tied up with sinew, the hair left on the outside, and tanned on inside. This was full of acorns when found, but since [then] the acorns were dumped out and the hair has been eaten off the outside by moths. In the way of food were found stores of squawberries, acorns, acorn flour, roasted mescal, dried meat, etc. The party looted the caves, bringing back much material; but the objects which Mr. Curtis showed me were all he has left. He used the cowhides to make pack bags of, which he has at his ranch now. Several parties have since been up to these caves so that they are now probably well stripped.

At different places Curtis has found the camps of these Apaches. They build brush structures of various shapes, and sometimes even put up a crude rock-mud wall. Their basketry is crude and bears designs in 2 colors, red and black. At one place in a mt. valley the ground was marked off by stakes as if for some game. A meat drying camp was located also, where much meat had been dried on pole frames still standing. At this place there was a crude sledge made with 2 half circles of poles for skids, and sticks laid between them, with a handle in front and behind for the purpose of pushing or pulling the meat from camp to drying racks.

Art with sledge used in moving meat from place to place, in the Apache ridgetop camp in the Sierra las Espuelas, 1931.

Nowadays the boys only use bows and arrows as the men are able to obtain guns and ammunition through stealing. That they are able to obtain useful articles in some way or other is shown by the finding of a pair of field glasses of U.S. Army type which had been lost by the Apaches in a cornfield, near a Mex. town on the west side of the Sierra Madre, while raiding it.[75]

[In a later diary entry, Grennie writes that the binoculars had belonged to a cowboy from a local ranch who had been killed by the Apaches.]

The costume worn by the men he [Bill Curtis] described as being a gee string, moccasins with rawhide soles and buckskin uppers which came as far as the knee, and a headband of buckskin painted red. In cold weather a shirt, or jacket with sleeves, on which they leave the hair, tanning the inside only, is worn. The women wear buckskin, or, if possible, get cloth to make dresses of. He said he has seen quilts stolen by these Apaches which have been stripped of their lining to be used for dresses, the cotton batting left lying upon the ground. One instance occurred in which the Apaches raided a burro train of tobacco. They stripped the cloth wrapping off the tobacco, and left the latter lying there, only taking the cloth.

[This story is still told in the villages of the Bavispe River valley. In 1923 two men, named Jesús Pedrego and Antonio Olivas, were ambushed on the road from Bavispe to Casas Grandes. Their bodies were found, mutilated in such a way that everyone thought the killers were Apaches, though they could also have been killed by enemies made during the Revolution. The neighboring villages of Bavispe and San Miguel took different sides during the ferocious fighting that engulfed the country.]

The last time the Sierra Madre Apaches were in the U.S. was about 3 years ago when they rode up into the southwest corner of New Mex., bringing two steers shod with rawhide which they rode. These steers they left there after raiding a ranch and running off some horses.

[The story of the Apache raid of 1924 is still told along the border. The steers mentioned above, a well-remembered detail, bore the brand of the Palomas Ranch. The Apaches were camped for a while on Big Hatchet Mountain in the New Mexico boot heel while they rustled livestock from the nearby Diamond A Ranch. Eventually their camp was discovered and they fled, leaving everything behind. They were almost certainly people from the Sierra las Espuelas ranchería.]

On asking about the possibility of seeing some of these Apache camps, etc., he [Bill Curtis] said to come along down to his ranch near Colonia Oaxaca, that he was going on down for a month, and could leave me at his place to look around, as there was fine hunting and fishing, and one or two Apache camps fairly near.

NEIL'S COMMENTARY

The inventory is intriguing. Caching valuable objects and food in storage caves was common Apache practice, not only as a way of keeping things safe from the elements and animals, but also as a hedge against the future. In this case it implies that the Apaches knew they would be away from the camp for periods of time, either as part of a seasonal migration or simply out of prudence in case of unexpected discovery.

The cache reveals that they were eating standard Apache fare, that they were roasting mescal, making acorn flour, and jerking meat. It reveals that they made decorated baskets of the standard Apache types: dish baskets, burden baskets, and pitched water bottles. It reveals that they were skilled in making bows and arrows, and that they had the time to play games. They had the skill and inclination to make objects of beauty, perhaps even of ceremonial significance, such as the "flat stick about 12 in. long which had on it paintings of horses, cattle, deer, done with great skill."

It wasn't long after Grennie's meeting with Bill Curtis that the two of them left Douglas and drove to Bill's ranch for the first of two extended visits. During Grennie's first visit in the fall of 1930, he went with Bill to several of the villages of the Bavispe Valley, where he gathered a wealth of oral history and entered it all in his diary. It wasn't until his second trip about a year later that Bill was able to take Grennie to the two abandoned campsites.

The larger one, in the Sierra las Espuelas was a ranchería with dwelling sites spread over more than a mile of canyon bottoms and ridgetops. When this stronghold was discovered by Curtis and Fenn in 1926, the Apaches instantly abandoned it. The occupants moved south and built a smaller, more compact camp on the Sierra Chita Hueca. Discovered by cowboys in 1929, it too was abandoned.

Barney, Margot, Seth, Kathy, and I found the Sierra las Espuelas camp on a frigid day in January 1997. Some three years later a slightly different group of us is back for a thorough survey of the place. As usual, I keep a daily diary, which begins on May 3, after leaving Tucson early in the morning in a caravan and arriving at the headquarters of the ranch where the Apache camp is located.

NEIL'S DIARY

May 3, 2000, Rancho los Huerigos

The hacienda is a large, elegant building with a more or less contemporary Spanish colonial flavor. Our caravan of three vehicles arrives late in the afternoon after a long drive from Tucson. Seth and I are in a Toyota 4-Runner on loan from the Southwest Center at the University of Arizona; Barney is driving his heavily loaded Suburban, a battle-scarred veteran of several hundred thousand miles of unforgiving Mexican roads. Diana Hadley's pickup is the third vehicle. I have been in contact with Carlos, the owner of the ranch, who is pleased to have a site of historical and ethnographic interest on his property. Carlos is a prosperous, cosmopolitan businessman from Juárez whose family has owned very large ranches in this area for many years. He speaks perfect English, having gone to the University of Arizona.

Although he is not here at the moment, Carlos has notified his nephew Rogelio, who manages the place, of our arrival and purpose. If we need them, he has arranged to put pack mules and horses at our disposal for hauling equipment to the high campsites. The main camp is in an arroyo bottom not far from the end of a road leading up an access canyon some ten miles away across the valley from the ranch headquarters. We can make a base camp at the road head and walk to this site, and two others that are nearby. About a mile and a half farther, and a steep 1,000 feet higher, there are two other camps—too difficult a scramble for a daily commute. We will have to haul equipment, food, and water from the base camp to these sites and stay there while we work on them.

In the evening we devote a lot of time to a discussion of pack animals and the logistics of using them when we move our campsite to the upper reaches of the ranchería. To undertake this part of our expedition, a cowboy known to us only as "El Indio" is to arrive in the morning. He spends a lot of time in the wild western end of the ranch on horseback, mending fences, chasing strays, and keeping an eye on the stock tanks. He is the ranch's expert packer, and we will wait for him before we leave in the morning. When he comes and we have decided about animals, we will drive from the headquarters straight across the valley, then enter Las Piedras Canyon, drive to the end of the road, and camp.

When Grennie and Bill arrived in 1931, they came across the mountains by horseback from Bill's ranch in the west end of Pulpit Canyon, near the old Mormon village of Colonia Oaxaca.

GRENVILLE'S DIARY

Oct. 27, 1931, Las Piedras Canyon

Rode by Las Varas ranch, where a large mescal outfit is being put up, and turning north there, followed up Sandoval Canyon for about 7 miles.[76] From here we went up over a little divide, and down on to the llano along the edge of the mts., in Chihuahua. These plains have very little brush on them here, except for some places in which mesquite, desert willow, etc., grow along the arroyos.

We hit the llano near a place called the Vacas, where there is water and a large prehistoric ruin. From here, followed along the foot of the mts., stopping at some windmills on the flat for noon, from which place we could see a lot of smoke rising from one of the high peaks of the S. Espuela.

NEIL'S DIARY

May 4, 2000, Rancho los Huerigos

We have a forest fire of our own. There is an immense conflagration working its way across the Sierra Madre toward us from somewhere near Colonia Oaxaca in the Bavispe Valley, about forty miles to the west. The people at Los Huerigos are quite sure it was started at a notorious marijuana-growing operation by the men who work there—drunk or drugged-out.

While waiting for El Indio, we pass the time watching the smoke from the fire. Though it is still far away, the blowing smoke is so thick as it pours out of the mountains that we can't even see the mouth of Las Piedras Canyon only a few miles away. We wonder if we might end up being smoked out of the canyon, not to mention being chased out by flames.

GRENVILLE'S DIARY

Not long after, we left the llano and turned up Las Piedras Canyon, heading back into the S. Espuela to the west. There is a road up this canyon for about 6 mi., over which the Nogales ranch outfit used to haul fence posts which they cut in the canyon. It is in a fork of this canyon that the Apache ranchería is situated.

We rode up to the mouth of the branch canyon in which the Apache camp is, and here had to make a dry camp, as it was getting dark, and none of us three cared much to travel that country after dark. The mts. in this locality have little water except in the rainy season.

NEIL'S DIARY

At the best of times there is hardly any water in the Sierra las Espuelas, but the region has been in the grip of a drought for over a year. There has been no rain since last fall. We are carrying over fifty gallons of water—weighing four hundred pounds—in the back of Barney's van. If we use pack animals to carry our gear to the high camp at the ranchería—most of which will be our water—we may also have to pack water for them to drink when they get to the top of the ridge.

When El Indio does not show up, we realize that the pack animal plan is probably not going to materialize. Perhaps it's just as well. We can travel light to the top of the hill, carry up enough water ourselves for two or three days, and we won't have to worry about an uncertain rendezvous with El Indio and his pack animals four days from now in order to get all our gear back out again.

GRENVILLE'S DIARY

Riding up this afternoon Bill told Art and I how he and Moroni Fenn came to run on this Apache camp here. They were looking for a lost mine, and the story about this mine is rather interesting. It seems that back in the nineties sometime, a party of Frenchmen, of whom there were a good many in Mex. at that time, were prospecting in this part of the country.

They had been warned before of Apaches being in the Espuelas, but had apparently disregarded this information. After some time these

Frenchmen ran onto a rich gold-bearing ledge, and started in to work it. They had worked here for about a month, when they ran out of grub. One of the party was sent out to get provisions, and when he returned he found all his companions killed by the Apaches. He immediately left there with what gold he and his partners had cached, and made his way to California, where he lived the rest of his life. Here he made friends with a man, and to this man he told his story of the mine, etc., also giving him a map of the mine's location. This man, in turn, gave the map to his son, an electrician.

In about 1914, this son and a friend of his, an engineer of some sort, decided to spend their summer looking for this mine. The two friends came down and crossed the border below Columbus, where they hired a Mex. to take them to the mouth of the canyon in which the mine lay. Here they paid him off, and he went on south to Carretas. The other two came on up the canyon and found the mine. Here they worked for a while, panning in the wash below the ledge. One day they came back to their camp to find everything gone, taken by the Apaches. (I forgot to say that about a mile or two below the mine, in the bottom of the canyon, the two friends had come upon an Indian camp, on their way up. There was only one very old man in the camp with whom they were unable to converse. So being afraid of the place, they gave it a wide berth, circling around it and proceeding on up the canyon.)

After their camp had been raided by the Indians they had to leave, so took out over the mts. with two large nuggets, and some smaller ones which they had cached. The two fugitives came out finally in the Animas Valley, New Mex., half starved and about played out. From here they went on back to California where they deposited their gold at the mint in San Francisco. The two never returned to the mine. The engineer was killed, and the other was badly crippled by high voltage in a power house. This crippled one, however, made friends with an old peg-legged man, whom he in turn told about the mine. The map had been destroyed, but the cripple gave directions as closely as possible, and the peg-legged man set off on his search. But he never could find the mine, and as the electrician was unable to go with him, he had to rely entirely on directions by letter, etc., which were not very satisfactory. Moroni Fenn helped the peg-legged man look for this mine, and it was this that led Bill and he to the Indian Camp, after both peg-leg and electrician had died.

The location was described thus: "You strike a canyon in the mouth of which is a marshy area. This *cienega* may be passed on either side. Up this canyon goes a road for some ways. After a while a side canyon takes off to the right, and following on up this you strike the Indian camp in the bottom of the canyon. About a mile above this camp is a brushy flat, about 1.5 acres in extent, and on the left side of the wash. At the upper end of this flat is a rock which looks like a monument. Right across, and up on the side of the canyon, is the mine, the shaft passing into the rock ledge for about 15 ft. The only place you can pan gold is right at the flat." Bill and Fenn knew that the mine lay someplace between Carretas and the U.S. line, and as Las Piedras Canyon filled the description almost perfectly, they went up it, and this is how they came on the Apache ranchería there, but never found the mine, as have no other people either.

NEIL'S DIARY

This gold mine story is one of the most compelling and important in Grennie's diary—not only for its narrative appeal, but also for what is to be found between its lines.

First of all, it is probable that the French miners knew exactly what they were doing. Either they had been told precisely where to look for gold by someone who already knew about it, or they knew enough about geology to know where to look themselves. They found the gold-bearing strata without wasting much time, and they did so despite warnings about danger from Apaches—as if they had a destination in mind and were convinced that finding it was worth the risk. An ill-advised gamble, to say the least.

Second, it is clear that Apaches were known to be living in the Sierra las Espuelas by the 1890s, if not well before. The anecdotal evidence of this story is corroborated by history: in 1893, a U.S. Cavalry unit pursued marauding Apaches south across the border after an attack on several ranches in the Sulfur Spring Valley. Accompanied by several Western Apache scouts, among them a man named Sherman Curley who was later to befriend my father, the U.S. soldiers jumped a renegade Apache camp just west of the Sierra las Espuelas. During the course of the fight, Curley recognized one of the Apaches, identifying him as Adiłnadzi·d, one of the men who was with Geronimo at the time of his surrender in 1886, but who stayed behind in Mexico. Adiłnadzi·d escaped, wounded, but two Apache girls were captured. One was adopted and raised by the well-known Douglas cattleman and sheriff

John Slaughter, and she came to be known as Apache May. The other one went back to San Carlos with the cavalry and the scouts, and she eventually settled in the mining town of Miami, west of San Carlos, married to a Mexican miner.

This campaign was only one of several of the 1890s in which Sherman Curley served, pursuing renegade Apaches across the border into the Sierra las Espuelas and beyond. The Apaches that Curley and the soldiers were after had killed people in Arizona, so it's conceivable they might have been involved in the slaughter of the French miners. In any case, these or other Apaches settled in the Sierra las Espuelas, and when the two miners returned in 1914 to find the gold mine, they stumbled into the Apaches' camp as soon as they entered the canyon.

Starting almost from the time of Geronimo's surrender, there is ample circumstantial evidence of free-roaming Apaches in Mexico, but they were so seldom encountered—so elusive, and their camps so well hidden that it is no wonder they came to be thought of as a phantom people. They were thought to be so constantly on the move that the existence of a permanent campsite was simply not considered.

GRENVILLE'S DIARY

Bill says he had heard of there being wild Apaches in these mts., but had never really believed till the time he came on this camp. He had met an old American prospector in San Miguel, Sonora, who claimed to have seen them one time. This prospector was up in the Sierra Espuela. He had run across two human skeletons, and started to find Indian tracks on top of his own. One day he saw two or three Indians, but was not able to parley with them. This was enough for him, and he left the mts. right away. He told Bill they looked more like Apaches than anything else.

When they were cutting posts in Las Piedras Canyon, the Mexicans there had their camp completely cleared by the Apaches in broad daylight. These Mexican post cutters moved out right away, and started cutting in another canyon, some distance to the north of here. The same thing happened in this canyon again, and all post cutting was postponed indefinitely in that locality. But the exact location of the Apache ranchería here was never known until Bill and Moroni stumbled on it.

NEIL'S DIARY

We have given up on El Indio, and we head out across the valley to the mouth of Las Piedras Canyon. Baking in the sun for the last six months, the road is hard as concrete but the daily pickup traffic on it has worn the ruts down, grinding them to powder inches deep, fine as talcum, that boils up in the airless morning as thick as the smoke pouring out of the forest fire in the mountains. It takes about thirty-five minutes to cross the valley. The cattle are baking in the sun, cooking on the hoof, eating mesquite leaves and not much else. They don't look great.

We get across the valley to the outlying ranch where we stayed three years ago. It has a small bunkhouse, corrals, a stable, and a diesel engine mounted on a concrete pad that drives a deep well pump. Rogelio turns it on, and it bellows into life filling a stock tank for a burro and a jenny and a good-looking horse. Rogelio comes over every day to feed and water these animals as there is no one else to do it. Rogelio says that the ranch to the north is owned by an infamous Ciudad Juárez drug cartel. They have been stealing his livestock for years, but are so powerful and so ruthless that nothing can be done about it. Los Huerigos is evidently one of a dwindling number of legitimate ranching operations in the mountains close to the border. The amount of money to be made from growing drugs is so unimaginably vast that the temptation to do so is nearly irresistible.

Leaving Rogelio at the buildings doing chores, we start driving up the canyon to the main camp.

GRENVILLE'S DIARY

Oct. 28, 1931, Apache Camp, S. Espuela

Got up here to the main camp, in the bottom of the canyon, about noon, and spent the afternoon in going up on the big ridge to the west where the big corrals are, and in looking for the small corrals on the other side, which we were unable to find. Found out that the smoke we saw coming from the mts. out on the llano is caused by a small forest fire on a mt. to the north. As there have been no lightning storms lately, and as few Mexicans or Americans ever go in this part of the mts., there is a good chance that this fire may have been started by the

Apaches. There are lots of deer and bear signs here, as well as some of mt. lion.

NEIL'S DIARY

This is still prime bear habitat. (When we were here in the winter of 1997, there were mountainous piles of very fresh bear scat in the middle of the road, but like the Apaches of old, the bears themselves were nowhere to be seen.)

We stop at the end of the road and it is only a short walk to the main camp; on the way we see heaps of dry bear scat. It's old so the bears must be somewhere else as there is not enough water to keep them here. That must also mean there was not enough water for Apaches living off the land: perhaps this was only a fall and winter camp.

Walking ahead, Seth and I get to the camp first. We stop by the first of the stone houses so we can see how the people who have never been here react as they come to it. The first arrivals walk right past it, then turn, stop, and stare. Coming next, Diana spots it right away and her jaw drops in amazement. First one, then another, then another, then another of the stone houses materializes out of the underbrush. All of the brush fences and gates and corrals have long since deteriorated, and the pathways have all grown up. All that remain are the stone house walls, far more mute and mysterious than when Grennie was here seventy-five years ago, when thatched roofs, stretched cowhide, entire brush shelters, log cabins, and stacked building materials were still in place.

The smoke in the canyon is not nearly as bad as it looked from the ranch buildings, but there is a thick, high haze in the air, and we can see the smoke billowing high to the south at times. We are too deep in the canyon to have any real idea how far away the fire is, but now in the late afternoon we get a draft of hot air, smelling of smoke and fire and the light goes all yellow.

GRENVILLE'S DIARY

The country right in this vicinity is very broken by steep ridges and canyons and rocky ledges, etc. The canyon bottoms are very brushy as are also the northern slopes. The southern slopes are more open and grassy, being dotted with blue oak. There are a few ash trees in the draws and sheltered places, a great deal of silver leaf oak; and on the high ridges and in deep draws some piñon and juniper grow, along with pine. On the highest parts of the mts. there are good stands of yellow pine.

These Espuela Mts. are nothing more than a series of canyons and high ridges, with a few high peaks among them, which stand out because of the large timber growing on their sides.

We didn't get back to the main camp in the canyon, which we had made our stopping place, till a good bit after dark. Tomorrow am going to get the photographs needed, and try to draw a general map of the ranchería, as well as plans of the different camps and houses.

NEIL'S DIARY

Grennie was a student of terrain. His diary never fails to note geology, vegetation, and animal sign, and his sense of distance and direction was remarkably accurate, as we are to find out from his maps and descriptions—so accurate that the very occasional inaccuracy will throw us completely for a loop in the coming days.

GRENVILLE'S DIARY

Oct. 29, 1931, Apache Camp, S. Espuela

Spent today in taking photographs, making drawings and plans. Went up canyon to caves in the morning, and up on top of mt. to corrals and over on other side of there to the small corrals which we were unable to find yesterday. On the general plan the whole outlay of the ranchería is shown.

Coming up this side canyon from Las Piedras Canyon on trail (no. 20) for about 3 miles, you strike a brush fence across the bottom of the canyon (no. 1), and from here on you are within the ranchería.[77] The approach up the canyon is very rough, and difficult to get over on account of the thick brush and rocks. The trail never was good, and when we went over it, it was almost entirely grown up

About ¼ mile above this first brush fence the canyon forks, a small canyon taking off to the left. Just in the right fork of the canyon here, is the main camp (no. 3).

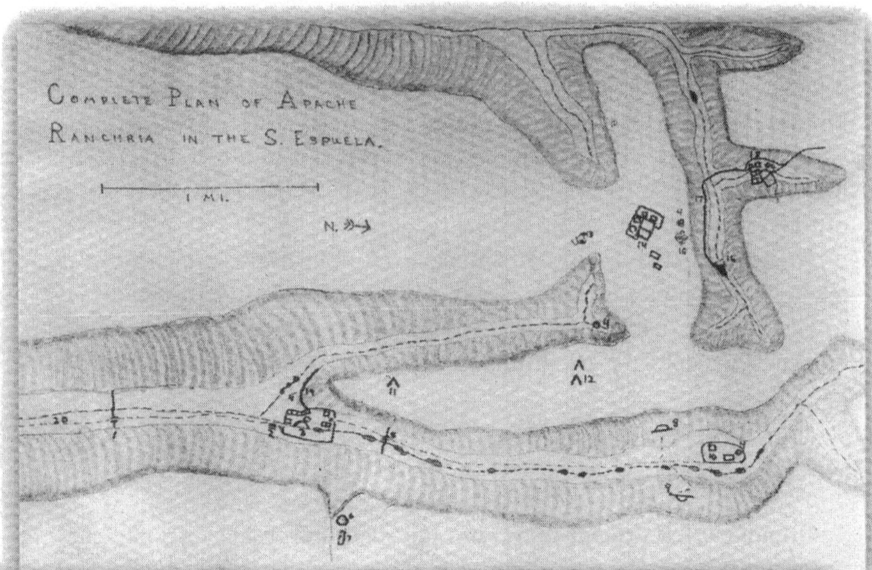

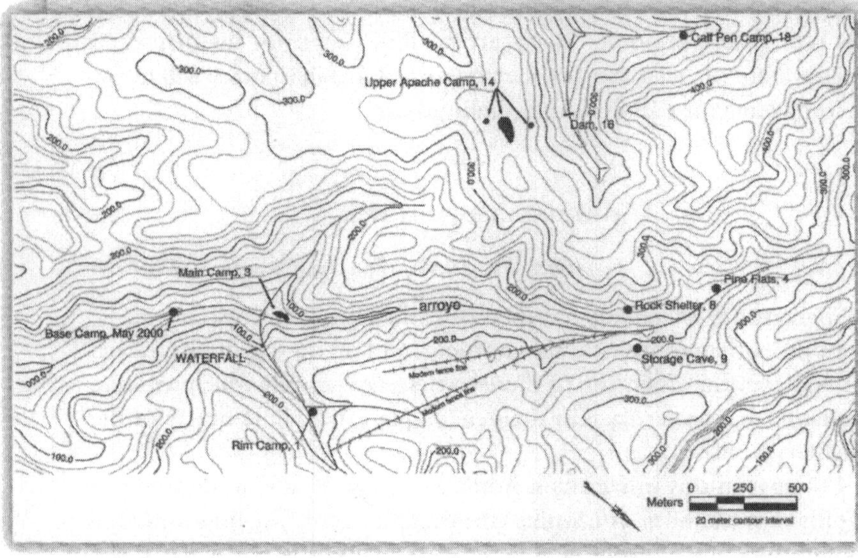

(Top) Apache ranchería in Sierra las Espuelas, complete plan. (Key: 1. lower brush fence; 2. gate to ranchería; 3. gate to arroyo camp; 4. mescal pit; 5. brush fence; 6. rim camp corral; 7. rim camp stone house; 8. rock shelter; 9. storage caves; 10. storage caves camp; 11. brush shelter; 12. lookout site; 13. potholes used for tanning; 14. main camp on ridge; 15. bones pile; 16. rock and mud dam; 17. trail to calf pen camp; 18. small pen (calf pen) camp)

(Bottom) Apache ranchería in Sierra las Espuelas, complete plan, May 2000 survey.

NEIL'S DIARY

May 5, 2000, Base Camp

Our own first full day of surveying begins with a division of labor. Our most time-consuming job will be the mapping of the main camp in the arroyo bottom. It is only a fifteen-minute walk from base camp, so while the rest of us are fine-tuning plans and priorities, Austin heads for the main camp alone. The preliminary phase of the survey is a one-man task consisting mostly of simply figuring out how to tackle the job.

Austin identifies the features to be mapped and the extent of the camp. There are four surviving stone houses, the remains of the tanning pit, the main arroyo to one side, a steep bank at the back of the camp, a streambed created by floodwater through the middle of the camp. After careful scrutiny of the whole layout, Austin decides he should map the contours of this site as well as the locations of all its features. He can do the entire job using the simplest of tools: compass, tape measure, hand level, and surveyor's staff. Austin loves to do this and always refers to it as play, never as work.

Try as we might to change her mind, Diana has to go home. She knew this was going to be a quick round-trip, but even a glimpse of the site after hearing so much about it from me and Barney is worth the long three-day journey. Her daughter Sadie, married to my young cousin Sage Goodwin, is expecting a baby any day now. They are living in Tucson, and Diana has promised herself not to be gone more than two days. She is no stranger to solo trips in the Mexican outback and heads her pickup back down the bone-jarring, vehicle-wrecking road. I suspect she's seen worse.

There are two nearby satellite camps within the ranchería that we have not located yet. One is the storage cave camp up the arroyo. Barney and Alan will look for that. The other one, which we call the rim camp, is somewhere on the more or less level ground above the canyon rim, some seven hundred feet in elevation above the arroyo bottom where the main camp lies. There was originally a trail that led directly from the main camp to the rim camp, but we have seen no sign of it, so Seth and I will have to rely on Grennie's map and description to find it.

When I was here three years ago there was not enough time to take it all in, but now there is more time, and the layout of the ranchería is beginning to sink in. Grennie's description of Bill's discovery of the camp becomes even more vivid to all of us as we move through the landscape ourselves.

GRENVILLE'S DIARY

On the ridge between the forks of the canyon, at no. 11, is a brush shelter, used for a lookout house, and so placed that the whole canyon, for more than a mile below, can be easily watched.

In this same picture can be seen the high, dark ridge to the right, from whose top Bill and Moroni Fenn first saw the main Apache camp. They lay here and watched for an hour with field glasses, before descending the slope to the canyon and camp.

On the way down this slope they suddenly heard a mule bray loudly, and soon saw him. He was side hobbled, and had both ears cut so they hung down on the sides of his head. Further back on this same ridge are two other brush shelters, which appear to have been used as temporary camps (no. 12).

Just above the main camp is another brush fence—across the bottom of the canyon (no. 5). A short distance below this fence, a trail turns off and goes up the side of the canyon, and out on the rim to a stone house, and small brush corral (no. 6). The Apache that Bill and Fenn had run onto had probably been working on this house, and was just coming from there.

Bill and Fenn were in the canyon right where the trail came in, when they looked up on the side of the canyon, and saw this Apache riding down towards them, mounted on a buckskin horse and leading a gray, entirely unaware of the two white intruders. Bill and Fenn let him get almost to them, at a place which you can see just at the foot of a little rocky cliff on the side of the ridge, indicated by mark, then they made a noise.

The Apache saw him immediately and Bill says he can still remember that Indian's face, very broad and shiny, with black staring eyes. The Indian was a big man, but active. He whirled his horse around and still leading the gray, rode off around the little rocky cliff as fast as he could go.

NEIL'S DIARY

With Grennie's map and description in hand, Seth and I try to reconstruct this encounter, first to figure out where it took place, then to figure out how the bolting Apache, mounted on one horse and lead-

Location of Main Camp, Lookout Hill to left. (Photo by Grennie Goodwin)

Main camp in arroyo; measuring house number 8; left to right: Alan Ferg, Austin Lenhart, Barney Burns; Sierra las Espuelas, May 2000.

Neil Goodwin; Sierra las Espuelas, May 2000. (Photo by Seth Goodwin)

ing another, would have rushed back to the rim camp house—probably to pack up and leave, as he and the others in the camp always had known they might have to do if discovered.

First we climb out of the canyon onto the rim and look in all the places where we think the camp might be and find nothing. Then we look in all the places we doubt it would be and find nothing. We scrutinize every unnatural-looking rock alignment and every pile of stones. We are utterly puzzled, and the more we try to fit Grennie's map to the terrain the less sense it makes. We even consider the possibility that Grennie never saw it and just put it on the map where Bill said he thought it was, but a careful parsing of Grennie's written description convinces us otherwise. He saw it. It had to be up here somewhere.

We have radios for keeping in touch, and Alan comes on the air to announce that he has found the storage cave camp. The caves were very hard to find—high up on the side of the canyon, one on each side. In fact, one is only a narrow ledge under a rock overhang where the Apaches had camped at times. The other was actually a pair of caves. These were the caves in which the 1926 raiding party led by Bill and Moroni Fenn found so much cached material.

GRENVILLE'S DIARY

Another mile or so up the canyon, and on the right side going up, is a small open cave which was used for storage. It is situated in a pink colored tufa ledge. Across the mouth has been built a stout stockade fence about 9 ft. high. At one end of this cave was another small chamber entered by a door which had been sealed with rocks and mud, but was now broken open. Inside this were some sticks and the remains of some prepared mescal.

This little chamber had been enterable from outside, as well as [from] inside the larger cave, but a good stone and mud wall had been built across this outside entrance to close it. Right outside this wall were the remains of a pole structure of some sort, probably a cache of some sort. It was in this cave that so much of the material was found by the raiders (see general plan no. 9).

A little way down the canyon, on the opposite slope, was a large, overhanging bluff, fairly high up, under which Apaches used to camp (no. 8, general plan). About 80 yards up the canyon from the storage cave, and on a little pine flat to the left, were two houses, of the type no. 6. These were surrounded by a brush fence, (see no. 10, general plan).

In the canyon bottom here were pools of water at intervals, and extending less frequently down to the main camp.

NEIL'S DIARY

Although there was much more to go on when he was here than there is now, Grennie never speculated, at least in print, on the reasons and functions of this and other satellite camps. The fact that there were pools of water in October, long after the rainy season, makes this an attractive place for a camp, though, as with the main camp downstream, vulnerable to surprise discovery and attack because it has no commanding views. Were the storage caves filled and sealed only by the people who lived in this particular camp, who had perhaps gone away, leaving their valuables safe in the caves, or were they placed there as a joint enterprise of the entire ranchería? The placement of material in the cave suggests the former: a seasonal departure on the part of only a few, since there were other people in the ranchería at the time of its discovery.

Alan makes a quick sketch map of the storage cave. It still has much of the rock-mud wall described by Grennie and has an access doorway built into it to keep the wall from being damaged as things were moved in and out of the storage chamber. It had been sealed with mud and rocks when the Apaches left. The "stockade fence" is still there, the poles wrapped with wire. It is inside the mouth of the cave and was likely intended to keep bears and other animals out of the cache. Alan makes careful note of all that is now left of the Apaches' 1926 plan for the future.

As suggestive in its own way as this storage cave is—with the structural remains and the material wealth it once contained—the small rock shelter across the canyon has its own eloquence. It is hardly more than a narrow ledge under an overhang with a small level strip of ground in front of it. Alan says that it is way up a very steep slope, and at the end of such an arduous scramble it is hard to imagine anyone wanting to camp up there; but, of course, that is precisely why the Apaches used it, knowing that no one coming up that slope could surprise them.

While Alan is exploring the storage cave camp, Seth and I give up on finding the rim camp for today. We return to the main camp in the

The storage cave at the Apache ranchería; Sierra las Espuelas, 1931. (Photo by Grenville Goodwin)

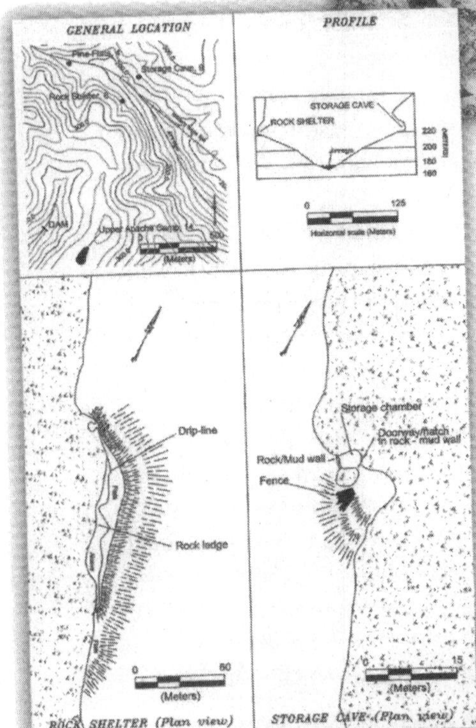

Apache ranchería in Sierra las Espuelas, storage caves, May 2000 survey.

Storage caves from across the canyon; Sierra las Espuelas, May 2000. (Photo by Alan Ferg)

arroyo, where we find Austin deep into the mapping. Austin has the site crisscrossed with tape measures and has a host of little red flags in the ground, big nails with red tape marking datum points.

Seth takes a radio and goes out to scout above the camp. He goes to the crest of the ridge, to the location of the lookout post at no. 12 (on Grennie's map) and from this vantage point spots what looks like a well-used game trail on the east side of the canyon—very probably the one where Bill and Moroni had their unforgettable encounter with the Apache on his way down from the rim camp.

All day I've been feeling the presence of the Apaches more than anything else—occasionally the presence of Grennie, but mostly the presence of the Apaches. It's because we're looking for their houses, because we're trying to find where they lived, trying to see some sign that they might have left behind. Every time something turns up—even vestigial traces such as those Alan found at the storage caves—it adds to the picture of the lives of the people who lived here.

At this time of year there appears to be absolutely no water. What were the Apaches doing in the dry season? What were their cattle doing? I assume the cattle weren't here at all, that they went somewhere else or that they were slaughtered, skinned, and jerked before the dry season. My own experience of being here engenders a new kind of understanding for the people who lived here; somehow they managed to do it for decades without being discovered. In addition to subsisting on stolen cattle, to a certain extent they were also living off the land: they were roasting mescal, grinding large quantities of acorns, collecting and storing a variety of wild plants. There is evidence that they had firearms, but they also used bows and arrows—conceivably for small game. In the piles of bones at the camps, those of deer are conspicuously absent—virtually all are cow or horse bones. Grennie wondered if the lack of game animal bones was due to a lack of ammunition or because the sound of gunshots would have betrayed the Apaches' position. Perhaps, but I think this was primarily a high-volume cattle-rustling operation, and there may have been little need or incentive to hunt for wild game.

Part of the mix in the mystery of this place is the distinct possibility that these people may not all have been Indians. The oral history we have been collecting over the years consistently tells of people who collaborated with the Apaches. There is an additional consistent theme in the oral history to the effect that the Apaches living in these northern camps (as opposed to the small scattered camps of Apaches south of

Carretas Pass) had close ties with the people at San Carlos. I should add that in all of Grennie's field notes gathered over a period of years at San Carlos and Fort Apache, there is no corroboration of this. That does not mean he did not hear such stories—only that he did not write them down. When I pose questions on this matter to people I meet at San Carlos, I am told there is a very good chance that such contact existed; but so far I have heard nothing more concrete than that. ✣

May 6, 2000, Base Camp

In the morning we decide to leave Austin mapping at the main camp while the rest of us go to look for the rim camp again. We go up the trail Seth had spotted from the opposite side of the canyon yesterday. The sides of the canyon are so steep in most places that this is clearly the only trail fit for a horse. It is still in use as a game trail and winds up the steep canyon wall, coming out on top of the rim rock from which point the land slopes gradually upward. We spread out and sweep uphill to the height of the land, then east across the level ground on the hill all the way to a dry streambed of water-sculpted rock. It leads down a short way to a precipice three hundred feet above the main camp and would make a spectacular waterfall after a heavy rain. We find no sign of the camp though. We watch Austin far below us, then we come back looking at all the possible level spots on the rim rock, finding nothing again—finding as well virtually no place where there would have been any water, except for the dry streambed, which has a number of rock tanks upstream of the pour-off.

Back at the main camp Austin puts us to work plotting the exact plan and cross-section of the stone wall of the large round house. Meanwhile, he is setting up to plot contour lines for a topographic map of the camp. It takes three to do this, using datum points, red flags at the contour break points, compass headings, a surveyor's hand level mounted on a tripod, and a vertical staff. Austin uses the level and calls out compass bearings, Barney holds the measuring staff, and Alan writes Austin's and Barney's figures down.

Studying Grennie's diary while all of this is underway, I realize for the first time that he and Bill spent only a day and a half here—hard to believe considering how spread out the place is and how hard it is to get around from camp to camp . . . not to mention the amount of surveying, measuring, pacing, and photographing Grennie managed to do in such a short period. His maps, diagrams, detailed descriptions, and inventories are all remarkably accurate and thorough.

GRENVILLE'S DIARY

I have waited to describe in detail the main camp, the big corrals on the ridge, and the small corrals and calf pens, as these three places have more to them than do the other camps.

The main camp consisted of 8 houses, and two brush shelters (nos. 14). Two of the houses had been burnt down by Bill's raiding party (nos. 9).

House no. 10 was of was of type 7, but had no beds [see house types, pp. 233 & 234].

House no. 11 is the one shown as type 7, and had two frame beds in each of its ends. These beds were naturally small and cramped on account of the size of the house. House no. 12 had stone walls, and is of type 2.

House no. 13 was built against the bank, half of upright poles, and half of rock and adobe walls. This house was about 7 ft. high, flat roofed, and well built. It had a chimney which was blocked up, and was the only house which had one in the whole ranchería. This, along with a house of similar dimensions in the little corral camp, were the largest structures which the Indians had built (type 4).

House no. 8 was of type no. 1. The roof of this house was burnt off, but the walls still stood. On the top of the walls of this house were two tin conical bells, such as the Apaches and other Indians attach to the end of buckskin fringes on dresses, etc., and which produce a jingling effect when in motion. There were also three pieces of hematite, paint rock.

House no. 15 is of type 2.

This main camp is enclosed by a brush fence (no. 2). There are two entrances, no. 1 in the creek bed and no. 3 in the brush fence, on the up canyon side of the camp. Right near the lower entrance is a pile of boards, all hand hewn from pine trees, and a frame with some peeled logs piled on it (no. 16). These boards were about 6 ft. long, by 5 to 10 inches wide, in most instances, and some ½ to 3 inches thick. They, along with the logs, had apparently been placed there for future use in building houses, etc.

In this camp was also a rigging for soaking hides, in the process of tanning (no. 6). A cowhide was hung on a square frame of logs, and used as the water container. Under it was a foundation of rocks to hold up weight. The water was obtained from a pool in the creek bed, which appears to be permanent. In this pool in the bottom, is set a small wooden box, which must have been used as a spring box from all appearances (no. 4).

There was a small, brush-walled corral in the camp (no. 5). This had apparently been used for stock which was kept up for use. One of its sides was bounded by the steep bank of the arroyo, and thus was not fenced.

Upon the other fork of the creek bed, around the hill, was a small mescal pit (no. 7). From this mescal pit to the house no. 12 ran the remains of a brush fence, which originally went further on around the hill from the mescal pit (no. 17).

These pits were all small and none over 5 ft. in diam. The main trails are all shown, though most of them are barely traceable now. Bill says when he first came here in 1926, they were all plain, and that the brush, which has grown up so thickly in the camp now, was then cleared away, and the surrounding ground tramped clear of grass, etc.

NEIL'S DIARY

In 1976 I interviewed Moroni's younger brother Alvah, who had been one of the party of 15 who returned to raid the camp in 1926 after its initial discovery. He said that one of the trails was as much as 75 feet wide and had been used for driving cattle between camps. That the ground was so well worn and the trails so clear indicates substantial traffic—both of people and of livestock. The mention of hewn planks, stored for "future use in building houses" indicates an active, thriving, possibly expanding community. There was a tanning operation at the main lower camp, as well as one at the high camp, as we shall see from Grennie's next series of notes. The care and time that had gone into the planning and construction of everything indicates not only a long-term and well-maintained facility here, but also, as of late 1926, a confidence that it would continue to operate for some time to come.

As Austin, Barney, and Alan map the place, features that we were unsure of or had never noticed before, become apparent. An unnatural-looking pile of rocks near the remains of house no. 13 is without a

Drawings by Grenville Goodwin from his 1930–31 Sierra Madre diary. (House-type numbers match those referred to in text.)

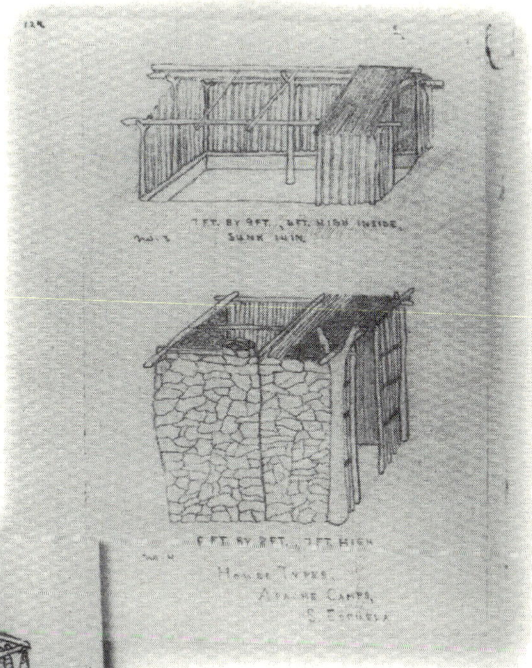

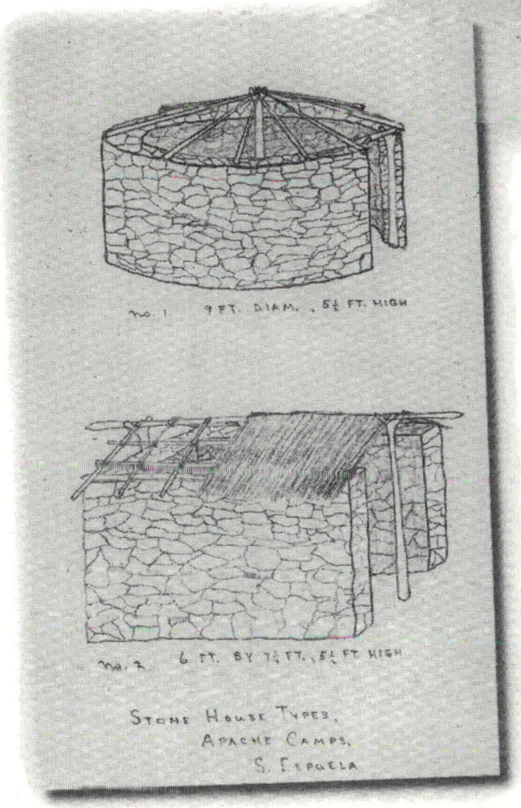

House types, Apache camps, Sierra las Espuelas.

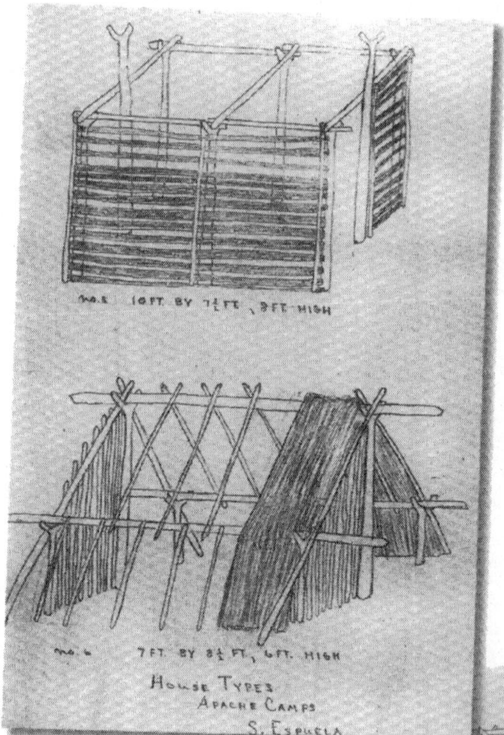

House types, Apache camps, Sierra las Espuelas.

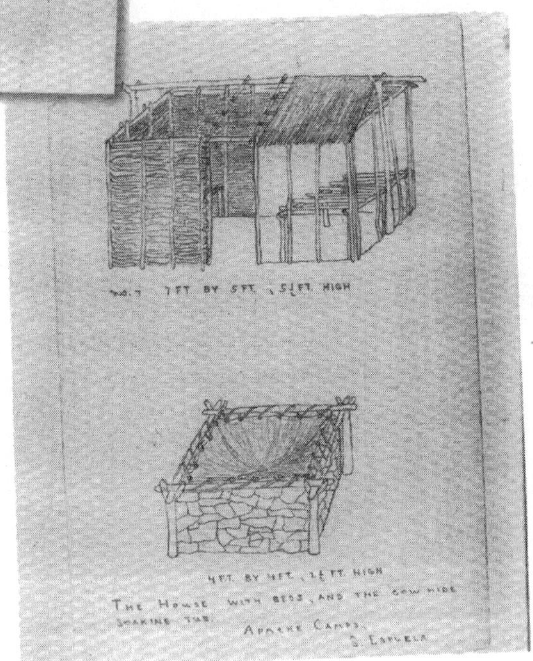

House type and tanning vat, Apache camps, Sierra las Espuelas.

doubt the remains of the tanning pit, no. 6. We notice insect activity at a deep pit in the gravel of the streambed. There are big hornets: tarantula hawks, mud daubers; there are bees; there are half a dozen beautiful black-and-orange butterflies—all drawn by the dark stain of moisture in the bottom. The hole has probably been enlarged and deepened in recent months by bears trying to get to a small permanent seep of water a few feet below the bone-dry surface. I am sure this is the "permanent water" Grennie referred to, and it was probably where the spring box was set, filled with clear water in October when he was here. Half-buried near the bank of the arroyo, we find two very old, heavily weathered logs that have been cut at each end with an ax and notched near each end as if for use in building a small log cabin. These might well be all that's left of one of the smaller structures in the camp.

These items are duly noted by Austin and plotted on his map, and when the last of them is done, we remove the dozens of small red flags that mark all the features on the camp. We roll up all the tapes and remove the big nails flagged with red surveyor's tape that he has been using as datum points—points of reference from which distances and compass bearings of everything in the camp have been measured, written down for eventual plotting on a computer-drawn map. ✣

May 7, 2000, Base Camp

After two days Austin is done with the survey of the main arroyo camp, and last night we made plans to move our camp up on the ridge where the main corral camp is. Since we don't have pack animals to get our gear and water up there, we will do it ourselves, but in two trips.

There is still one galling piece of unfinished business—the elusive rim camp. We work things out. Seth and Alan will hike to the high camp to cache several gallons of water. We will all hike there tomorrow with gear, food, and more water for a stay of two or three nights. There is as much work to do there as there has been here at the lower camp, if not more. The fire is an unknown at this point, though we are constantly aware of the smoke billowing from the south over the mouth of the canyon to the east. Barney and Austin and I will have another go at the rim camp. We are going to explore some open grassy areas to the right of the waterfall, and we are going to walk up the streambed leading to the dry waterfall as far as we can go.

While Seth and Alan are on top, they will get a good look at the fire and will be able to do some preliminary exploring of the upper camp

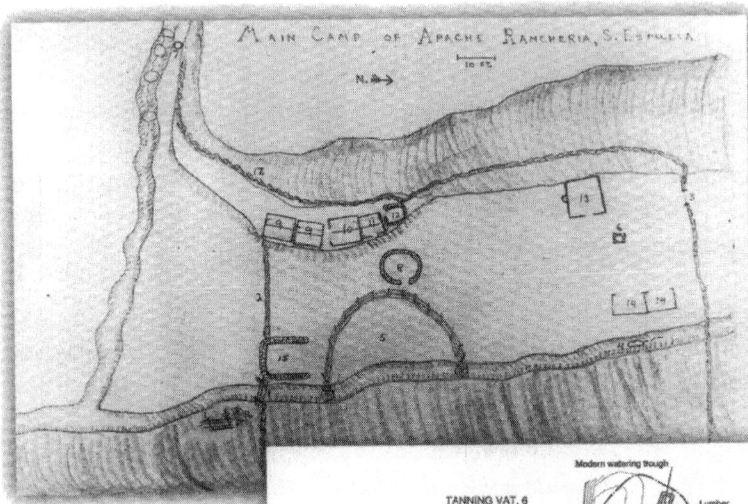

Sierra las Espuelas ranchería, main camp in arroyo. (Key: 1. gate to camp; 2. brush fence; 3. gate; 5. corral; 6. tanning pit; 7. mescal roasting pit; 8. stone house; 9. houses; 10, 11. houses; 12. stone house; 13. stone house; 14. houses; 15. stone house; 16. pile of logs; 17. brush fence)

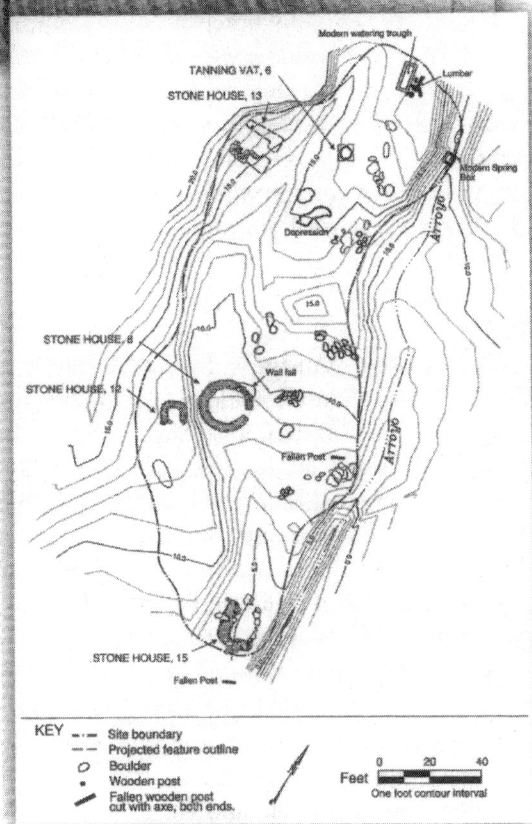

Sierra las Espuelas ranchería, general map of main camp in arroyo, May 2000 survey.

area. When we were there three years ago, we had time to study only the two stone houses, but there is a great deal more to this site, judging from Grennie's maps.

As Barney and Austin and I set out, we reread Grennie's description of the rim camp.

GRENVILLE'S DIARY

A trail turns off and goes up the side of the canyon, and out on the rim to a stone house, and small brush corral (no. 6). (The Apache that Bill and Fenn had run onto had probably been working on this house, and was just coming from there.)

This stone house (no. 7) appears never to have been finished. It was just being built when the camp was raided in 1926. The walls are well set up, and there are two doorways. The logs for the roof are there, peeled and ready to put in place.

NEIL'S DIARY

Alvah Fenn told me in 1976 that when he, his brother Moroni, Bill Curtis, and several others returned to raid the ranchería it was December and cold. They approached the camp, stopped some distance from it, then built a fire for warmth, waited till midnight, then sneaked in and surrounded the camp. Based on what else he was saying, he may have been talking about the rim camp—the one place that for sure had been occupied when Bill and Moroni stumbled on the place. They must have assumed that if any people were in the ranchería, they would be in this camp. In fact, of course, they found it deserted, as was the entire ranchería. Alvah thought the Apaches might have smelled the smoke from their fire.

As we scour the slopes looking for the rim camp, it is clear, in this thick brush and loose footing, no one was going to do any silent night-sneaking. My guess is that, if the Apaches had in fact been there, they would have known about Alvah and his party long before they built a fire and would have been gone in a flash. But in all likelihood they left the minute it was discovered by Bill and Moroni.

The rim camp is the only one that Alvah talked to me about, though he had seen them all on that and subsequent visits. He told me several times that if I went back there I would find it "just like he left it"—an unfinished stone wall, a pile of peeled logs, just as Grennie said, ready for making a roof.

As we climb to the waterfall, I split off to the right and cross the arroyo to look at the open grassy areas beyond it—not a likely place for the rim camp but we are now ready to search in places we don't think the camp would be. I am following a game trail through brush when the radio comes to life. It's Barney, excited, talking a blue streak. He has found the rim camp . . . only about 2⁄10 of a mile up the arroyo! He almost walked right past it, so heavily overgrown was it with brush. Seth and I had come within a couple of hundred yards of it on our first day out, but that's as good as a mile in this thick brush—visibility being only twenty or thirty feet.

I backtrack and hurry up the streambed from the waterfall. The location of the camp really doesn't correspond to the map Grennie drew, because he came by the trail that the Apaches themselves were using and it probably never went anywhere near the waterfall—a trail most of which has long since disappeared—except for the part of it that is still a game trail leading up out of the canyon.

Barney and Austin were just sitting there. Barney said no one had gone inside yet. He didn't say that they were waiting for me, but that is what he meant and I am touched by this. Not because it is considerate, generous, even respectful, though it is those things, but because it expresses Barney's sense of joint enterprise, that if experiences are to be truly valued, they are to be shared. And I think about how Seth would have savored being here—not only to see the rim camp, but also because of Barney's small but memorable gesture.

We spend a long time mapping and photographing the place while keeping track of Seth and Alan by radio. They make good time to the top, taking about two hours with the water load. They are up there for a few hours, taking in all the different features, including a few things we had not seen before—one of which might be the bone pile marked on Grennie's map.

As Alvah said, the house at the rim camp was "just like he left it." It is also like all the other stone houses: ovoid in plan with no right angles. There are two framed doorways with the wood still in place. Some of the roof beams are still lying on the ground, just as Grennie had found them, just as Alvah said they would be as well—ax marks very plain. The house is dug slightly into the side of the hill and might have had a very good view out across the canyon if some of the trees had been cleared in front. Off to the side was the probable location of the corral: a small, open, grassy area.

After we were through mapping, we went up the canyon and found signs of very old ax work: trees felled and left where they lay. This was probably work interrupted and abandoned forever when Bill found the camp in 1926. Without knowing the background, anyone seeing the ax work would not give it a second thought. But since we know all work on this camp was stopped and the place abandoned upon discovery,

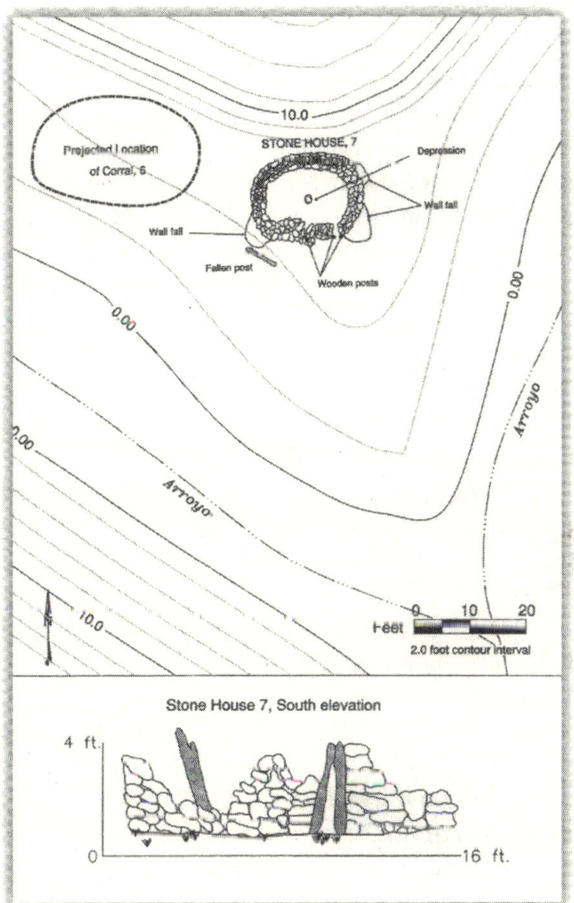

Apache ranchería in Sierra las Espuelas, rim camp, May 2000 survey.

we can imagine that the stunned Apache man probably rushed back to this spot, gathered up—what?—wife, children, anything valuable, and rode away at once, along with all the others here, mulling over, perhaps, the advisability of doing away with Bill and Moroni first. From what Bill told Grennie, he and Fenn did not follow the network of trails to the other campsites within the ranchería until later when they came back with reinforcements. When they did, it apparently took them a few days to find all the dwelling sites in the ranchería.

It is tempting to speculate on the rim camp. Why was it being built? Who was building it, and why is it so far from the other camps? The builders would have had to haul water or depend on rock tanks downstream for seasonal water as there was none permanent nearby, though there might have been some much farther upstream. Still, what was this? Such solitary isolation from others is not the Apache way. Was this a satellite camp made up of a family group? Had the standard Apache gregariousness undergone some revision due to the extreme stress of fugitive life in the Sierra Madre? Since this camp was never finished, it leaves little behind to tell us how it was to have been used, but the double doorway is unique, an intriguing, confounding arrangement, and surely one with a definite purpose. What could it mean? The house is so small, there is hardly any room for two chambers.

I do not believe that this was the only occupied camp at the time of discovery. The trails in the ranchería were well-traveled—probably by a number of people and animals. Then there is the memorable bit of sign-reading in the bluebirds—a detail repeated to me by Alvah. He said that Bill and Moroni, after the encounter with the Apache on the trail up the side of the canyon, continued for a short way. They noticed a flock of bluebirds in the canyon below, flying upstream, then settling in a tree, then taking flight again as a flock, settling again, then flying. Both Bill and Moroni knew that bluebirds would do this if they were disturbed by something moving along on the ground below. What Bill and Moroni saw made them certain that other Apaches were moving up the canyon bottom below them and that was when "they got out of the mountains in a hurry."

As we talk to Seth on the radio, we get bulletins on the fire. It is still a long way off, though not so far that we can't see where it's coming from. We're thinking that it will take days and days to reach us.

We all gradually straggle into camp and review the day. Alan reads from the diary the descriptions of the upper camp and the inventory of things that came from the storage caves. Now that we've been here for a while, these descriptions take on new meaning and new life with every reading. Taking measurements of things forces us to look more closely at them. We plan to be up by 6:30 and on the trail by 8:00 for two nights and three days on the top of the hill at the camp Grennie refers to as "the main corrals."

GRENVILLE'S DIARY

The plan of the main corrals is on page 135 [of the diary]. These corrals were extremely well-made of posts and barbed wire, the fence being one of five strands, and the gates regular pull shut ones, the most common kind in this country. There were two of these corrals, side by side (no. 2 on plan). One had a large snubbing post in its center (no. 3). Their length and width would be about 30 paces by 20 paces.

On the south and west sides of the corrals were two brush enclosures in which houses stood.

No. 6 was of the circular kind, type 1.

No. 8 house was of type 6, and was completely in ruins.

No. 7 house was type 3. It was the best made house in the whole ranchería, and still in excellent condition. It was in this house that Bill found the reloading outfit.

Houses nos. 9 were of type 6, and quite large. These last were a little way to the northeast of the corrals.

At no. 1, near the edge of the ridge and to southeast, are some pot holes in a group of large boulders there. These pot holes the Indians had used for tanning hides in, when they contained enough rainwater, and they still had a quantity of pounded oak bark in them.

Right north of the corrals was a mescal pit, near the edge of the ridge (no. 11). Near this was a large pile of the bones of cattle, horses, and mules apparently slaughtered there by the Apaches, for food (no. 10).

Along the south side of the brush enclosure around the corrals were some drying racks (no. 5) on which meat was hung, in the process of making jerky.

Near house no. 7 was the sled Bill told me about last year, used in hauling meat out to the drying racks.

An excellent view could be had from the top of the ridge, in all directions, and this, strange to say, was the only camp which commanded such a position

NEIL'S DIARY

May 8, Main Corrals Camp

As we climb to the upper main corral camp we follow a game trail up the ridge that Seth and Alan found yesterday. Halfway up there is a large concrete dam, built years ago by a previous ranch owner—perhaps the Palomas Land and Cattle Company before 1950, though it is more likely to have been done in the 1970s, after the ranch was sold and broken into smaller properties.[78]

From the dam we go more or less straight up the hill toward the high camp. Guided by Seth, we top out after an hour or so right in the middle of the camp. We are immediately struck by the quantity of small obsidian nodules on the ground. I had not really noticed on our last trip just how prevalent the obsidian was. The little black nodules, frequently called "Apache tears," are everywhere in the ranchería proper. They are most highly concentrated where the corrals were, and are not to be found at all outside the limits of the camp.

Three years ago we collected a number of these and sent some of them off to be analyzed by Steven Shackley at Berkeley. He is assembling a database of obsidian samples from all over the region—easy to do, in theory at least, as each source has its own chemical fingerprint. These he found to be from an unknown source. The obsidian is a mystery—how it got here and where it came from. A careful examination of the entire ridgetop over the next three days will reveal no local source for it—no deposits, no place where it is weathering out of the rock. This is not a volcanic landscape. The only thing we can imagine is that the obsidian was brought here by the people who built this camp.

Alan has an interesting theory: the traditional Apache protection against lightning is "Black Metal," which could be construed as obsidian. Anyone living up here is very vulnerable to lightning. Occasionally Apaches will place toy models of animals in corrals to protect the real animals. Could the obsidian be a combination of the two: the placement of lightning protection in the animal holding pens to protect them?

In a subsequent conversation, a Chiricahua friend tells me that black stones would have been used in a dwelling site considered as home. Stones of another color, probably yellow, he said, would have been used while traveling away from home.[79]

We begin walking the site, marking all the features and the artifacts with red flags: everything from piles of stone and fence posts to bits of wire, chipped stone, rusty metal, and broken glass.

Austin's first task is to figure out the size of the ranchería in order to get a scale for the map. We decide first to account for all the features on Grennie's map and plot them as well as possible. Then we'll see if a pattern develops because it is hard now to look at what remains of posts and wire and rock piles and know what we are looking at. So we will plot the dots, such as they are, and then connect the dots.

First we go to the place where Seth and Alan found bones yesterday, but there is some doubt: there aren't enough bones for the immense pile that Grennie described. Unable to find any other bones on this side of the ridgetop, Austin decides to use Grennie's map to find the bone pile. Attempting to do so might also be an interesting test of Grennie's mapmaking accuracy. Austin takes a compass bearing and scales the distance on the map from the stone houses to the bone pile: north-by-northwest, three hundred yards. Austin aligns his compass and strides off north-northwest, we all scurry behind him. Austin is a big guy who goes through the brush like a bulldozer on automatic pilot. Three hundred paces later he comes out on the north rim of the ridge precisely at the small bone pile we were so dubious about. We're not so dubious now.

There is a lot to take in up here. The most arresting features are the two round-to-ovoid stone houses that we found three years ago. But there once was a great deal more: several log and brush houses; big, sturdy corrals; meat-drying racks; fences; and myriad smaller items—all painstakingly listed by Grennie in his diary. These things lend human context and mystery to a place that is inherently dramatic with its sweeping views of the Carretas Plains to the east and range after range of the Sierra Madre to the west and south.

What makes this place even more affecting, not to say ominous, is the conflagration to the south. This is the first good look I have had at the fire. At this point it looks to be about thirty miles away, but all day long there has been a wall of dense yellow-brown smoke blowing eastward. The winds are very strong up here, and they must be fanning the flames furiously. We can see where the smoke is coming from—a series of valleys several ridges to the south and west. That is just the northern edge of it; the body of the fire stretches out of sight way to the south. It has burned its way right across the Sierra Madre in the last three weeks and now is approaching the Carretas Plains.

With one eye on the fire, we return to the task of flagging everything that looks man-made. Soon we learn to spot the stubs of posts that were once fences or house corners or roof supports.

At the northern edge of the camp there were once two similar houses labeled as no. 9 on Grennie's map, and we think we may have located some of the wall and corner posts of these houses. They are just stubs sticking up out of the ground in an open area, and they are ringed with rocks. Piling rocks around posts is often done here in addition to or instead of digging a hole. Austin measures and plots them all.

We start identifying the corners of the big corrals—often big posts with lots of boulders piled around them. Once we are fairly certain of these, Austin uses Grennie's map and compass headings to predict where other corners might be. He follows headings and paces as he walks; sure enough, features start coming out of the underbrush, including one of the barbed-wire corral gates—completely intact. Similar to a typical pasture gate, it is made of five posts joined by barbed wire and is meant to be stretched across a fence opening. It is discovered bit by bit hidden under a tree. We might never have seen it but for Austin's facility and ingenuity with maps. It causes great excitement as first one then another part of the fence is discovered; everyone dives under the tree, and soon all five of us are on our bellies scouring the duff for clues.

At one of the big stone piles there is barbed wire wrapped around a big stone, the end coming out and ending in a loop that probably was once wrapped as a guy wire around a corral corner post. We found a similar situation at another of the rock piles.

Seth and Austin team up to take more accurate measurements. Barney and Alan are out hunting for artifacts in front of the stone houses. In a bush I find an old galvanized steel canteen that had been mended with wire. It could have been left by either the Apaches or some cowboy or one of the other visitors the place has had over the years. The canteen is a regular round galvanized one, but it has two holes in it either from being struck by a sharp rock or from being stepped on by a horse as it lay on the ground on top of a sharp rock. Alan wondered for a moment whether it might have been punctured ritually, "killed," as is often done with ceramic pots when the owner has died.

Other small odds and ends turn up: there is a small piece of beaten copper or brass that might once have been a coin, which Barney found over near one of the stone houses. There is a piece of machined brass

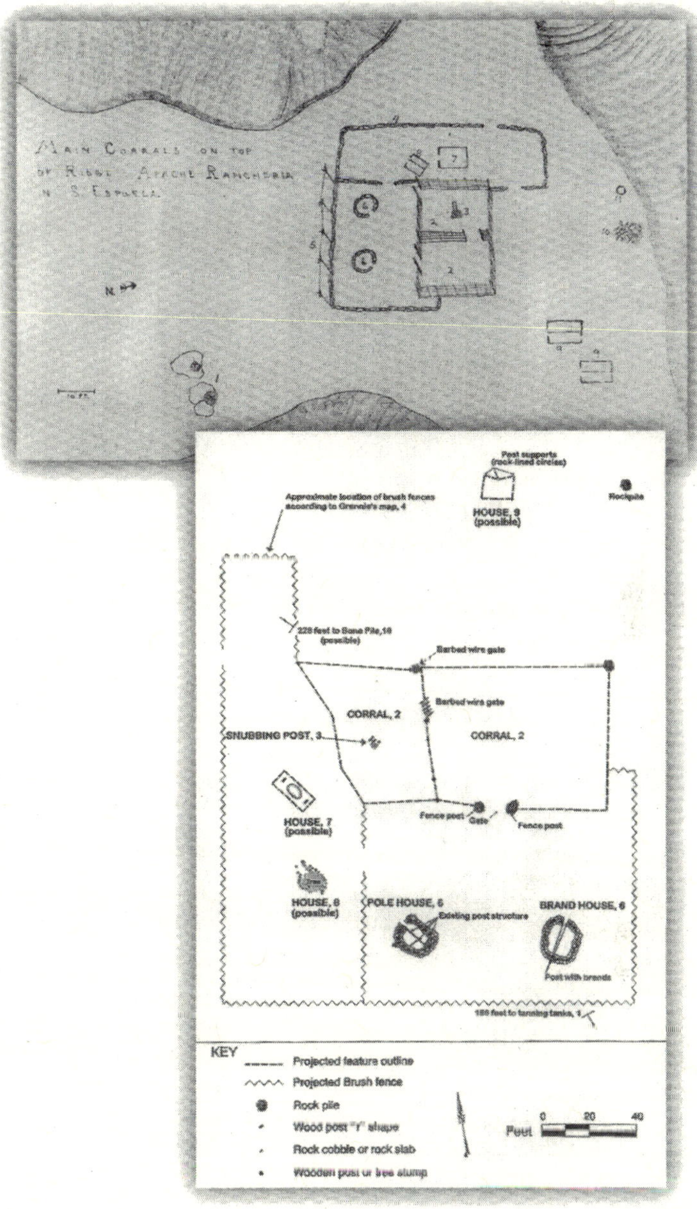

(Top) Sierra las Espuelas ranchería, main corrals on ridge. (Key: 1. potholes for tanning; 2. corral; 3. snubbing post; 4. brush fence; 5. meat drying racks; 6. stone houses; 7. house; 8. house; 9. houses; 10. bone pile; 11. mescal roasting pit)

(Bottom) Sierra las Espuelas ranchería, main corrals on ridge, May 2000 survey.

(Top) Remains of house number 7, main corrals, upper camp, Sierra las Espuelas, May 2000. (Photo by Seth Goodwin)

(Bottom) House number 7 at the Apache ridgetop camp; Sierra las Espuelas, 1931.

Bill and Art at house number 6 at Apache camp on the top of a ridge; Sierra las Espuelas, 1931.

Alan Ferg at house number 6 (Brand House), main corrals, upper camp; smoke from forest fire in distance, Sierra las Espuelas, May 2000. (Photo by Seth Goodwin)

Barney Burns at house number 6 (Ridge Pole House), main corrals, upper camp; Sierra las Espuelas, May 2000. (Photo by Seth Goodwin)

Grass and pole house, number 9, at the Apache camp in the Sierra las Espuelas, 1931.

from some instrument or clock or military hardware; there is a piece of aluminum that has had pieces cut from it with a cold chisel. We find two cubes of iron cut off the ends of horseshoes, and then a tiny treasure: a single earring of beaten copper, next to other pieces of beaten copper and brass.

Just before 6:00 P.M., I go to have a closer look at the fire and it seems to be quite close—maybe three or four ridges away. We come back after supper, and against the darkening sky we can see flames on the horizon—probably no more than eight or nine miles away, maybe even less. The wind is pushing the fire directly west and it looks as if the flames are heading for the mouth of Las Piedras Canyon. We decide to pack up at first light in the morning and leave for base camp, then drive out as fast as we can so that we don't get trapped in the canyon.

Because there is still so much to do, we decide to do archaeology in the dark: a tight clot of extremely busy people in a rush to find red flags and take bearings and measurements by flashlight under the great bowl of the night sky—the stars made dim by the smoke, the flames winking on the horizon. ✣

May 9, Main Corrals Camp

The crack of dawn. The wind has died down and the fire on the dis tant mountains seems quiet. There is less smoke on the nearest mountain ridges to the south, and we decide that it is probably safe to spend the day up here.

Seth and Barney and I will try to find the calf pens. Austin and Alan will remain at the main corrals camp to finish mapping and inventorying artifacts and features. It is the highest part of the ranchería, commanding a 360-degree view and the only place from where we can tell what the fire is doing. Alan and Austin will keep us posted.

GRENVILLE'S DIARY

The big corrals lay about two miles from the main camp, right square on top of an open, level topped ridge (see no. 14, general plan). Right to the north of here is a deep, dry, steep-sided canyon, which is really the head of Las Piedras Canyon, as it makes a big swing around to the north, and then east, and ends up at this place.

NEIL'S DIARY

We drop off the north end of the plateau and quickly find game trails that lead to a sheet of bald rock that pitches down to the arroyo that will lead to the calf pen camp.

The going is quite different on this side of the hill than on the other side. The footing is good, the woods are more open and we can walk much of the way on bare rock—both on the way down and in the creek bottom itself, which is carved out of bedrock. There is also a fairly wide trail paralleling the stream that once was maintained by cowboys mending fences, checking water, gathering cattle, and is now maintained only by bears.

GRENVILLE'S DIARY

Right in the bottom of this canyon, across the creek bed, is a rock dam, built to hold seepage water, which comes to the surface at that place. This dam is made of rocks set in adobe, and is about 4½ feet high, by 10 or 12 feet long, built directly on bed rock (see general plan, no. 16).

NEIL'S DIARY

We soon come to the place where the Apaches had built the low rock-and-mud dam described above. In its place is a large concrete Mexican dam, now completely silted in and neglected. At the bottom there is a clean-out that has standing water in it coming from a permanent seep around which there are many insects, as at the small seep in the main camp: bees, hornets, and the same beautiful orange-and-black butterflies. This is the third large concrete dam we have found—all in remote locations, and all built in the 1960s and '70s. At least one of the dams—the one on the way up to the main camp—we can date by the apparent vintage of the automobile bumpers embedded in the concrete and projecting out of the top of the dam. They appear to be bumpers from the 1950s, recycled here ten to twenty years later as reinforcing steel.

It is only much later—in a conversation with Al Fenn, the nephew of Moroni Fenn, with whom Bill Curtis discovered this ranchería in 1926—that I discover that the dam we have just found is on a different ranch property from Carlos's place. Al knows the owners of this neighboring ranch well and tells me that he even helped them to repair the dam in about 1975.[80]

GRENVILLE'S DIARY

About half a mile below this dam, there is a little draw, going up to the right, and a quarter of a mile up this draw are the small corrals and calf pens (see general plan, no. 18). From the draw, running down the left side of the creek bottom, and crossing over, and up the side canyon to the small corrals, is a brush fence, part of a large pasture fence apparently (see general plan, no. 17). This fence also runs up the side of the ridge from the small corrals, and clear to the top of the high hill at that place.

NEIL'S DIARY

We find the junction of the little draw as expected, and ascend following fairly well-defined bear trails, seeing the occasional ax mark along the way, indicating that cowboys or someone had reason to come up this way not all that many years ago. We start getting into pine trees as we climb, and we start seeing much older ax work on the trees, indicating that we may be getting warmer.

The arroyo widens into a small bench with fairly steep sides above to both right and left. We see one, then two, then three charred trees—some standing upright, some lying on the ground. Then it registers: the charred wood forms familiar patterns. These are not trees, but posts that once stood in the corners of houses and corrals. This is the camp. I go a little further and, looking to the left, see the little stone house behind a thick screen of brush, enduring undisturbed for all these years.

The moment of discovery of one of these houses is as it always is: the sense of having to look no longer; the sense of having found the long-dreamed-of; the sense of completing another station in this long pilgrimage.

GRENVILLE'S DIARY

The plan of the encampment at the small corrals and calf pens is on page 136 [of the diary]. There were two small, low fenced brush corrals here, about 20 paces by 18 paces roughly. The fencing was made mainly with poles and stood some 3½ to 4 feet high (nos. 12), and had two outside gates and one inner gate (nos. 13).

No. 9 was a small pen, apparently used for calves, and no. 8 was a structure for the same purpose, only with roof. Four houses were in the camp, two of them on the west side of the arroyo.

House no. 2 was of stone, and of type no. 2. It was in this house that Bill found the bows and arrows he told me about, hung up under the roof.

House no. 1 was of type 6. It has completely fallen down.

House no. 3 was of type no. 5. It was the largest house in the whole ranchería, and appeared never to have been entirely completed.

House no. 6 was of type 7. There were a pile of logs at no. 4, peeled, and put there for use in building most probably.

At no. 7 was a kind of roofed-over cache. The houses, calf pens, etc., on the east of the arroyo were linked together by two sections of brush fence, put there to keep stock out.

There was a small mescal pit at no. 11.

No. 10 is the brush fence going up to the mt., already described. It might be well to add here that the brush fences in this ranchería are exactly like those in the Chita Hueca ranchería.

NEIL'S DIARY

We can now account for all of the different features of this ranchería. The stone house is somewhat dug into the side of the hill, and a lot of brush has grown up inside it. The masonry is well laid, as it is in the other houses; there is one door on the south side of the house and a crotched post in each of the four corners to hold up the roof.

Grennie took a picture of the house in 1931 from above, and Seth and I work into position so that we may photograph it from the same position, standing exactly where he stood. We spend a lot of time photographing each other so that the moment would be preserved, Seth looking just as Grennie must have—all long, rangy limbs.

We then map the whole place: all the posts, the parts of the big main house, the corrals. We find empty loops of barbed wire that once were wrapped around posts, a wide strap of rusty sheet iron wound around a tree trunk then tied in a knot. The only charred pieces of wood in the camp are the posts that first told us we had arrived—telling us also, we thought at first, that the place was probably torched by Curtis/Fenn et al. when they raided the place, but a close reading of the diary indicates that only two houses were burned and those were at the main lower camp. And Grennie's photos show that the little stone house here still had its roof when he was here. In all likelihood it was one of the many forest fires that have swept through these mountains since 1931 that charred the posts. The lack of other charred wood in the camp meaning, no doubt, that the place had been cleared of large trees and brush by the Apaches for pastures and corrals. The thick growth of underbrush and small trees has sprung up since the last big fire.

It is a very cramped-in place, though originally it was more open. Even so, it must have been claustrophobic—a bit of a trap because the sides were so steep, though you could scramble out on foot if you had to. The trail from the main camp did not originally come up the arroyo

Apache ranchería in Sierra las Espuelas, small pens in canyon below ridge. (Key: 1. house; 2. stone house; 3. house; 4. gate; 5. fence; 6. house; 7. lean-to; 8, 9. houses; 10. pasture fence; 11. mescal roasting pit; 12. corrals; 13. gate)

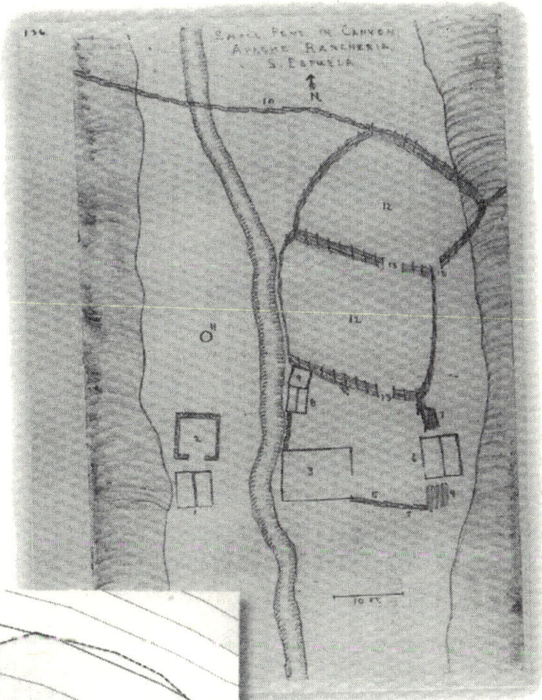

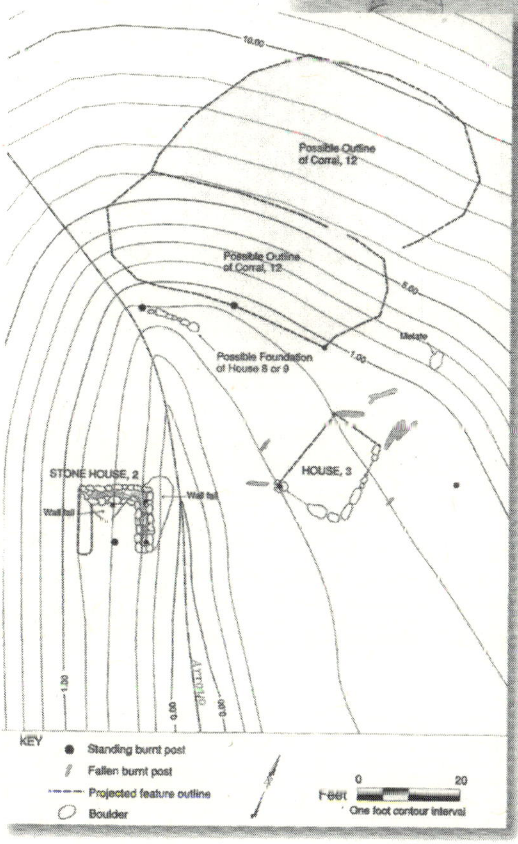

Sierra las Espuelas ranchería, small pens in canyon below ridge, May 2000 survey.

Seth Goodwin at the calf pens camp; Sierra las Espuelas, May 2000.

as we have come, but went out across the contour of the side hill to connect with the main canyon. From here it would have been only a short trip back to the main corrals.

We spend a lot of time trying to figure out what the people were doing up in this place, as we always do when we find one of these satellite camps. Why are these dwelling sites located where they are? Why are they so far apart? What kind of relationship did the inhabitants have with one another? Were the camps seasonal or work-specific? Or did they have something to do with the social organization of the entire band and its ranchería? Were these family groups? Could there have been some ethnic mix or some hierarchical stratification?

One thing all but one of the dwelling sites have in common is at least one stone house in a distinctive masonry style. Each of the dwelling sites has a mescal roasting pit. And each has what appears to have been ongoing construction: peeled logs, never-completed houses, stockpiled materials.

Grennie must have had a reason for calling these "calf pens"—perhaps it was the size of the corrals and the presence of a shed in one to shelter the calves. Instead of being dry, all the camps probably had water, and this one had the best—the dam up the canyon collecting water from the permanent seep, which was also easily accessible from the main corrals camp. Other camps had access to big rock tanks that would have held water for a long time after rain. Apaches were known to carry water in skin containers with them when they traveled, and they used waterproofed basketry to carry water from springs to campsites.

We keep in touch with Austin and Alan all day on the progress of the fire, and the reports are good: the fire is sputtering. We head back but by the time we get into the main corral camp about 3:00 the fire is raging again. The ridge line is ablaze just to the south of us, and as far as we can see beyond that, smoke is pouring out of canyon after canyon. There are flashes as clusters of pine trees are engulfed in flame then disappear behind clouds of inky smoke. It looks as if the fire is moving north and might be about to drop into Las Piedras Canyon, though well to the west of where we will enter it on our way out, and unlikely to trap us.

Somehow the fire has become a member of this whole enterprise. It seems like a messenger telling us not to take the place for granted, that our time up here has to be limited. As we make the decision to leave this afternoon, both Seth and I see the same thing: two ravens flying very low above us. We both notice the shadows as the ravens glide over—silent for once—and we both find the sight arresting, as if we were meant to see these ravens in a way different from all the other ravens we have been seeing and hearing today.

As soon as he sees the shadows streak across the ground, Seth thinks it an omen, a sign of some kind. For me, seeing the ravens fly over, seeing their shadows racing ahead of us is one of those "bird experiences" that I have from time to time. Like them, this one is enigmatic, powerful but inchoate, seeming to be full of unformed promise. Seth feels it as a confirmation, a ratification of our decision to leave.

I think of the bears as the winter custodians of the place and the ravens, the summer ones.

As after our first visit here three and a half years ago, we all feel that this is hallowed ground. This and the other camp a few miles to the south are the only places I know of for sure where the Sierra Madre Apaches made a physical mark that remains. That we know something about the mark they made gives an eloquence to these remains that would otherwise be mute.

If there were more here, if we did not have to tax our imaginations so heavily to build a picture of those who lived here, the spiritual dimension might have been less powerful, simply by being more concrete. As it is, we are all trying to assemble the clues into a coherent narrative and that brings our minds to bear intimately on the minutest details of the place.

By four in the afternoon, we have tended to the last chores: final photographs, artifact and feature locations, measurements, compass bearings, house sketches, removal of red flags. Just before leaving, Barney says there is one more thing. He has brought a bag of tobacco with him specifically for a parting gesture. He makes an offering by spreading the tobacco on the ground and letting the "smoke," the essence of the tobacco, cleanse him, thanking the place and its spirits for what they have given to us. He says it is a Hopi and Acoma smoke cleansing ritual. Seth and I both give our thanks to this special place. He told me later that he was overcome with emotion. It is touching to me that he has such a compelling connection with this place and that it represents such a powerful bond with his father and grandfather.

It takes us about an hour and a half to get down to the main camp—the footing really treacherous on the steep slope. We try not to hurry as we watch the smoke rolling overhead. It doesn't take long to pack up our base camp and begin driving out. We stop on a grassy oak savanna near the mouth of the canyon and find that the fire is in the next drainage to the south, still moving east toward the Carretas Plains. We will be safe here for the night. In the dark, we watch the fire winking and licking, and we talk about the Apache ranchería.

GRENVILLE'S DIARY

The house types both here and at the Chita Hueca ranchería are hard to account for, they not being of the true Apache type, with the exception of the temporary brush shelters, which are probably Apache. House type no. 1 is the nearest approach to the true Apache dwelling that I have yet seen. It is an interesting thing that the stone walls these Apaches have built, are very well laid up, in adobe usually, and are quite thick, being from two to two and a half feet through. All top layers of roofs here are of bear grass thatching, with a covering of adobe at times.

NEIL'S DIARY

May 9, Las Piedras Canyon

Not only are most of the house types unknown among reservation Apaches, they represent an amazing variety. Grennie himself records 10 separate house types, including log cabins of two kinds, various brush shelters, and stone houses of at least three kinds. Although the Chita Hueca ranchería (about thirty miles farther south) was built presumably by these people when they abandoned the Sierra las Espuelas camp, it is worth noting that it has no stone houses and the log cabin type found at Chita Hueca is not found in the Sierra las Espuelas camps. What convinced Grennie that the two camps were built by the same people is the fact that the corrals and brush fences are made in exactly the same way.

Since we know next to nothing about the people, does the variety of houses tell us something about their background? Were the house types chosen out of personal preference; for certain functions, for use in different seasons; for ease and personal familiarity of construction on the part of the respective builders?

Some house types were built at each dwelling site in the ranchería—most notably the stone houses, and the stone houses are so similar that they seem to constitute a single building style. Four of the five camps have at least one stone house, built as a rectangle with rounded corners, the rocks chinked with adobe, roofed with wood and beargrass—often covered with mud. The fact that they used mud and adobe indicates a plentiful water supply within hauling distance.

When the camp was discovered, someone, probably the man Bill and Moroni encountered, was building such a house at the rim camp. As Grennie observed, many of these houses must have been very snug in the winter. Could it be that the stone houses and the log houses were meant for winter use primarily and the other, more drafty ones meant for warm-weather use?

There appears to have been permanent water in at least two places—the dam in the canyon near the calf pens, and in the arroyo near the main camp; and water could have been carried from these places to the various dwelling sites. At least one pitched water-carrying vessel had been found in the storage cave, sounding much like the typical Apache *tus,* a tightly woven juglike container, holding about two gallons, with a narrow neck and handles for carrying on the back with a tump line. In spite of the stone houses, there appear to have been many typically Apache items: the pitched water bottle, dish baskets, burden baskets, moccasins, bows and arrows, acorns, roasted mescal, and some of the brush shelters. If the place had not been so thoroughly stripped by raiders and then by the Apaches themselves, we would know much more.

Grenville's Diary

The Apaches have not been back to this camp for at least two years or even three. They did come back after the raid in 1926 at some time or another, but never to stay, merely to clean up, and this they did thoroughly. Not a thing was left in the houses, or about the camps which was moveable. Every scrap of stuff, whether useful or not, was taken away. It seems as though the Apaches had made a point of doing this, maybe to give the idea that they had moved away, never to return. That they still come back to the S. Espuela is known though, and they certainly must have other camps in the mts., not so far away to the south, west, or north.

Neil's Diary

Alan has made beautiful drawings of the two stone houses at the high camp, and the more we look at it, the drawing of the one with the ridge pole is showing us something we never saw before. The one thing

Burden basket found at the Apache ridgetop camp in the Sierra las Espuelas, 1931.

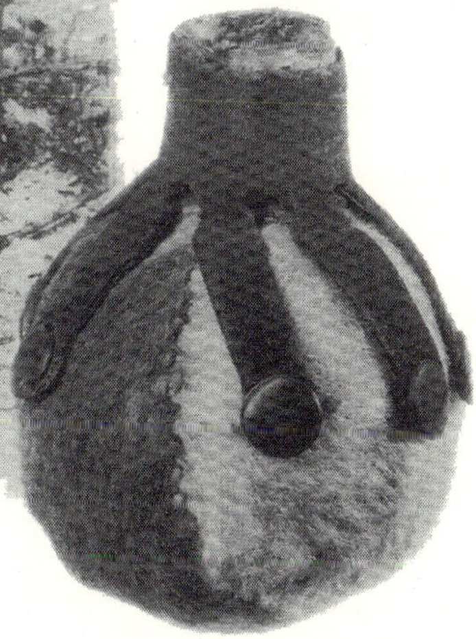

Small leather bottle found at the Apache ranchería. (Courtesy Arizona State Museum, negative #64288)

that has never made sense about this site is that Grennie said there were two round stone houses of type no. 1, and he made a careful pencil drawing of this type, leaving no doubt that it had a conical roof structure supported by a pole in the middle. Moreover, both of these houses at the high camp had doorways facing northeast. His map shows them clearly: both round, with doorways facing the same direction.

What we have found are two stone houses (no. 6), just where his map said they should be. One of them is clearly type 1. The other one is of type 2: more or less rectangular with rounded corners, a doorway on the north side, a roof structure consisting of rafters resting on a ridge pole supported at each end by a crotched post. But Grennie said nothing about such a house at this location, and judging from the care and thoroughness of the rest of the maps and diagrams, this is not a mistake that he would have made.

As we look at Alan's drawing, we realize we are seeing this house for the first time. It is not rectangular; it is more of a dented oval. It looks as if the stone wall to the east had been rebuilt. There is a wooden post in the middle of the east wall that makes no sense—unless it is actually a door frame for the original northeast-facing doorway of the house, such as we find in the other stone house, the brand house. The stonework is different on that side from the other side. As we puzzle over this new wrinkle, Seth suggests that it must have been rebuilt at some time. Could it be that after 1931, someone came back and reconstructed the house, closing the opening in the northeast wall, making a new one in the northwest wall, and replacing the original central post and radiating rafters with a ridge-pole roof?

This theory seems completely plausible, leaving us with the tantalizing question: Who did it? The Apaches? Some cowboys? Whoever it was went to some trouble and was setting up for a stay of some length. This place was a refuge, remote and infrequently visited: a perfect hideout for anyone who knew of the reliable water sources in the canyon bottoms but who chose not to camp near them and risk discovery. There is no way to be completely certain, but I feel the most likely people to have gone to the trouble of rebuilding the stone walls and the roof of this house were people who needed a hideout for some period of time: who but the original occupants of the place—who but the Apaches?

One drawback to this theory is that the place was compromised, its security blown. There was no telling when unwelcome visitors would arrive, as they frequently did, tending to ranching chores or having a look at the hidden camp as a curiosity, not to mention searching for the gold.

Whoever it was, the rebuilding must have occurred soon after Grennie's 1931 visit, judging from the weathering of the wood ridge pole and rafters and comparing them with the wood we know was there in 1931. Moreover, it was not likely to have been much later than the early 1940s because the Palomas Land and Cattle Company changed hands in 1941. At that time it was bought by a group of American investors, and they put in many improvements; they stocked the ranch with 25,000 head of cattle, strung a thousand miles of fencing, and began to develop water sources. All this work would have flushed out any clandestine occupants of the high country, if there were any at all at that late date.

Al Fenn, the son of Alvah, has told me of the frequent visits he and his father have made to the area, in a vain search for the lost gold mine.

Al's first visit was in the 1940s, and at the time this house had a ridge pole. He spent a night or two sleeping in it because the rock wall provided a windbreak.[81] Could some earlier rider who had to spend a few days in this exposed spot—while mending fences or gathering strays—could he have been the one who rebuilt the house?

All we know is that while Grennie was there, so were the Apaches, not far off, watching everything that happened in the Sierra las Espuelas, determined never again to be taken by surprise in this particular neighborhood.

GRENVILLE'S DIARY

Oct. 30, 1931, Las Piedras Canyon, S. Espuela, Chihuahua, Mex.

We packed up and came on out this morning. At the mouth of the canyon, where it enters the Las Piedras Can., we ran on two Americans, friends of Bill's. Their outfit consisted of four pack animals, and two mounts. We gave them a bad scare, they having guilty minds, and being in the smuggling game. They had come south over the mts. from near the line, just got in that very morning, and were waiting for a load of illegal goods being brought to them from Casas Grandes. We all sat down in the sun to talk for a while.

NEIL'S DIARY

Now that we've seen all the dwelling sites and have a better idea of the terrain between them within the ranchería and the terrain beyond them in neighboring canyons, we notice something else that's puzzling—prompted by this encounter of Grennie's with the smugglers.

These men had probably come south from the border up the Cajón Bonito, a regular thoroughfare for smugglers in those days, and for travelers of all kinds over the years. The cajón tops out at the Continental Divide not far from where Las Piedras Canyon begins and drops down on the other side toward Chihuahua. It is near the head of Las Piedras that the small side canyon (where the calf pen camp is located) comes in from the north, meaning that the Apaches were at risk of discovery by anyone on the route taking it into his head to do a little exploring up this side canyon. If someone had done that, they would have seen evidence of occupation and, exploring further, as Bill and Moroni eventually did, they would have stumbled onto the calf pen camp.

Seth observes that this ease of access to the cajón might have been no accident if, as many have said, the Apaches were in the smuggling game themselves. From the number and size of the corrals, the very large piles of bones, the amount of dried meat, and the hide-tanning basins, it seems very possible that this was a high-volume cattle-rustling operation with a "commercial" agenda. The inhabitants would steal from the ranches—mostly Palomas—produce hides and dried meat, and then sell or trade this output to others who would take it back to the States, or down-canyon to Mexico. The folklore suggesting such a scenario is commonplace even today. The Apaches had figured out a way to "launder cattle" as Alan said later. For this purpose the setup was perfect. The folklore that we have gathered suggests at least two similar scenarios for this commerce: the Apaches would sell or trade hides and jerky, either (1) to non-Indian middlemen; or (2) to other Apaches who came down secretly from San Carlos for a rendezvous at the border to exchange goods for contraband hides, dried meat, and possibly even the prized, sure-footed little Mexican ponies.

Grennie recorded a story about a man who claimed to be a bear trapper in the 1920s, who would disappear into the mountains from his cabin on the Carretas Plains for days at a time. He never seemed to catch any bears, so people suspected him of trading with the Apaches. Grennie also heard that red human hair was found in a pinecone used as a hairbrush in one of the two camps he visited. Both the captive Apaches, Lupe and Carmela, mentioned white men living with one of the small bands, and there is plenty of other oral history of white men who ran with the Apaches.

This circumstantial evidence, combined with the remarkable variety of building types at the camps, begs the question (virtually unanswerable now): is there some correlation between the diversity of houses and the diversity of the ethnic or cultural background of the people who built them? Or were the inhabitants all Apaches, but so conversant with the house types built by rural Mexican subsistence farmers, Indian and non-Indian alike, that they freely borrowed and improvised to suit their shelter needs? ✥

The structure of the preceding part of this section—alternating between my father's and my diary entries—necessarily means that many of the conclusions and new insights derived from this trip are scattered, appearing in the narrative at the points when they occurred to us. I'm going to gather them together for recapitulation as a conclusion to this piece, and I'm going to use our new survey maps of the place to help with the interpretation.

In the 1880s the Sierra las Espuelas and the Carretas Plains were heavily traveled by Chiricahua Apaches and pursuing military forces guided by Western Apache scouts who knew where the Chiricahua were likely to camp.

Apaches were known to be in the Sierra las Espuelas in the 1890s; the French miners were warned and paid the price of disregarding the advice. It is clear that the mine is not in Las Piedras Canyon, but in one of the many parallel canyons running into the Sierra las Espuelas from the Carretas Plains. A raiding party of Apaches killed three Americans in 1896 and was tracked to a camp a few miles west of the Sierra las Espuelas. Here the Apaches were attacked by soldiers and Apache May was captured. Possibly these were of the same band that wiped out the French miners sometime during that decade.

When the next party of miners arrived in 1914, they found an Apache camp in the canyon and were eventually robbed of everything. This raises the question: was there also an Apache camp there when the French party came through, or did the Apaches move in only after attacking the miners' camp?

On the Nogales Ranch (for a time the headquarters of the Palomas Land and Cattle Company), fence post cutters had their camp stripped by Apaches in about 1915 while working both in Las Piedras Canyon and the one north of it. The old prospector that Bill met had encountered Indians in the Sierra las Espuelas who looked more like Apaches than anything else. After finding two human skeletons and then moccasin tracks on top of his own, he got out fast. It seems as if the Apaches wanted outsiders to know they were intruding and were warning them off—were telling them they proceeded at grave risk, until of course, the ranchería was discovered and the Apaches' home base was no longer safe.

What we do not know is how long Apaches had been living in permanent camps with such an investment in infrastructure as we found at the Chita Hueca and the Sierra las Espuelas rancherías. Apaches frequently built masonry structures, such as defensive walls, low rock walls for dwellings, and of course, tent rings.[82] While in hot pursuit of Sierra Madre Apaches in 1896, Lt. N. K. Averill attacked a camp so well defended by rock redoubts that he said "it would be absolutely impossible to get at them by day."[83] The so-called "small stone house culture" of the Sierra Madre had not been attributed to any identifiable people. Because it is found high in the mountains between Nácori Chico and Casas Grandes in the heart of *Ndéndaa'i* Chiricahua Apache strongholds, could it be that Apaches are responsible? Carl Lumholtz describes this culture in *Unknown Mexico,* and the houses at times sound exactly like what we have been seeing at Las Piedras: "about ten feet square, with no particular attention paid to the corners." Associated with these houses is very simple pottery. Apaches made some pottery, but not much. The small stone house culture is a real mystery, and there is a good chance it is mixed in among other stone-structure cultures dating from much earlier periods.[84]

Even more enigmatic is a site near the headwaters of the Gila River in west-central New Mexico in the heart of what once was Warm Springs and Bedonkohe Apache territory. It's at about 7,500 feet in altitude—the same elevation as the Sierra las Espuelas ranchería. The site consists of twenty-five walled enclosures of stone—some rectangular, some perfectly circular, some of them joined together, some freestanding. The masonry is largely collapsed, so it is hard to tell if it was originally as well laid as that which we found in the Sierra las Espuelas. The site was partially mapped and photographed by Bureau of Land Management (BLM) archaeologists in the late 1970s. There were no artifacts on the surface, and the BLM has done no excavation, so the cultural affiliation of the place remains a mystery. It bears no resemblance to known prehistoric sites and no determination has been made as to the age of the site. It is tempting to hypothesize an Apache origin for this place, but without further investigation, an attribution is impossible to make.

When Bill and Moroni found the Sierra las Espuelas ranchería in December 1926, they had no idea how many people were there. They saw one man and were quite sure there were others close at hand. They found new construction underway at the rim camp, and they found other materials that were apparently stockpiled for use in construction—meaning that the people there were planning for the future: they intended to stay and keep doing what they were already doing. In addition, there was at least one storage cave with many valuable items, meaning again that the people were planning for the future. The stored food consisted of acorns, acorn flour, squawberries, roasted mescal, and dried meat, signs of a more or less traditional Apache hunting, gathering, and raiding subsistence.

The ranchería contained as many as eighteen houses, though we don't know how many were in use at the time of discovery. We also don't know how long the ranchería had been in use, but Grennie's opinion was that the place had been in use for a "long time"—perhaps twenty years. The facts that there were clear trails connecting the dwelling sites and that the ground was trampled down around all the dwelling sites and corrals indicate substantial activity on the part of both people and livestock. The scale and distribution of the corrals, including a snubbing post in one of them, indicate a volume cattle-and-horse-handling operation—larger in scale than would be required for the mere subsistence of a small number of residents. The residents were processing enough jerked meat at any given time to require the construction of a sledge to move it from the corrals (which must have served as a slaughterhouse) to the meat-drying racks; and possibly to move the bones to the pile at the edge of the mesa.

Somehow the Apaches were able to steal cattle from the Palomas and other ranches and drive them into the mountains without being tracked and discovered. We don't know quite how they did this, though it must have been by taking only a very few at a time. There are only two canyons leading to the main corrals: the canyon where the main camp is located and the canyon where the calf pen camp is located. The Apaches might also have found a way to drive them up onto the mesa top and across the mesa to the main corrals.

There seems to have been permanent, year-round water in at least two locations: at the main lower camp and at the dam near the calf pen camp. We found standing water at the latter and a seep at the former in May of one of the driest years on record. Even so, we can't be sure that this was truly a year-round camp. The presence of snug, well-insulated, well-sealed dwellings (some of which had interior chimneys and fireplaces) indicates that it was occupied in winter—a time when water would also be plentiful. The fact that there were a number of less substantial dwellings suggests warm-weather use as well.

Is the masonry technique found in all five of the camps a style in use by several ranchería masons, or is it the work of a single mason? The walls of several of the houses are parallel, as in a rectangular house, but the corners are rounded rather than squared off. Easier to build perhaps, and just as durable, to judge from the condition of the walls after all this time. It's not likely that the masons in this ranchería learned how to lay stone from Mexicans, who would probably have built traditional right-angle corners with interlocking stones.

After the place was discovered in 1926, the Apaches deserted it at once and later came back to remove everything they could carry. Grennie notes, however, that it was known that they had returned from time to time as of 1931, and the probability that one of the stone houses at the main corral camp has been rebuilt since then means that someone came back for a more substantial sojourn—quite possibly one of the Apaches themselves.

We can make some guesses about the way the various camps were used, drawing almost entirely on Grennie's interpretations—but many questions remain. Were the camps like traditional Apache "local-group" dwelling sites built around kinship ties, or were they work-specific, or some combination of these? Is any paradigm of traditional Western Apache or Chiricahua social organization even valid here?

Why was one man or group building a new house at the rim camp location—was this a new local-group site? Was the storage cave camp with its large cache of supplies and material just another dwelling site, and was the cache the property of the whole ranchería or only of the people in that isolated camp? The amount of stored material suggests that some of the inhabitants were temporarily absent and planned to return.

The stockpiling of building materials and the suddenly interrupted construction of at least one of the buildings suggest a working confidence in the future, tempered, of course, by the understanding that discovery would require immediate abandonment of everything.

Could the whole place have been populated by only a small number of people who moved around from camp to camp when certain tasks had to be performed, such as: slaughtering, skinning, tanning, and drying meat at the main corrals camp; preparing food and other equipment for storage at the storage cave camp; calving, nursing, and feeding calves at the calf pen camps, and so forth? My guess is that some of these operations would have had to be overlapping, suggesting simultaneous occupation of at least some of the camps by separate groups of people.

And what of the artifacts that we found on the surface of the ground at the main corrals camp? That the obsidian nodules are to be found there and nowhere else has some significance, I suspect, but I can only guess. Barney found a concentration of worked metal objects in the open between the two stone houses, suggesting a metal-working site: brass beaten into what could only be items of jewelry; conical metal bells like those Grennie found at the main arroyo camp; sheet aluminum that had been cut with a cold chisel; a bit of machined brass that came from some scavenged instrument, a clock, perhaps; odds and ends of raw material, such as the cut-off ends of horseshoes.

The Apaches were able to supply themselves with a quantity of barbed wire of several different varieties—stolen from neighboring ranches. Grennie's description of the corrals and fences as "well-built" suggests some experience in making them. The snubbing post in the very ruggedly-constructed main corral suggests some sort of a long-term horse-handling operation.

The maps made by Austin of the ranchería speak for themselves, but they are instructive in many ways. The first is as a gauge of the accuracy of Grennie's 1931 maps. The thoroughness of his mapping and inventory of the place is especially notable given that he was at the site for only a day and a half—hardly enough time to visit all of the dwelling sites, let alone gather enough data to make so many accurate measured drawings, take so many photographs, and make note of all the features such as corrals, fences, and dwelling types. Austin discovered that Grennie's compass bearings and measurements of individual features were reasonably accurate, though his measurements of the distances between them and of the overall site dimensions were not always reliable.

There is ample evidence that there were numerous Apache camps in the Sierra Madre from the border south for a hundred miles or more. The Apaches invariably sought shelter in caves or in simple brush houses that they made in several different but typical patterns. This camp is very unusual in that it has stone and log houses. These features augment the growing body of evidence that Apaches did build masonry structures, however. We hear frequently of small stone houses being found in the Sierra Madre by local cowboys and hunters in Mexico.

So far, however, we have seen nothing else that looks like the stone houses in this ranchería. If they are unique they may reflect a way of life and subsistence agenda substantially different from those of the rest of the Sierra Madre Apaches. Perhaps there was an admixture or influence of non-Apaches among them sufficient to give the site its remarkable diversity and complexity. In any case this ranchería and the one to the south at Chita Hueca suggest the possibility of an undocumented Apache way of life in the Sierra Madre that can be fleshed out only through further exploration of other similar sites. ✥

Where Did They Go?

chapter nine

The people who built the rancherías in the Sierra las Espuelas and the people of the other scattered bands to the south were the last holdouts, the survivors of the longest war waged against an indigenous people by either the U.S. or the Mexican government. They had somehow survived in the Sierra Madre, doing what they had done for centuries; but their way of life was a death warrant. They were going against the grain of history, living in a way that had eventually brought down all the other resistant Native American people. We know from the testimony of Lupe and Carmela that they were afraid, that they never felt safe; but I also wonder if another kind of life was even imaginable for them.

In Mexican eyes they were outlaws, but as far as the Apaches were concerned, they were answerable to no law not of their own making. They may also have felt that there was no turning back, that there would never be amnesty, that they had no choice but fugitive defiance to the end. As mythic-heroic-romantic as that may sound, from what we can piece together of the behavior of the Sierra Madre Apaches, and what we know of the warriors of the 1870s and 1880s, it may not be far from the truth at least for some of them.

After Grennie made his last visit to the Sierra las Espuelas camp in 1931, there were reliable but diminishing numbers of reports of contact between Mexicans and Apaches throughout the 1930s. But by the end of the decade, there was no more recorded contact, and it seems that they had simply disappeared—either through death or migration or, perhaps, a kind of metamorphosis.

When I began this project, I assumed their disappearance simply meant extinction—from bloodshed, starvation, capture, or misadventure. Mexican folklore on the fate of the Sierra Madre Apaches is fairly consistent in supporting the assumption that any surviving Apaches eventually fled north across the line and back to the reservations.

Mexican oral history and Apache oral history are, I find, mirror images of each other. At Fort Apache and Mescalero, and especially at San Carlos, they say no Apaches ever returned for good, but that somewhere south of the border they survive in secret enclaves, some still speaking the language, even wearing traditional clothing. It is a persistent oral tradition, and over the years I have heard it from a variety of sources.

Two Western Apache men, the father and uncle of a woman I know, went to Ciudad Juárez in the 1940s. While speaking to each other in Apache in the street they were accosted by a man who spoke to them in their own language. They turned around and replied to the man in Apache, and they spoke for a long time that way. With the man there were two women. He said that there were other Apaches living in Mexico, that they lived in certain places, that they had fields and planted crops and were more or less integrated into Mexican society, but that they stayed out of the way and tried not to attract attention to themselves.

There is more: I know of a young woman who was born and raised in Colorado by parents who were immigrants from Mexico. In due course, her paternal grandmother moved up from Mexico to join the family. When the grandmother arrived, she spoke in a strange language with her son, the young woman's father. This language was Apache, and she learned it by hearing it spoken at home. Her Apache-speaking father and grandmother were born in a settlement in the mountains west of Chihuahua City where "everyone is related to each other." This was a household, perhaps even a village, in Mexico where the Apache language was spoken as recently as the 1950s.[85]

The family of this Mexican Apache originates in a region of the Sierra Madre to the south and east of Nácori Chico. It is a domain so vast and wild that even today there are virtually no roads. The people who live there are for the most part Mountain Pimas, Indians who for centuries shared the Sierra Madre with the Apaches.

It wasn't until I reread material gathered by anthropologist Tom Hinton that enough of a pattern emerged to suggest this area as a possibility for at least one of the Apache escape hatches. While Hinton was traveling through this part of the Sierra Madre on horseback in 1955, he met a mining engineer named Neil Parker who told him about finding Indians who described themselves as Apaches while on an extended exploratory pack trip in 1948. Parker spoke with one of them at length. He wore buckskin clothing, a G-string, moccasins, and long hair, and spoke some Spanish. He said there were about thirty families living in isolated camps and that they were partially descended from Chiricahuas led by the old chief Nana who broke out of American reservations in the 1880s, and partly from renegades who left the reservation at later dates. They lived in groups of three or four families, planting small patches of corn and living in wickiups of grass.

Tom heard a similar story from another American named Gordon MacMurray, who said that while in the Sierra Madre in about 1920 he had seen some people who told him they were Chiricahuas. They had broad faces, large features, and long hair tied with a red sash. They were mining for gold and there were Mexicans among them. Most interesting of all, MacMurray said these people called themselves O-o-pas.

How often a snatch of someone's language can tell us who they may be. The Piman word for Apache is *ohbi*, with the *i* silently aspirated. More than one Apache is o*h'ohbi*. In fact the term is a general one that means "enemy," but since Apaches were the most common enemy, it usually refers to them.[86]

I was told a story by a man who met a self-described Apache in the Guyanopa country, close to Mountain Pima territory, in the 1970s. This man said that "Apache" meant "enemy" and he was no one's enemy, but just wanted to live in peace.[87]

These stories give added meaning to the claims of two smugglers Bill and Grennie encountered and camped with for two days after leaving the Apache camp in the Sierra las Espuelas. They said that the Mexicans of the Aros River district claimed that the Apaches had their headquarters in this region. The Aros River flows through the heart of Mountain Pima country.

None of these stories should be taken at face value, but considered in light of what I have heard firsthand about Apache descendants emerging from the vast wilderness east of Sahuaripa and west of Chihuahua City, they suggest a possible hypothesis. Not only could Apaches lose themselves in Mountain Pima country, they could lose themselves among the Pima people—and they could have been doing so since the final days of the Apache Wars in the 1880s. It is conceivable that this was a pattern: as military, vigilante, and development pressure in the northern Sierra Madre drove the Apaches farther south, they simply settled anonymously among the Pimas.

Whether or not this hypothesis is supportable with more investigation, one thing can be said with certainty: there is by now, after all these years of warfare, captivity, assimilation, and survival instinct, a good deal of Apache blood in northeastern Sonora and northwestern Chihuahua. In fact, there are probably four different strains of Apache descent in northern Mexico. The most well known is comprised of the descendants of *Apaches mansos* (in Spanish: "tame Apaches") who have lived at peace in towns such as Janos, Casas Grandes, Bavispe, and others since the eighteenth century. Another is comprised of the descendants of Apaches captured by Mexicans during the warfare of the nineteenth century. Others are descended from people who remained in Mexico after Geronimo surrendered, but eventually settled peacefully in remote locations, such as Mountain Pima country. And the fourth group, if it exists at all, would be descended from the last holdouts, the Sierra Madre Apaches. There are none living as they did in the 1930s, but their descendants may have done what others had done before them: drifted in among the Pimas or other Indians, or into remote ranches, settled down, assimilated: a kind of metamorphosis.

Since the completion of *The Apache Diaries*, another theme of Apache heritage has been surfacing. I am beginning to hear accounts of people claiming Apache descent now living in communities in Mexico. One man arrived in El Paso from a Tarahumara village in Chihuahua bearing a fascinating tale. He made contact with a colleague of mine who telephoned me immediately. This man's story was so compelling that I took a plane the next day to El Paso to hear his story. The details will remain confidential for now, but he said he was on a mission to make contact with Apaches on American reservations. He had been sent by the people of his community who had been living ostensibly as Tarahumaras for 120 years, but who were in fact descended from Apaches who had settled among the Tarahumaras toward the end of the Apache Wars. They had concealed their true identity all this time, but had finally considered it safe to reveal their true heritage and to effect a reunion with Apaches north of the border.

Colleagues of mine have been told of other Apache groups absorbed by and living among the Tarahumara Indians on the north rim of Copper Canyon. Others have heard of an underground community of Apaches in El Paso and Ciudad Juárez.

In October 2000, a group of people in Chihuahua identifying themselves as Apachean people, and calling themselves Chihuahua Apache, launched an initiative that resulted in a weeklong gathering in Chihuahua City. It was to be both a reconciliation between the state of

Chihuahua and the Apache people, and a chance for Mexicans of Apache descent to effect a reunion with Apaches on American reservations. During the week of October 14 to 20 Apache individuals and delegations from the Mescalero reservation, the Navajo Nation, and the BIA descended on Chihuahua City. There were Mexican officials, a delegation of one hundred from another ancient Apache enemy, the Tarahumara Indians. Most notable, there were thousands of Mexicans who were drawn by a sort of romance that has apparently replaced the universal Mexican fear and loathing for Apaches of earlier generations. Reported in exhaustive detail for an entire week in Chihuahua newspapers, the gathering became a public event of enormous proportions.

As much as I wanted to go myself, I couldn't; but people who were there tell me there are good reasons for this about-face in Mexican attitudes toward the Apaches. The living memory of the nineteenth-century wars, even the events of 1930s, is virtually gone and is being replaced with revisionist myth and legend. Educational policies born of the Mexican Revolution, intended to engender a certain pride in Mexico's Indian heritage, are beginning to take hold and mold public attitudes. Newspaper articles made special note of the fact that, because of the centuries of mutual kidnapping, Apache blood runs in the veins of many Mexicans, just as Mexican blood runs in the veins of many Apaches.

What's more, Mexicans are beginning to feel pangs of guilt for the atrocities suffered by indigenous people at the hands of the Spanish and Mexican governments. This sounds a hopeful note for the future—I can only hope that Mexico finds a better road through the minefield of racism than the United States has. I should add that by no means all Apaches or all Mexicans felt this gathering was assembled in good faith. Some traditional Apache elders felt that not enough was offered by the government of the state of Chihuahua to induce them to forgive and forget the wrongs of the past. Some Mexicans, though perhaps only a very few, saw no reason to extend the olive branch to the Apaches who had so terrorized the northern frontier of Mexico. Some even recalled the 150-year old Mexican perception that Apaches were used by the United States government as a tool for terrorizing and destabilizing Mexico following the Mexican War of the 1840s. These ancient mistrusts die hard.

The Chihuahua Apache group believes that the closest thing to an Apache community in Chihuahua today is made up of descendants of true Apaches who have married into the mountain Pimas and who, among the Pimas, are known simply as *los apaches*. This confirms a long-held belief of mine, stated in *The Apache Diaries* and again earlier in this chapter: other members of Chihuahua Apache are recording their own oral history, and once they share that with the public, another chapter will be written in the Apache epic.

Last year I spent several hours talking with a man in southern Arizona whose parents, he stated, fled the Sierra Madre in the 1930s, a time when terrible things were happening to the Sierra Madre Apaches. His parents moved out of the mountains and then traveled north from one Indian community to another, some of them in Baja California, until they settled among Mexican Indians on the border near Yuma.

A newspaper reporter in Tucson told me of contact in 1986 with a woman who had grown up in Tombstone's Mexican community but whose mother was in fact an Apache. She said that her mother, like many other Apaches, had settled among Mexicans in U.S. border towns. Born in 1918, probably in Mexico, the woman and her family came to Tombstone when she was two years old. Her mother spoke Spanish and Apache, but the woman told the reporter she remembered hardly any Apache, having been strictly instructed by her parents never to utter a word of that language. She said that the anti-Mexican prejudice she encountered was ferocious, and she fled Arizona to escape it at the age of eighteen, settling finally in San Diego in about 1940. What a cruel irony. It was worth their lives to hide their Apache identity in Mexico, so hated were Apaches by the Mexicans. But in order to survive in the United States, they had to assume the identity of the hated Mexicans and then endure the Arizonans' scorn for Mexicans.

There were other Apaches in Tombstone, all playing the "Mexican game" as she called it. They knew each other and had secret methods of communication, using hand and eye signals, but beyond this small circle, the true identity of these Apaches was secret. The children of their community would be taken every year to secret rendezvous sites in the Huachuca Mountains on the border between Douglas and Nogales for instruction in Apache traditions from elders who would come north from Mexico.

These very recent stories are intriguing, and they are consistent with patterns I know to be true: concealed identities, assimilation, and migration. But even as I pursue them and write them down word for word,

I am skeptical. And my skepticism is nothing compared with that of some American Apaches, who are so hounded with people claiming to be long-lost relatives that they tend to believe none of them—and with good reason. Most of them are claiming Apache blood so that they can become enrolled in the tribe and take advantage of tribal entitlements.

Until I can dig deeper into the oral traditions about which I am hearing, I can have no idea of their historical veracity; but, like all folklore, all oral history, however much we may find them wanting in accuracy, they repay us richly in another coin. The accounts of emerging Apaches in Mexico tell us that Apache heritage is now something to be claimed publicly—albeit very cautiously—in Mexico for the first time.

There are two simultaneous processes of erosion underway: an erosion of the Mexicans' hatred of Apaches; and erosion of Apaches' fear of reprisal or revenge for acts committed during long-ago warfare. This relaxation of tension may have been encouraged in part by the events of the centennial observances of 1986, when Chiricahuas came forward for the first time since 1886 to take their place in history. Lasting for several days, the events were staged both at Fort Bowie, where Geronimo was held following his surrender, and in the town of Bowie, where he boarded the train as a prisoner of war for exile to Florida. Chiricahua elders told the stories heard from their parents who had been taken prisoner with Geronimo. It was a powerful experience for all of the Chiricahuas and it helped to heal a shame that had lasted one hundred years. One of the things the Chiricahuas did that they had not done—at least in public—for one hundred years was to begin making trips to Mexico, to revisit sacred sites and strongholds. The publicity surrounding these visits may have encouraged what appears to be a kind of tentative, emerging "Apache Pride" in Mexico.

I am waiting for someone to come to the surface who is descended from people who somehow survived the holocaust of the 1930s in the Sierra Madre. The captive children I know of are all gone. Are there any others? ✣

NOTES

1. Edward H. Spicer, "A Dedication to the Memory of Grenville Goodwin 1907–1940," *Arizona and the West* 3 (1961): 203.

2. Morris E. Opler, ed., *Grenville Goodwin Among the Western Apache: Letters from the Field* (Tucson: University of Arizona Press, 1973), 11.

3. *The Silent Enemy* was released as a feature film in 1930. Its production is described in Kevin Brownlow, *The War, the West and the Wilderness* (New York: Knopf, 1979). Douglas Burden became a naturalist of some note and explored and collected specimens for the American Museum of Natural History in New York.

4. Grenville Goodwin, "Clans of the Western Apache," *New Mexico Historical Review* 8: 176–82.

5. Edward H. Spicer, biographical note in Grenville Goodwin, *Western Apache Raiding and Warfare* (Tucson, University of Arizona Press, 1971), 3.

6. Jesús Fuentes Yáñez, *Correrías apaches en Nácori Chico* (Hermosillo: Instituto Sonorense de Cultura, Dirección de Culturas Populares de Sonora, 1991), 46. The extermination of the Apaches had Sonoran government sanction.

7. Apache scholar Philip Greenfeld of San Diego State University, has analyzed the word *bui* and states that if the word refers to "owl," it appears to derive uniquely from the Western Apache dialect with no corresponding word in Chiricahua or Mescalero Apache, indicating the possibility of a significant admixture of Western Apache among Bui's people (personal communication, Oct. 20, 1997).

8. Helge Ingstad, *Apache—Indianerne: Jakten På Den Tapte Stamme* (Oslo: Gyldendal, 1939), 112. Private translation by Liv Bjørnard, 1976.

9. Tom Hinton, unpublished field notes, recorded June 17, 1955, archives of the Arizona State Museum, University of Arizona.

10. From an article written by Dixie Harris, Jack's wife, *Douglas Daily Dispatch*, July 16, 1932.

11. *Douglas Daily Dispatch* July 13, 1932.

12. Ball and Sánchez, "The Last Apaches," *True West* 29, no. 1 (1982).

13. Nácori Chico interviews Mar. 19, 1996.

14. Tom Hinton, unpublished field notes, recorded June 16, 1955, archives of the Arizona State Museum, University of Arizona.

15. Rodolfo Rascón, *El Imparcial,* Oct. 19, 1993. It is possible he was carried in a cradle board. Hip displacement is fairly common among older Apaches today who were carried in cradle boards while young. Philip Greenfeld, personal communication, September 22, 2000.

16. Rascón, *El Imparcial,* Oct. 19, 1993.

17. Rascón, *El Imparcial,* Oct. 19, 1993.

18. Opler, *Goodwin Among the Western Apache,* 47.

19. He must have been captured as a young man, perhaps during fights such as those at Sahuaripa in 1883 or at Casas Grandes in 1882. Only captive women were reported from the battle of Tres Castillos in 1880.

20. These were not tarot cards, but rather old-style Mexican or Spanish playing cards. See Philip J. Greenfeld, "Playing Card Names in Western Apache," *International Journal of American Linguistics* 37 (1971), 195–96; Virginia Wayland, "Apache Playing Cards," *Southwest Museum Leaflets* No. 28 (Highland Park: Southwest Museum, 1961).

21. See chapter 5 for the full text of this letter.

22. In the narratives of Sherman Curley and others who served as Army scouts in the 1890s, there is ample mention of campaigns in pursuit of the "renegade" Apaches, or *hai'i'ähä,* in southern Arizona and Mexico.

23. Chapter 8, "An Apache Ranchería" contains a detailed description and interpretation of this unusual site. When it was discovered in 1926, it was occupied by a group of Sierra Madre Apache and was thereupon immediately abandoned. My father was guided to it in 1931 by Bill Curtis.

24. 1954 letter from Evelyn Riesman to my mother quoting the anthropologist Charles Kaut. Kaut told me (personal communication, November 8, 2000) that in his letter he had been referring to a time when he read a passage from *Myths and Tales of the White Mountain Apache* to an elder of the Cibecue community, who listened in reverent silence.

25. *Shi-cho* is the Apache for "grandmother" as well as "grandson." Grennie and Anna Price called each other by this name. Literally "my daughter's child" or "my mother's parent," it is the term for relationship through a female person and is therefore a very significant relation in a matrilineal society such as the Apache.

26. Grenville Goodwin, "Report on the San Carlos Indian Reservation," July 20, 1937, p. 21.

27. "Curator, Arizona State Museum," to James B. Kitch, June 3, 1931 (unsigned letter). Arizona State Museum archives.

28. Tulipai is a mild illicit homebrew. No liquor of any kind was allowed on the reservation.

29. This is a reference to a sand painting done on May 30, 1936. The ceremony was held by medicine man John Robertson for "the sick woman at Mark Dwain's."

30. C.F.3 is a man's tag-band name. The army gave all Apaches tag-band numbers, and the Apaches often used them when referring to one another. See Carl Eric Granfelt, "Apache Identification Tags," *The Military Collector and Historian* 26, no. 1 (1974), 18–21; also Goodwin, *Social Organization of the Western Apache*, 577.

31. Dan Thrapp, *The Conquest of Apachería* (Norman: University of Oklahoma Press, 1967), p. 230.

32. Goodwin, "Report on the San Carlos Indian Reservation," 142.

33. Pasco was a white policeman or BIA official.

34. Sam Hinton was probably a local rancher or farmer.

35. Goodwin, "Report on the San Carlos Indian Reservation," 142.

36. Diary notes, p. 140.

37. See Phyllis de la Garza, *The Apache Kid* (Tucson: Westernlore Press, 1995), 133, for what is probably a description of this incident as reported in the *Silver Belt,* a Globe newspaper. It took place on October 11, 1890.

38. De la Garza, *Apache Kid,* p. 28.

39. Charles Kaut, personal communication, November 8, 2000.

40. The averted gaze is good Apache etiquette, and these girls would have avoided looking directly back at Jan.

41. Statement of an elderly Apache from the introduction of an early draft of *Social Organization of the Western Apache.*

42. From an undated statement written by Harry Hoijer and sent to my mother to be used for the original introduction to *Social Organization of the Western Apache.*

43. Goodwin, *Social Organization of the Western Apache,* p. xvii.

44. "Curator, Arizona State Museum," to James B. Kitch, June 3, 1931 (unsigned letter). Arizona State Museum archives.

45. Opler, *Goodwin Among the Western Apache,* 24; from a letter written April 4, 1932.

46. Opler, *Goodwin Among the Western Apache,* 22; from a letter written March 22, 1932.

47. Goodwin, "Report on the San Carlos Indian Reservation," 34.

48. See Goodwin, *Social Organization of the Western Apache,* 92.

49. Goodwin, *Apache Raiding and Warfare,* 41.

50. Goodwin, "Reminiscences of Charlie Norman," unpublished notes, item 28, p. 2.

51. Goodwin, "Reminiscences of Charlie Norman," p. 110.

52. *Hadn'tin,* cattail pollen, a very important element in many Apache ceremonials.

53. Goodwin, "Songs," pp. 35–37, from unpublished notes, Arizona State Museum.

54. Goodwin, "Report on the San Carlos Indian Reservation," 19.

55. Goodwin, "Report on the San Carlos Indian Reservation," 127.

56. Goodwin, "Report on the San Carlos Indian Reservation," 138.

57. Goodwin, "Report on the San Carlos Indian Reservation," 126.

58. Goodwin, "Report on the San Carlos Indian Reservation," 129.

59. Opler, *Goodwin Among the Western Apache,* 22.

60. Grenville Goodwin to Elizabeth Sage Hare, November 11, 1932.

61. See Keith H. Basso, *Wisdom Sits in Places* (Albuquerque: University of New Mexico Press), 1997.

62. The only letter that hints at knowledge of Grennie's illness is one written by the interpreter Richard Bylas in July 1934 after Grennie's recovery. He simply says he is "glad you're well and able to spend a summer in New Mexico."

63. It was beginning to be common practice among ethnographers in the field to keep such a diary as an *aide-mémoire* that provided the context and chronology of daily events.

64. Long after the repeal of prohibition in 1933, laws remained on the books making it illegal for an Indian to possess, buy, or drink liquor off the reservation. The law was not repealed until the 1950s. San Carlos Reservation is "dry."

65. See also Morris E. Opler, "Remuneration to Supernaturals and Man in Apachean Ceremonialism," *Ethnology* 7:356–93.

66. Goodwin, "Report on the San Carlos Indian Reservation," p. 129.

67. The hoop is a very important and potent part of ceremonial symbolism and has elements of the rainbow, of lightning, and of the snake.

68. His name is variously spelled as Roberson, Robson, Robison, and Robinson. Robertson seems to be correct.

69. Diary, p. 71. John Robertson made a number of *gá•n* masks for the Arizona State Museum, all of which have been recently returned to the tribe under NAGPRA repatriation policies.

70. "Section 14" refers to one of the categories by which Grennie was organizing his research. In this case it had to do with "sun, moon, sky," etc.

71. For a thorough discussion of an Apache puberty ceremony, see Keith H. Basso, "Gift of Changing Woman," Anthropological Papers 76, Bureau of American Ethnology Bulletin 196. Washington, D.C.: Bureau of American Ethnology.

72. *Na-ai-e-es* is the Apache term for the initiate girl's godmother, a woman who guides and advises the girl through the ceremony and who plays an important part in it herself.

73. This was a brutal, apparently unprovoked attack on a Mexican family in which several people were killed and from which only a boy twelve years old survived. See Neil Goodwin, *The Apache Diaries* (Lincoln: University of Nebraska Press, 200), pp. 170–72.

74. This was another apparently unprovoked attack. See N. Goodwin, *The Apache Diaries*, pp. 40–41.

75. This town is probably one of the villages of the Bavispe Valley, or possibly one farther west, such as Moctezuma or Oputo.

76. By "mescal outfit" Grenville is referring to a still for producing one of the fiery local forms of white lightning from the fermented heart of the mescal plant.

77. These numbers refer to features on Grennie's original maps. In the new maps we have made, we use the same feature numbers.

78. The current owner, Carlos, and his nephew Rogelio say that much of the dam construction was done after their family acquired the ranch in the 1970s.

79. Personal communication, October 25, 2000.

80. Al Fenn, personal communication, October 9, 2000.

81. Al Fenn, personal communication, October 9, 2000.

82. Bruce R. Donaldson and John R. Welch, "Western Apache Dwellings and Their Archaeological Correlates," in *Mogollon V*, edited by Patrick H. Beckett, pp. 93–105 (Las Cruces, N.Mex: COAS Publishing and Research, 1979).

83. Report to the Adjutant, 7th Cavalry, May 9, 1896. Records of the War Department, Office of the Adjutant General, No. 38312 file with 29451.

84. Carl Lumholtz, *Unknown Mexico* (New York: Macmillan, 1902), 43–49.

85. Interviews at Fort Apache and Tucson, October 1997.

86. Bernard Fontana, personal communication, May 22, 1998.

87. Billy Martineau, interview, June 10, 1987.

ABOUT THE AUTHOR

In 1996, Neil Goodwin undertook a life-long dream of completing some unfinished work of his late father, the anthropologist Grenville Goodwin. Part mystery, part memoir, the work focused on a small elusive group of Apaches who had not surrendered with Geronimo in 1886. Neil traveled widely in Mexico and the American Southwest gathering information and exploring the Sierra Madre, and the result was *The Apache Diaries, A Father-Son Journey*, published in 2000. *Like a Brother* was conceived as a sequel to that work and is a further exploration of Grenville's years among the Apaches in Arizona and of their mysterious kin in Mexico. Neil works as a film producer and lives in Cambridge, Massachusetts, with his wife Margot. He returns to the Southwest frequently to pursue the ongoing research that his father began in 1929.